Don Mosey, well-known Test Match commentator and former BBC cricket correspondent, has followed Botham's career first-hand from the very beginning. He saw Botham's first major innings in county cricket at Taunton in 1974, went with him on his first big tour, was with him during his captaincy of England in the West Indies, and watched those dramatic performances against Australia in 1981. Don Mosey has already written a highly acclaimed biography of Geoff Boycott – described by the *Financial Times* as 'probably the best profile of a cricketer ever written'. His account of Botham's life is approached with similar frankness.

Don Mosey

BOTHAM

Foreword by Trevor Bailey

SPHERE BOOKS LIMITED

A Sphere Book

First published in Great Britain in 1986 by
Methuen London Limited
Published in a revised and updated edition by
Sphere Books Limited, 1987
Reprinted 1989

The photographs in this book are reproduced by kind permission of the following: Patrick Eagar: 1a, 2c, 8a; All-Sport Photographic Limited: 1b, 2b, 3a, 3b, 4a, 4b, 5b, 6a, 6b, 7a, 7b, 7c, 8b; Associated Sports Photography: 2a; Don Mosey: 5a.

Reproduced, printed and bound in Great Britain by
Cox & Wyman Ltd, Reading

ISBN 0 7221 6167 0

Sphere Books Ltd
A Division of
Macdonald & Co (Publishers) Ltd
27 Wrights Lane, London W8 5TZ
A member of Maxwell Pergamon Publishing Corporation plc

CONTENTS

ILLUSTRATION ACKNOWLEDGEMENTS

The photographs in this book are reproduced by kind permission of the following: Patrick Eagar p.1 (top), p.2 (bottom), p.8 (top); All-Sport Photographic Ltd p.1 (bottom), p.2 (top right), p.3, p.4, p.5 (bottom), p.6, p.7, p.8 (bottom); Associated Sports Photography p.2 (top left); Don Mosey p.5 (top).

FOREWORD

Trevor Bailey, of Cambridge University and Essex, was the first of England's genuine Test all-rounders in the post-war period. Since then he has kept a keen and experienced critical eye on the game as administrator, cricket correspondent of the Financial Times *and one of the expert summarisers on BBC Radio 3's 'Test Match Special'.*

It is noticeable how the football manager who was himself a creative ball-player always makes sure that his team contains a number of decidedly *physical* players, while the manager who in *his* playing days was a robust defender who did not believe in taking many prisoners tends to worship the artist. Therefore, as our respective styles were so dissimilar, I am one of Ian Botham's greatest fans – nobody being better-equipped to estimate the worth of a Cavalier than a Roundhead!

The life of an all-rounder at school and club level has no serious problems, but it becomes an increasingly more difficult and demanding job in county cricket when one is expected, sometimes seven days a week, to provide a goodly quota of runs and wickets. It is easy to understand why many county cricketers with all-round ability become either batsmen who can take wickets or bowlers who can make runs. They decide to specialise because the all-rounder will not make as many runs as the pure batsman of similar ability or take as many wickets as the pure bowler. Thirty overs of bowling is not the ideal preparation for a big innings, while, conversely, making a century must take something out of any bowler, especially a quickie, even if he has been blessed with the physique and stamina of Ian Botham. However, I believe (like Ian) that the advantages of concentrating on both departments more than outweigh the disadvantages. The biggest attraction is having the opportunity to be centre stage and a key figure throughout the match. And with two strings to one's bow there is a chance to compensate for failure with the bat by taking wickets, or vice versa.

All-rounders provide the balance which is a vital factor in every team sport. The ideal cricket side should contain five frontline bowlers and a wicket-keeper, which leaves only five places for pure batsmen. I have deliberately placed the attack first because this will be the deciding factor in most matches other than limited-overs games. A good Test pitch should have pace and bounce and encourage spin at later stages so that the perfect attack, especially when it is recognised that fewer than 100 overs in a full day is unfair to the paying public, should consist of three pace bowlers and two spinners.

However, a Test team containing five bowlers and a wicket-keeper is likely to be short of runs unless one – ideally more – of that sextet has ability with the bat, which is why Selectors are often forced to include a sixth batsman. This would not be necessary if there were two all-rounders able to add to the run potential without reducing the attack's penetration. As a result, a great all-rounder like Ian is the key figure in any side, and everybody likes to be indispensable. The complete all-rounder is so proficient in both departments that he justifies selection in either, which is easy to achieve in the early stages but becomes hard at county level. It follows that the all-rounder able to meet these requirements is even rarer in Test cricket. The honest county bits-and-pieces player is frequently not good enough in either department; consequently, Selectors are inclined to pick an international specialist batsman who can turn his arm over adequately or a specialist bowler capable of making runs. This applies especially to England, as the overseas all-rounder leads a less demanding existence, but nevertheless there are at the moment more exceptional Test class all-rounders than ever before.

Since Ian Botham made his début for England against Australia in 1977, when he displayed his insatiable appetite by gobbling up five wickets, he has been an integral part of the team, worth his place both for his bowling and his batting. He is our most spectacular, dynamic and successful all-rounder in Test cricket this century, his only serious rival – the immortal W. G. Grace – coming from the previous one. My assessment is made on his ability, not on his record in international cricket, even though this stands (after the winter 1986 tour to the West Indies) at a tremendous 4577 runs and 354 wickets, because figures can be misleading. There has been a surfeit of international matches and many – especially during the World Series in Australia – have been sub-standard and do not mean too much. Although Ian has already captured more wickets than any other English bowler, not by the widest stretch of imagination is he the best bowler we have ever produced. While he has scored (up to the start of the 1986 season) almost as many runs as Tom Graveney, he is certainly not as good a batsman. Ian is, however, very definitely our finest all-rounder and match-winnter.

The outstanding feature of Ian's bowling in Tests has not so much been the size of his haul but his remarkably high striking rate, so that he can with justification be called the man with the golden arm. There are various reasons for this. Firstly, he is essentially an attacking bowler whose prime objective is to remove rather than contain opposing batsmen. This is an increasingly rare attribute in the age of limited-overs cricket and explains why he is, relatively speaking, less impressive as a bowler in the one-day game than in the five-day. He certainly would not be my choice to send down the last five overs in a limited-overs match when the opposition, with wickets in hand, required something like seven runs an over. On the other hand I would fancy gambling with him when a game appeared to be irretrievably lost. In Test matches, Ian's bowling record is exceptional. Possibly even more impressive than his total haul of wickets is the number of occasions he has captured five or more in an innings. Just how remarkable it is may be gathered from the fact that Mike Hendrick (who was a high-class, reliable seamer in the same era) *never* took five wickets in an innings in any of his twenty-three Tests, yet in limited-overs cricket he was usually a more effective bowler because he gave less away.

Secondly, in his early years Ian's most effective delivery was a late away-swinger. He quickly realised that it paid any swerve bowler to keep a full length and invite the batsman to drive him through the covers, which at his pace was a very tempting bait. He also acquired a good inswinger, making him even more formidable.

Thirdly, he has an outstanding physique which, allied to his economical run-up, has meant that he has been able to operate for very long spells. Indeed, once he is taking wickets it is very hard to prise the ball out of his hand and, of course, the more one bowls, the greater the opportunity of taking wickets.

Fourthly, Ian's hunger for wickets – not maiden overs – can be seen in the way he has always been prepared to experiment with a slower ball, by using the width of the crease, and with the bouncer. There have been times when it has seemed that Ian has overdone the bouncer – at times it has looked distinctly inviting – but it has brought him many wickets. He has been helped by a number of batsmen, probably influenced by the protection of the helmet, who attempt to hook even though they have taken note of the two men back on the boundary.

I saw Ian during the 1982–3 Australian tour and immediately wondered what had happened to his bowling. He appeared to have lost his outswinger even in conditions encouraging swerve, his bouncer lacked venom and on the few occasions when the ball did beat the bat it did not hit Bob Taylor's gloves with a real thwack. What was wrong? The answer was that he had lost his timing, a fact which became immediately apparent when, at the end of a very long spell and using only an abbreviated run-up, he produced two outswingers – admittedly only at medium pace.

What had happened was that he was not getting his body as far round as once he had done, nor was he releasing the ball at the right moment, and this was worrying because England could ill afford to lose their chief wicket-taker in his prime. Some critics immediately wrote him off, which was stupid, and fortunately Ian proved them very wrong against Australia in the summer of 1985. After a winter's rest from cricket (1984–5) he came back into the England team in a new role – as their fastest bowler who charged up to the wicket and relied on pace rather than swing and hurled the ball down. Although not fast in the Malcolm Marshall sense, he was distinctly sharp and had most of the Australian batsmen in trouble. He sent down more overs than any other bowler and picked up 31 wickets in the process.

The one question about our new strike bowler was: would he have been able to bowl quite so quickly for England if he had bowled rather more for Somerset, for whom he took only 11 wickets at more than 42 runs apiece? However, this is the present trend. During the previous Aussie tour Bob Willis bowled 252 overs in the Test series, taking 29 wickets, but only managed 138 overs for Warwickshire, for whom he captured 13 wickets. His county that season, like Botham's in 1985, finished bottom of the County Championship. Would Bob Willis have been able to bowl so fast and for so long for England (taking 323 wickets) if his haul for Warwicks had not been so small – a mere 353 in thirteen seasons at 24.84 apiece?

It could well turn out that Ian Botham will be remembered more for his batting than his bowling. It is certainly more spectacular, as genuinely successful hitters are even rarer than great all-rounders. Every team desires somebody who is able to transform the complexion of a game in a short time by his aggression with the bat, and every spectator wants to see him in action. What makes Ian's batting so unusual is that he is essentially a *correct* hitter, not an old-fashioned slogger. The difference is that he possesses a correct defence, and hits straight and not across the line. He scores centuries as well as flamboyant thirties and can destroy an international attack in a very short time, his two best examples probably being against Australia at Headingley and Old Trafford in 1981. In my career I encountered very few hitters, and nobody in the same class as Ian Botham, who has not only scored hundreds in Test cricket but in 1985 made five for Somerset, all in very quick time. The nearest approach England has had as a batsman-hitter at international level was Gilbert Jessop before the First World War.

Why is Ian such a successful hitter in terms of runs scored, and why have not more players adapted to his methods? There are several reasons. First and foremost, Ian is technically a correct player. His straight-bat strokes, whether used for defence or offence, are mainly with the full face, while – possibly even more important – his feet are in the correct position and his down-swing, from the top of the full back-swing, is copybook. There are exceptions, the most notorious being his reverse sweep, but most of his cross-bat strokes are made with the bat parallel to the ground. When feasible he normally cuts *down* and rolls his wrists. Why does he bother to indulge in the reverse sweep when he possesses such a large repertoire of safer and more effective strokes? I assume it stems from his inability to resist a challenge, as can be seen so often when he will still attempt to hook even though the odds are not in his favour.

Secondly, Ian hits the ball exceptionally hard off either foot, which makes trying to contain him even more difficult. It also reduces the risk involved in hitting sixes (for which he has a partiality, as he showed in 1985 when he struck the highest number ever in an English first-class season). Whereas the normal player needs to time his stroke perfectly to register a six, Ian will not infrequently mis-hit one. A perfect example of this occurred at Headingley in a Test when he went for the sweep and, though he top-edged the ball, it still sailed safely into the crowd instead of being caught just inside the boundary. When Ian really middles the ball it will finish not just over the boundary line but high up in the stands or even out of the ground.

In consequence, he is still prepared to loft a bowler into the crowd even when fieldsmen have been stationed back on the ropes – regarding them as yet another irresistible challenge. Sixes, especially really big ones, have always provided a special attraction for spectators. Like a fast bowler sending a stump somersaulting out of the ground, or a boxer landing a knock-out punch, a six possesses a positive, primitive appeal – it's something everyone would like to do but only accomplishes in his dreams. And Ian's ability to hit so many gives him great box-office appeal.

Thirdly, it is a hard and frustrating business bowling at Ian in full flow. There were two types of batsmen I disliked bowling against: (1) the player who looked so secure that only dynamite would remove him – someone like 'Slasher' Mackay, Ken Barrington or Eric Rowan; (2) the man who had the infuriating ability to score off the good ball – like Sir Donald Bradman, Denis Compton or Clyde Walcott. Ian Botham falls into the second category and, as bowlers do not bowl as well when runs are being scored quickly against them, it follows that Ian's aggressive approach has frequently upset bowlers' rhythm. It has also disturbed opposing captains to such an extent that after a couple of boundaries they have set fields suitable for a Botham bombardment in full flow, rather than before it had really started.

Fourthly, throughout his career with Somerset he has had the good fortune to play alongside and watch Vivian Richards, who for several years has been the best batsman in the world. Anybody must learn *something* from Vivian, and Ian must have learned a great deal from the maestro about dismantling attacks, scoring fast and the art of improvisation.

Finally, he was born in an era where it has been easier for a hitter to establish himself and to justify his selection for county, and later country, in that capacity than at any other time since the 1914–18 War. Ian served his apprenticeship in Somerset at a time when limited-overs cricket had become in many respects more important than the County Championship (once the *only* tournament) as the Club had a much better chance of winning one of the three one-day competitions.

He was thus able to discover quickly how effective he could be in demolishing attacks and how valuable that was to his side. In the one-day game he was able to play the free sort of cricket which was natural to him. And in addition it has to be said that, if one excludes the overseas players in the County Championship, much of the bowling he faced was insipid. It is difficult to remember when the overall standard of English bowling on the domestic circuit has been much lower – one genuinely fast bowler, Bob Willis, who did not bowl all that amount in county cricket, about a dozen good seamers and an even bigger shortage of young slow bowlers.

Excluding the West Indies, Test attacks have been limited, too. England were forced to include an honest county seamer like Robin Jackman when he was past his best, while the Australian bowling line-up in 1985 was the weakest they have ever sent to this country, consisting really of one fast bowler who was never fully fit and a novice. Though it may be easier to be a hitter these days, this in no way detracts, in my view, from Ian's performances. He has won many matches, including Tests, by the speed with which he acquires his runs, while it would be impossible to quantify the pleasure he has given those fortunate enough to be present. As well as his bowling Ian has given us superb, all-purpose fielding: he is a brilliant slip for both pace and, far more difficult, spin; a fearless expert in any of the suicidal bat-pad positions; a spendid cover and outfield who is much quicker over the ground than one expects; a possessor of a very safe pair of hands, and he has a swift, accurate throw. Like most bowlers, he is an especially brilliant fielder to his own bowling whether he is preventing runs or securing another wicket. I cannot think of any member of the seam-bowling brigade who has been his superior in this respect.

Trevor Bailey

1 THE BEGINNING

Few people looking back over a cricketing century and more than 1000 Tests would dwell for more than a second or two upon a couple of days in mid-June 1974 as having any significance at all – England scoring a not-unexpected victory over India at Old Trafford by 113 runs on 11 June, and the players then dispersing either to enjoy a few days off or, if their counties were still involved, to plunge straight into the quarter-finals of the Benson and Hedges Cup on the 12th.

But those two days in June were, in fact, quite dramatically important in a way which has affected modern Test cricket history to a remarkable degree: 11 June was Geoffrey Boycott's last day in international cricket for three years – thirty Tests were to go by before he wore England's colours once again – and 12 June was the day when a burly 18-year-old all-rounder was drafted into Somerset's side against Hampshire at Taunton because Alan Jones, the frontline fast bowler, had developed a slight groin strain. The following morning most of the country was talking about how Ian Botham had turned seemingly certain defeat into a win for Somerset. Three years and forty-six days later these two cricketers – who could scarcely provide a greater contrast in styles or personalities – were to come together on 28 July 1977 at Trent Bridge, Nottingham. Boycott ended what had become known as his self-imposed exile for thirty Tests to return with his thirteenth century, and Botham (about whose selection there were divided expert opinions) took five Australian wickets for 74, bowling in his first Test innings. No one knew, and very few could have suspected, the impact that these two men in their different ways were to have on Test and county cricket in the next decade.

It was nineteen minutes past five on that final afternoon in 1974 when England beat India in Manchester, where the traditional rain had washed out five hours thirty-eight minutes playing time and the new regulations, allowing an extra hour's play in the evening if more than an hour had been lost during the day because of the weather, were invoked for the first time. Boycott, weighed down by his inexplicable failure against the Indian medium-pace bowlers Solkar and Abid Ali and the burden of skippering Yorkshire in an increasingly hostile atmosphere, morosely considered scores of 10 in the first innings and 6 in the second and asked Alec Bedser, the chairman of Selectors, not to consider him again for Tests until he had sorted out his personal problems.

And while that conversation was taking place I was driving down the M6 and M5 towards Taunton with my 'Test Match Special' colleague Henry Blofeld for the following day's Benson and Hedges game, which Henry was covering for the *Guardian* while I watched it on behalf of Radio 2. Henry is a lively companion and the journey passed quickly and easily – so easily in fact that we achieved something which most people would regard as impossible: we went through Birmingham without even noticing it! I was due to have dinner in Taunton with the Somerset captain, my friend Brian Close, and after dropping Henry at the Castle Hotel I drove to the Crown and Sceptre, the pub which Brian used as his base while playing for Somerset, quietly pleased with my driving time of three and a quarter hours. It had started with a crawl through the crowds leaving Old Trafford, then merged into the homeward-bound rush-hour traffic making its way out of Manchester to the stockbroker-belt residential area of Cheshire. I was expecting a compliment from my friend, whose own high-speed driving exploits around the cricket circuit were (and still are) legendary. But no. At the pub I was greeted by a smiling group of Somerset players. '*You* are in trouble,' grinned Graham Burgess. 'When it got to half-past eight Closey snarled, "The so-and-so must have stopped for dinner on the motorway. I could have got here by now on a bike!" So he's gone off for dinner on his own and he's not pleased with you.' Resignedly – you simply cannot win with D. B. Close when it comes to driving matters – I trudged off in search of my friend, finally running him to earth at the Tudor Tavern which, significantly under the circumstances, was a favourite water-hole of Judge George Jeffreys when conducting his bloody assize three hundred years earlier. It was a reasonably appropriate spot for the dressing-down awaiting me, so it was simply a matter of waiting for the storm to subside before starting to talk a bit of cricket.

Yes – they should beat Hampshire tomorrow. No – he wasn't sure yet what the team would be. Barry Richards and Andy Roberts? Why worry about them in particular? They were just cricketers like everybody else, weren't they? Brian Close on the eve of any important game showed much the same sang-froid as Drake when the arrival of the Armada was imminent. There was a bit of a doubt about Alan Jones, but what was new about that? (Close, in his Somerset days, had more than his share of traumatic experiences involving that much-travelled and occasionally idiosyncratic fast bowler.) And so what was left of the evening passed pleasantly enough.

The following morning Jones's fitness test brought a negative result, and the scorecard showed that his place was to be taken by one I. T. Botham. No one knew much about him. Various bits of information were offered – his parents lived in Yeovil but he was not a native Zummerzet lad, he had been on the Lord's ground staff, he was only eighteen and a half – but with Richards and Roberts on view no one was particularly interested in a teenager who had been drafted into the game at the last minute. One simply went through the motions of getting basic details about him because that was part of the 'homework' necessary before any game began. No one really expected to have much to say, or to write, about I. T. Botham.

He took the wicket of the great Barry Richards, but in a limited-overs game one does not attach undue significance to just how the mighty are fallen. His bowling as a whole made absolutely no impact upon me whatsoever, as I can recall. But his fielding did. For so bulky a youngster he moved around the outfield with surprising speed. He anticipated brilliantly and moved on to the ball almost gracefully. But from Botham the batsman we could expect nothing. The game was lost when he went in at number nine, and when Tom Cartwright was out almost straightaway not one man, woman or child on that crowded Taunton ground could expect anything other than the formality of a Hampshire win. Seventy runs needed, two wickets left and the mighty Roberts, then at the height of his powers, still had the best part of seven overs to bowl. It was impossible. Only one person in the ground could have thought differently, and that was an 18-year-old boy with a mere couple of John Player matches representing his experience of big-time cricket. How he made us all look foolish . . .

It seemed impossible that so inexperienced a youth could be confident in that situation, yet he certainly *looked* confident. Even so, it simply had to be a false impression. An eighteen-year-old just couldn't hold out against the man who only the previous winter had been bowling in Tests against England and was recognised as the fastest bowler in county cricket. If Botham was conscious of this it was not immediately apparent. There were frequent consultations with his ninth-wicket partner Hallam Moseley, himself a West Indian-born fast bowler, and we all assumed that the more experienced man was imparting what advice was possible in a hopeless situation. On the contrary, we learned later that it was the 18-year-old explaining to a man seven years his senior and light years ahead in experience that all was not lost. He hit a six over square leg.

Roberts, smouldering at this affront to the dignity of a colleague, took up the attack from the other end and fired in a short-pitched ball which had to be the quickest delivery young Botham had so far experienced in his brief career.

It reared, hitting him in the face. Even in that moment he was shaping to pull, or hook the ball, but it simply arrived too quickly for him. He spat out blood and broken teeth when we all looked to see him prostrate on the ground, grudgingly accepted a glass of water which Close had sent out to him to give him at least a moment or two to recover what could be left of his composure, and carried on. He never flinched from anything Roberts or anyone else flung at him. He got his head behind the ball, he stroked it around – or flogged it when anything came short of a length or over-pitched – and the four he hit off the last ball of the penultimate over won the game for Somerset. Ian Botham scored 45 not out, won a Benson and Hedges gold award, and Somerset cricket had a new hero.

My last broadcast completed, I strolled over to the Taunton Cricket Club members' pavilion, met this young Lochinvar newly come out of the West, and said afterwards to Brian Close, 'You've got a future England player in your second team now.' He exploded: 'Don't be bloody daft. He's done well, the lad. But I don't want everybody telling him now he's a world-beater after one game. He's got enough confidence as it is. Now he's got to start learning what cricket's all about.' Close was, as usual, quite right. It *was* 'daft' to start talking in Test terms about a young man who had never even played one game of first-class cricket. But so overwhelming was the impression of inherent greatness in Botham's innings on that late afternoon of 12 June 1974, so marvellously impressive was his confidence in coping with an utterly hopeless situation and turning it into a winning one, so profoundly convincing was his belief in himself, that it was difficult not to get caught up in it all. His enthusiasm was infectious in the most wholesome way. There is a wafer-thin dividing line which separates that sort of self-confidence from simple big-headedness, and Ian Botham, as I saw him, was nicely on the right side of that line. He was a wholly likeable young man with an obvious ability to play cricket in any sort of company without being overawed. So I said to Closey, 'I'll bet you a fiver he plays for England.' Again he chopped me down. 'That's just plain stupid. Shut up about it,' he argued, and of course he was right.

It was quite impossible to make out a reasoned case on the basis of the only evidence available, and Close's cricketing wisdom and experience demanded that he demolish my naive argument, which was nothing more nor less than a *feeling* – a bit of intuition if you like. So the bet was struck at £5, and I suspected that Brian might be very happy to lose it in due course. There were fewer than 10,000 people in the Taunton ground that day, but in the years which followed it became virtually impossible to find anyone amongst Somerset's 435,000 population (not to mention nearly a million more in the artificially created Avon) who hadn't seen Ian Botham's performance that day in 1974, and most of them, it seems, came away with the same conviction that they had seen an England star of the future. Not too many of them, however, could produce a Somerset (and former Yorkshire and England) captain as a witness!

It is an interesting, and perhaps sobering, thought that Botham might well have been a Yorkshire player, performing alongside Geoffrey Boycott through the 1970s. His paternal great-grandfather came from York, where Bootham (not too far removed from the family name) is a place name of great antiquity. Indeed, Bootham Bar is one of the gated entrances to the great mediaeval city which still stand. His father, Leslie, was born in Hull but service in the Fleet Air Arm, which he joined before the war, took him away from his native county and young Ian was born when the family home was at Heswall, on the Wirral peninsula of Cheshire. Now, it is fairly well known that Yorkshire County Cricket Club prides itself on fielding players who, almost without exception, were born within the county boundaries (the fact that there are now no boundaries and, in effect, there is no county of Yorkshire these days as far as the bureaucrats are concerned is totally ignored, praise the Lord, by Yorkshire people), but what is not so well known is that the county club has no regulation which lays this down. It is largely a matter of custom and precedent. The best-known exception to the 'Yorkshire-born' concept would have to be Lord Hawke, who was captain from 1883 to 1887 as the Hon. M. B. Hawke, and then from 1888 to 1910 after succeeding to the title. He was also president from 1898 to 1938. His lordship was actually born at one of the family seats in Lincolnshire, but much of their land was in Yorkshire (covering the Roses battlefield of Towton, incidentally) and they were regarded as very much a Yorkshire family. Lord Hawke's case was clear, once it had been accepted that his cricket was good enough!

Other cases have, from time to time, been considered by the County Committee on their individual merit. There was no hesitation about accepting Geoffrey Keighley, for instance, whose bloodline was unarguably Yorkist but whose mother was enjoying the more congenial climate of Nice when he was born. Cricket historians can point to around a couple of dozen players who have played for Yorkshire without actually having been born on hallowed ground. Most of these enjoyed relatively brief careers wearing the white rose, and some were there by accident. It has always been up to the County Committee to decide the merits of each case when application has been made for aspiring players to be considered as Yorkshiremen. For example, in the mid-seventies the son of a Bridlington couple was accepted, although he had been born in the Caribbean where a business posting had taken his father, and more recently the son of a bank manager who had been temporarily domiciled in Durham during his wife's confinement was also ruled as being eligible to play for Yorkshire in due course, if selected. On the other hand the Committee gave the thumbs-down to parents of Yorkshire stock whose son was born in Australia, even though the boy lived only two years of his life there.

So how might an application from Les Botham on behalf of young Ian have been viewed? Given that his prodigious talent as a teenager had been recognised, it is difficult to see the request being turned down. There might have been some disapproving frowns at the young man's reputation for indiscipline, even as a raw youth; that was the report which followed him from Lord's after his period on the ground staff, and it was one to which he has significantly added throughout his career. 'Both' himself would almost certainly regard it as nothing more than a burning natural desire to express himself in his highly individual way, and that is all too clearly the way Selectors have regarded *him* in the 1980s. But for the purpose of exploring a fascinating but entirely hypothetical situation, let us assume that in 1974 Mr Botham senior, a good Yorkshireman whose service in the armed forces had involved postings outside the county of his and his forefathers' birth, had asked for young Ian to be registered as a Yorkshire-qualified player. Let us then take it a step further and picture the young giant being introduced into the Yorkshire side of 1974 rather than Somerset's. And finally let us indulge in a marvellous speculation on how the whole course of English cricket history might have been changed . . .

The rapport between Botham and Boycott which was for five years a feature of England's Test cricket can really only be explained as a classic case of unlike poles attracting. On the one hand, the most flamboyant batsman of our time to whom the smiting of sixes has always been as important as breathing; on the other, the most defensive-minded batsman of recent years whose grinding accumulation of runs has always been based on the simple principle of staying at the crease as long as possible. The two men are, and always have been, as unalike as two players of the same era could possibly be. And yet there was a strange bond between them, manifested usually in the form of a ponderously jesting badinage which masked a profound mutual professional respect. I would have given a great deal to have been able to sit with Boycott and watch Botham's innings against Australia at Old Trafford in 1981. It would have been possible, surely, to see Geoffrey marvel at the chances taken by Ian as he savaged the bowling – especially that of Lillee with the new ball – to hit a hundred off 86 balls? And what of Botham's view of Boycott at the wicket?

There was undoubtedly a wondering respect for the concentration of a man who could easily face 86 balls without scoring at all, or without even considering a scoring stroke lest it should give the ghost of a chance to the bowler. It is pretty certain that neither man would ever understand the philosophy of the other, and yet there was always a strange regard for each other when they were England team-mates.

What, however, would it have been like if they had worked and played together day in, day out, as members of the same county side? A different story – there can be no doubt about that. If Botham had joined Yorkshire in 1974 he would have walked into a dressing-room torn by dissent and discord, a gathering of strong characters, largely ranged against the autocratic and egocentric captain, rather than the talented but good-natured band of pilgrims he joined at Taunton. In Yorkshire Boycott was king, even if his rule was widely regarded by his subjects as despotic. He could not possibly have countenanced the swashbuckling intrusion of a young man whose entire cricketing personality exuded all the heroic qualities which Geoffrey's lacked. Botham was born to be every schoolboy's hero; Boycott could not have tolerated that alongside his own pedestrian personality. One of them would have had to go and in 1974, whether it was in Yorkshire or anywhere else, the man to go would have been Botham.

Can anyone consider without a shudder the thought of English cricket in the seventies and eighties without I. T. Botham? Whatever his faults, whatever the character-flaws we may find revealed in the course of his life on and off the cricket field, Botham has been the most colourful and dynamic figure in the game during the last decade. Almost alone amongst batsmen outside the West Indies he has stood at the wicket asking himself, 'Where can I score runs off the next ball?' rather than the more timorous, if practical, question, 'How can I avoid being out to this next ball?' His walk to the middle has, more than anything else in cricket, emptied bars and moved spectators on to the edge of their seats. His bowling – which has sometimes been terrible, at least since 1982 – nevertheless promotes an atmosphere of expectancy amongst the largest of crowds. His fielding (which in certain details offends the purists) is as spectacular as the more dramatic moments of his batting. If he is wrong to stand at second slip with his hands on his knees until the last possible minute, it means that his reactions have to be that much quicker when the ball flies from the edge of the bat, especially as he stands a yard or two ahead of first and third slips. So catches which to an orthodox placement would merely be good become brilliant when Botham takes them.

And that is the essence of the man – he *has* to be outstanding at whatever he does on a cricket field. When he translates that policy into terms of his everyday life the same principle applies, but because the context is often ill-chosen he has sometimes tarnished his own image in the eyes of men and women who love their cricket but also care for its good name. Yet his fans are not confined to the schoolboys and the young spectators who prefer their sport to come with fanfares and drum-rolls. The Revd Leslie Ward, formerly Canon-Treasurer of Wells Cathedral, was one of those who saw Botham at Taunton on 12 June 1974. In his view, 'Ian can be exhilarating and defiant with bat and ball, giving more joy in thirty minutes than many give in three full days. He can also appear careless and indifferent, especially on lesser occasions. This machine has many gears and we, his watchers, always expect over-drive. Yet despite our occasional disappointments a Somerset or England team without ITB at five or six would seem strangely empty.'

We shall hear more from Canon Ward in due course. His view of Botham is shared by countless thousands in every cricket-playing country of the world, but is it the whole Botham? Is it right that this blazing, God-given talent should be seen in isolation, that it should be regarded as a justification for lapses of a more personal nature? That is what his critics ask.

2 THE BOY

Ian Terence Botham was born on 24 November 1955 at Heswall, Cheshire. In Test cricketing terms of a contemporary nature, the date's only significance was that it marked the end of the first Test ever played between India and New Zealand, on the Fateh Maidan, Hyderabad, where, on the actual day of Botham's entry into the world, Bert Sutcliffe saved New Zealand from defeat with a not-out innings of 137. In terms of the future course of world cricket, however, it was a momentous occasion.

When father Les retired from the Royal Navy around three years later, the family moved to Yeovil because Les had taken up post-service employment with Westland Helicopters – a firm to figure as prominently in politico-economic controversy in 1985–6 as Ian Botham was to loom over the cricket–showbusiness fraternity. The Westland affair was to bring about the resignation of two of Mrs Thatcher's cabinet ministers; Botham's flamboyant rampage across the pages of cricket history was to have equally dramatic consequences in his own field. But there was no hint of controversy, only of prodigious sporting talent, as the burly youngster went first to Milford Junior School near the family home in Yeovil, then to Buckler's Mead School in a pleasant hilltop suburb where the art master, John Horwood, was to experience one of the earliest manifestations of Botham's urgent need to be in the top echelon of everything. 'Everything sporting, that is,' explains John.

> He did not make much impression on me as an art student, but I had inherited a good badminton team

> and two of the outstanding players were Ian and his close friend, Robin Trevett. They were a brilliant doubles pairing, but Ian didn't leave anything to chance. I have known him cross off every name on a team I had posted on the notice board and put 'Botham and Trevett' instead. Probably he is best described as a likeable rogue.

George Rendell taught French, which meant that ITB was very much a non-starter in his academic sphere, but he too came up against the likeable rogue in a badminton context: 'I took a team to play at Wells Cathedral School, and when we came to have our meal I discovered that the sandwiches for six had all disappeared. A frenzied search finally established that Botham had eaten the lot when I found him smoking a cigarette in the dressing-room. He was always full of life and zest, yet there always seemed to be an ulterior motive . . . like nipping off to the Green Dragon for a pint.' (Licensees must be particularly tolerant in the Yeovil area since this was some time before Botham left school – at fifteen!) But he seems to have had a persuasive air about him since his invitation to masters to 'come and join him' at the local did not bring him six of the best. 'There were times when I found myself almost agreeing to do it,' recalls George Rendell. Who can tell what might have happened with a more old-fashioned approach to schoolmastering? Might it have curbed a naturally adventurous spirit? Or might it have induced some kind of basic respect for authority which, as we shall see, generally seems to have been missing from the Botham make-up?

At Buckler's Mead credit for the earliest coaching of the young Botham goes, by general consent, to a man called Dave Burge, who left teaching soon afterwards. But Ivor Twiss, a science laboratory technician at the school, may reasonably claim to have been one of the first to spot his potential:

> I remember saying to the Head, 'He'll play for England one day.' I had never seen a young man hit a cricket

ball like him, and when he bowled the ball used to *fizz* off the grass. You were expecting to strike the ball and suddenly it wasn't so much that as the ball hitting the bat, and hitting it pretty hard too. He was clearly a phenomenon. As for his development, a lot of credit must go to the Somerset Schools Cricket Association. There was a man called Reg Pitman who brought all these lads together – Ian, Phil Slocombe, Nigel Popplewell, Peter Roebuck. He lived in my village of Huish Episcopi and he travelled miles at his own expense, looking at these lads, taking them to matches. He's never really been given the credit he deserved. He was dedicated to cricket and it was through his sides that Ian came up. But he really had this tremendous talent in every way at such an early age – batting, bowling and throwing. He threw like a bullet. I used to go out on the playing field and practise with him, even if it was only throwing the ball to each other. He could hurl it to an enormous height and I'd stand there, underneath it, knowing I was going to get some awful stick if I dropped it.

John Horwood was the brave soul who took a party from school, including Ian Botham, on a cruise in the Mediterranean: 'He couldn't stand conformity at any price – he always had to do his own thing. On that trip he had a cine-camera which he used to leave about all over the place, so to try to teach him a lesson I hid it on one occasion. I wish I hadn't. As soon as he missed it he turned the whole ship, the *Devonia*, upside down. Not only the school party but the whole crew as well were press-ganged into the search.'

Botham has rarely in his whole life backed down from any physical confrontation, so if we can find one figure who struck terror into his soul it is worth recording. To do so we have to go back half his lifetime to the days when the family garden bordered on the playing-fields of Yeovil Grammar School. Net practice was always observed closely – no doubt yearningly – by the adolescent Botham who probably resented the organised nature of the grammar schoolboys' cricket while he could only stand and watch. (This was before he could count on the good-natured informality of a knockabout with Ivor Twiss.) To some extent he was able to bottle up the resentment by retaining any cricket balls which found their way from a grammar school practice into the Botham garden. And then it gave him a certain gleeful satisfaction to use these balls for one-man practice sessions on the forbidden territory of the grammar school playing-fields. But to do this he had to brave the wrath of the one man he feared above all – 'Jasper', the school caretaker. Jasper, the name perhaps coming from the archetypal villain of Victorian melodrama, was in fact one Alfred Ellery, a fine figure of an ex-Guardsman, who patrolled his territory as regularly and meticulously as a sentry on duty outside Buckingham Palace. It needed only one stentorian shout of 'Oi' to send any trespassing youngsters, or indeed the grammar schoolboys themselves, scuttling into hiding. And the young Botham, whether venturing on illegal cricket practice or in autumnal pursuit of horse-chestnut conkers, was no exception. That is a favourite memory of Fred Horn who took the grammar school under-fourteens for cricket and spurred them on to greater efforts with a nod in the direction of the younger boy watching enviously from his own garden: 'Come on. That lad over there is better than any of you.' And when in due course his team came up against Buckler's Mead, led by the 13-year-old Botham, he found it was only too true.

And so the foundations of the Botham legend were laid in one corner of the engineering town on the Somerset–Dorset border. At four he was already playing with a cricket ball; at nine he had decided that his career was to be that of a professional sportsman; at twelve he startled the organisers of a throwing-the-cricket-ball competition in London with a distance recorded as 207 ft 9 ins. Nearly 70 yards! At twelve years of age! Today a huge framed photograph hangs on the wall of the school's office block (mercifully in his pre-tinted-hair days and with the blazer in respectably MCC colours) with an inscription which reads simply but impressively: 'Ian Botham (1966–71), Buckler's Mead School. Captain of Somerset and England.'

The headmaster of Buckler's Mead during Ian's final year at school was Alun Morgan, and in some accounts of the Botham life story he has been credited with denouncing our hero as likely to be 'a wastrel all his life'. It is not only a slight misquotation, it is a classic case of being quoted out of context, so let us put that particular part of the record straight. Mr Morgan can recall only one brush with the David and Jonathan pairing of Botham and Trevett on a disciplinary matter. In the course of what he recalls as 'a stern lecture for silly and irresponsible behaviour' he told them they would never achieve anything in life if they continued to adopt such an unhelpful attitude. What in fact emerges from a chat with Mr Morgan is far from a write-off of Botham as a wastrel; he is understandably proud of what his former pupil has achieved, and delighted with the links between school and the Botham family. Brother Graeme, and sisters Dale and Wendy, all followed Ian at Buckler's Mead. His mother has been chairman of the school's Friends Association and has served on the governing body. 'The school,' says Mr Morgan, 'has enjoyed a very happy and long-lasting association with the whole Botham family and has derived great pleasure from the incredible success of a very talented former pupil.'

It was through Mrs Botham that the school obtained the photograph displayed in the administration block. Ian himself presented to the school a cricket trophy, and the reciprocal gesture was an oak coffee table bearing the badges of the school, of Somerset CCC and England. This was the work of Ivor Twiss, from whom we have heard, but who modestly omitted to mention his craftsmanship at the time. In all, it adds up to a partly affectionate, wholly admiring relationship between a school and its most distinguished old boy. There remains one significant point to be elicited from the headmaster: 'In the course of reprimanding Ian and Robin on that one occasion, I indicated that I would be informing their parents of the problems they had caused. There is no doubt in my mind that Ian would much have preferred to be caned, but as I had banned corporal punishment upon my arrival he had to be content with pressure from home and school. It seemed to be a very effective ploy . . . but he hated it.' That is something we might perhaps reflect upon as this story develops.

Tom Cartwright, who joined the Warwickshire staff in 1952 as an opening batsman 'who bowled a bit' and developed into one of the outstanding English medium-paced swing and seam bowlers of all time (who also batted a bit!) left the county in 1969 to coach at Millfield School. The following season he became a Somerset player by special registration. In the winter of 1970–1 he went with Bill Andrews, then Somerset's coach, more or less as an observer to a coaching session in the Millfield 'barracuda', an inflated dome of a sports arena, where twenty or thirty young cricketers were showing what they could do. In one corner he spotted a burly youngster in grey trousers and blue shirt hitting tennis balls with Brian Lobb (a former Warwickshire and Somerset fast bowler who was helping with the coaching). Cartwright turned to Brian Langford, then Somerset's captain, and said: 'That's the most talented kid in this place.' The boy was built almost like a man at fifteen years of age, but Tom noted that he was beautifully co-ordinated and 'had something that was a little bit different'. Bill Andrews asked him to come and have a look at another boy who was batting in another net. This was Phil Slocombe, and the Cartwright view was that he was a 'coached' player while the youngster he had spotted, Ian Botham, was very much a natural. 'Who is that lad?' asked Cartwright. 'Oh, don't bother about him,' was the reply, 'he's just a kid from the sticks.'

'I want to know who he is, Bill,' insisted Cartwright. 'He's the most interesting boy I've seen here.' But the amiable Andrews was intent on showing off the youthful batting talent of Philip Anthony Slocombe, of Weston-super-Mare Grammar School and Millfield School. 'His name's "Bottom" or something,' was as much information as he could provide about Cartwright's choice of the most gifted natural player in the dome. But Tom remembered . . .

On 23 May 1971, Somerset were engaged in a John Player League game against Lancashire at Yeovil, where the county secretary's office was in a tent. 'Jimmy' James, a popular and efficient secretary of, successively, Somerset, Lancashire and Hampshire, was sitting there when the flap was pulled aside and a man looked in, followed by a youngster, well built with huge hands. The elder man said, 'This is my son Ian and he wants to play cricket for Somerset and England.'

The 15-year-old Botham impressed Jimmy with his size and his ambition – 'and England' did not go unnoticed, either. Close, before he became captain, and Tom Cartwright both took a look at young Ian and Cartwright in particular quickly sized up his potential as something out of the ordinary. As the boy was too young to be taken on to the county staff it was arranged that he should go to Lord's for at least a year there. However, Ian's father, Les, was determined that his boy should serve an apprenticeship in a trade so that if a career in cricket should prove to be out of Ian's reach he would always have some skills and qualifications to fall back on. He was, in fact, firm about this, and it took a good deal of persuasion before he allowed Ian to go to Lord's without having been indentured in a trade. After twelve months the chief coach (Len Muncer) recommended a further year on the ground staff at headquarters and at the end of 1973 Muncer telephoned Jimmy James. The conversation went like this:

Muncer: 'Are Somerset going to offer Ian Botham a contract for 1974?'

James: 'We have not considered it. He is a bit young and really needs more experience.'

Muncer: 'Well, we've taught him all we can and I am not sure we want to try and teach him any more. If Somerset do not offer him something, then some other county will.'

Jimmy reported this conversation to his Committee, who were faced with a major problem. They had a whole crop of youngsters of outstanding promise who had developed through the schoolboy channel and a young West Indian named Vivian Richards was just about to complete his twelve months' residence qualification. And there was little or no money in the kitty. After a lot of heartsearching the committee decided to offer a one-year contract to Vic Marks, Peter Roebuck, Trevor Gard, Philip Slocombe – and Ian Botham. It was a decision which Jimmy James saw as 'courageous' because Somerset's finances were far from healthy. They were taking a big chance but it paid off – my, *how* it was to pay off in the next ten years or so. In 1974, Somerset finished fifth in the County Championship, runners-up to Leicester in the John Player League, and made semi-final appearances in both Benson and Hedges and Gillette Cups. It was the shape of things to come.

Jimmy James recalls driving the healthy young Botham from Taunton to Macclesfield in Cheshire to play a match for Somerset's second team and stopping on the M6 at the Hilton Park service area north of Birmingham.

> I enjoyed a modest breakfast of tea and toast, while Ian demolished (the only word for it) the biggest plate of eggs, sausages, bacon and the rest that I have ever seen. He also needed an extra round of toast before we could get back on to the motorway to resume our journey. His first full season at Somerset was my last before moving to Old Trafford. I remember him as a very hard worker, both on and off the field. He was desperately anxious to be a success. He learned quickly and had a great admiration for Brian Close and Tom Cartwright, though he was never slow to express *his* opinion, even to those two seasoned professionals.

Fifteen years later, there is still a certain excitement in Tom Cartwright's voice as he remembers the 'terrific little group' of young players he coached at Somerset – Botham, Slocombe, Peter Roebuck, Vic Marks, Jeremy Lloyds,

Colin Dredge and later Trevor Gard, the wicket-keeper. And in the winter between Botham's two years at Lord's (1972 and 1973) he was able to work on the young man from Yeovil again. It was on one of these occasions that Tom asked, 'How much bowling do you get at Lord's?' Botham, with a touch of resentment, replied, 'Very little. They treat my bowling as a joke. They even take the mickey about it.'

'Right,' said Cartwright. 'I think you could be a more than useful fast-medium bowler and, if you are prepared to work, I am prepared to work with you.' Tom remembers the conversation vividly. Botham told him eagerly, 'Yes. I'd like to bowl, I want to bowl.'

'Fine,' said Cartwright, and Botham the bowler was born. He was a willing pupil. 'He might not be the brightest in some ways,' recalls Cartwright, 'but he had a very able brain for absorbing information and putting it into practice. I found him not only a willing pupil but an ideal one, and he learned to swing the ball both ways as quickly as anyone I have ever talked to.'

So much for the Cartwright influence. What of Botham's two years on the Lord's ground staff? It was here that we see a further development in that sporting personality which was always – except in certain circumstances – going to have its own individually rebellious character. Ian won the highest marks in the history of the ceremony for his resistance to the initiation rites of an MCC Young Cricketer! This was a time-honoured tradition involving a certain physical discomfort, not to mention affront to personal dignity, at the hands of a band of rather fit and physical young men quartered at NW8. They had a lot of trouble with 'Both'. At the end of his two years there his coach, Len Muncer, reported: 'An outstanding cricketer who shows a good deal of promise but does everything his own way. He needs a lot of guidance and is proving better with bat than with ball.' Botham himself would have argued then (as he will argue today at the suggestion that he might be less than the best at *whatever* he does), but most of those who have followed his career closely might feel that

Muncer's judgment was a shrewd piece of character assessment. Six years later, when Ian's international career was well and truly launched, Brian Close was to forecast that Botham's bowling would get no better and might actually deteriorate, but of his batting: 'There is no limit to what he might achieve.' The figures might tell a different story, but figures are not always the best yardstick and in terms of bowling that is very much the case with Ian Botham. In due course we shall consult a number of authorities on why and how his bowling changed, but in general terms most cricket pundits might agree that Close's prophecy hit the nail right on the head.

By the time Botham returned from Lord's (where, incidentally, his football interests had made him into a Chelsea fan) the Somerset Committee knew they had a young player of outstanding promise on their books, but they were not unaware that he might prove a bit of a handful as far as behaviour was concerned. They felt they could cope with that, but first came those golden years when there was not too much to worry about in terms of discipline. He had two mentors of entirely different natures. Close might be very much older than Botham but he was a very tough 41-year-old indeed, and as captain he would not tolerate any precociousness at all from a fledgeling, however gifted. Cartwright too was considerably older and immensely gifted both as a player and a teacher. There was so much in both men for Ian to respect, and that is what we shall see he has needed at every stage of his career. Respect for others takes different forms, depending upon the individuals concerned, and I think it can be seen throughout his life that when there was no one around to command his respect the wheels have come off his own life.

However, we are still in September 1973. Botham is back from his two years in London and he goes into Somerset's first eleven for the first time at Hove, in a John Player League match against Sussex. He is out, lbw, for 2. His bowling figures are no wicket for 22 and he holds one catch at deep square leg. The following Sunday, at the Oval, he gets no runs at all against Surrey, has one wicket for 14 and that comes from a full toss. Not, perhaps, the most glittering portent of future greatness, but wait! The catch at Hove dismisses Tony Greig, soon to become captain of England. The wicket he takes at the Oval is that of Geoffrey Howarth, later to be one of New Zealand's outstanding Test captains. Is there not something in that for the soothsayers to seize upon? One final point as we look for signs which hint at the future of this young man. He described his delivery to dismiss Howarth as 'a crap ball', a phrase which was to be applied from time to time in his career by Ian himself. But let anyone else apply it and great would be the wrath of I. T. Botham. Acceptance of criticism, however well-founded, was never to be his strong suit.

3 THE FOOTBALLER

There is no doubt that Botham was a rather more than useful association footballer as a schoolboy. He was big and powerful for his age and he was, as he continued to show in every aspect of his sporting life, a natural and aggressive competitor. Legend, and a certain amount of official biographical material, has it that he had to make a choice in his teenage years between football and cricket as a career. Bert Head (a Somerset man himself), then manager of Crystal Palace, received a scout's report on the burly youth from Yeovil which said he had 'all the skills' and he 'always wanted to be a winner'. Mr Head may even have offered terms to Botham to serve his apprenticeship as a professional footballer. Whether it would have been a successful career, given that he had started from scratch and learned his trade under professional supervision, is something we shall never know. It does, however, seem rather less than likely in view of what happened when Ian finally realised his ambition to play League football.

By this time he was married, living in the South Humberside (North Lincolnshire to those who prefer their geography untainted by modern terminology) village of Epworth, and thus his local side was Scunthorpe United. He was on friendly terms with the United players and it was Vince Grimes, also a notable local cricketer, who first brought about a closer personal relationship between Botham and the football club. At first, Ian was content to use the facilities there to help him keep fit when he was neither playing in the English cricket season nor touring abroad, but it is hard to see this as his only goal. There had to be a burning desire to get involved in the more competitive aspects of club activities.

There is an interesting Lincolnshire parallel here with Freddie Trueman, who in 1952 and 1953 did his National Service in the RAF at Hemswell. In fact it was from there that he went to play in his first Test against India at Headingley in 1952 and was 75 per cent responsible for that historic second innings scoreboard of 'India: 0 for four wickets', three of them to Trueman in eight deliveries. Fred was keen on his football and fancied himself as a goal-scoring forward, so that very shrewd manager Bill Anderson, at Lincoln City, signed him up to play, when available, on winter Saturday afternoons. The result was that City's reserve-team matches were soon attracting twice the 'gate' which watched the senior side.

Perhaps something of this was in the back of Ron Ashman's mind when the then Scunthorpe United manager signed Botham as a non-contract player in 1979. It couldn't do any harm, and it might conceivably do the club some financial good. And so it turned out after Ian's first appearance for the reserve side against Notts County, a game in which he was due to be marked by a renowned defender whose uncompromising attitude towards his duties had earned him the name of 'Killer'. Manager Ashman, finding himself short of second-team players, included Botham in his side with a whispered prayer that '"Killer" might not kill England's outstanding cricketer'.

Bob Steels, the experienced soccer reporter with the *Evening Telegraph*, describes Botham (with a smile which robs the remark of any venom) thus: 'As a League footballer he was a pretty good cricketer.' But very quickly he adds,

> As a team man, a club man, he was absolutely marvellous. He was the life and soul of the dressing-room. Even when he was not in the side I have known him go on the coach, on long trips to places like Hartlepool, and keep everyone laughing. It meant a great deal to a struggling side to have a world-famous cricketer on board, especially as he just wanted to be one of them,

one of the footballing boys. He wasn't quite quick enough off the mark as a striker and, much as he liked being in the thick of things up front, he agreed promptly when he was asked to play as a defender. And this was probably better for him. He had an absolutely fearless attitude – he would never dream of pulling out of a tackle – but his build was not really ideal for a professional footballer. Yet as a sportsman he had to be quite unique.

He was at the very top as a cricketer and Scunthorpe were in desperate trouble. Botham brought to them that same determination to win that he has always shown on the cricket field and that in itself lifted the side. He never tried to cash in on his fame as a cricketer. I have known him come out of the dressing-room with his team-mates and be surrounded by kids clamouring for his autograph. His reply was always the same: '*These* [indicating the Scunthorpe players] are the lads you want to sign your books. They've been out there doing it all.'

Injuries in the club kept him in contention for a second-team place after his first appearance and then, after one or two fixtures with the senior side as a substitute, Ian *started* a first-team game for the first time against Wigan on 12 March 1982. The result was a 2–7 home defeat! But he stayed in the team as a striker for the next three games. By the end of 1983 (with a cricket tour looming ahead) he had been converted into a centre-back with a moderate degree of success, and he took part in an FA Cup second-round victory over Bury which filled him with excitement. The Christmas fixtures also found him busily involved, despite the fact that England were due to set out on a three-month tour to Fiji, New Zealand and Pakistan – a tour which was to culminate spectacularly for Botham, though not as a cricketer – on 29 December.

Donald Carr, secretary of the Test and County Cricket Board, wrote to Botham asking him not to play to avoid risking the possibility of injury. Botham not only played, but he clearly did not hold back because he was booked by the referee, Mr Gilbert Napthe of Loughborough, for a tackle which was described by press men as 'more clumsy than vindictive'. No, Botham was always going to do it *his* way. When the tour party gathered at Gatwick on 29 December, Bob Willis, the captain, was asked if he had been concerned at the risks taken by his star performer. With that characteristic shrug of the shoulders which formed a major part of his answer to any question about Botham, the captain replied, 'Both's Both, isn't he? He's already turned up for one tour with his arm in a sling so I suppose you've got to be prepared for these things.' This was a reference to the start of a previous trip abroad when the injury was officially described as a result of Ian accidentally putting his hand through a glass door!

The 1984–5 season saw Botham the footballer playing largely in mid-week games for Scunthorpe reserves. This was not enough for his restless appetite for sporting involvement, especially at weekends, so he departed amicably to try his luck with Yeovil, in one of the less exotic areas of non-League football, while remaining registered as a non-contract player on Scunthorpe United's books. He left behind a lot of friends and no shortage of admirers of the way he had been content to be just one of the boys in a soccer camp. His novelty value had by this time worn a little thin with the footballing public of Scunthorpe, and they had stopped ringing up the local paper to ask if the cricketing star was included in the football side for next Saturday. But there is no doubt about the regard Ian built up amongst that public by his willingness to turn out with footballers much more modestly endowed with talent than he was as a cricketer, with little thought of rewards beyond a lot of bruises.

But we have moved ahead of ourselves with that short detour into soccer. Cricket was destined to be his game as far as Somerset were concerned from that June day in 1974 when he first changed the whole course of a match. He completed his part in that season's campaign with 441 runs at an average of 16.96, but, remember, at that time he was primarily seen as a bowler of the third-seamer type who could also bat a bit. His 30 wickets cost 24.63 and he marked up the first of his five-wickets-in-an-innings performances. He took 15 catches. In 1975 he played in twenty-two first-class matches (four more than the previous season, taking 62 wickets at 27.48, 18 catches, and scoring 584 runs with a highest innings total of 65. He was, it should be noted, still in the lower part of the batting order, but his reputation for giving the ball an almighty thump was growing. The following year (1976) his captain moved him up the order and he obliged by topping 1000 runs as well as taking 66 wickets (his first ten-in-a-match performance) and holding 16 catches. Ian Botham was by now firmly established as a county all-rounder of considerable accomplishments.

Brian Close was granted a testimonial by Somerset that year and, as another of my friends, Farokh Engineer, was taking one in Lancashire, I decided to stage a Celebrity–Amateur golf day at my home club in Morecambe. It was a happy occasion, with fifty-three sporting personalities from Test and county cricket, Rugby Union, Rugby League, association football and snooker – by far the greatest gathering of stars Morecambe had ever seen. Some enthusiasts wanted a practice round on the day before the tournament, and a four was made up of Philip Sharpe, Geoff Miller, Ian Botham and myself. 'Both' had recently taken up the game and announced that his handicap was 24. He stood on the first tee and drove his opening shot to the apron in front of the first green, a distance of around 320 yards. A startled member, watching originally with idle curiosity, gaped in disbelief and rushed across to ask: 'Who the hell is that?'

'His name's Botham,' I replied. 'He's a promising young cricketer from Somerset.'

'Cricketer?' muttered the member. 'He wants to forget about playing cricket!' The stakes for our practice round were hastily adjusted and I broke it gently to 'Both' that there would be a handicap limit on 'the day' of 18. He protested, but the rule stood. He came home on Sunday with 44 Stableford points to win the competition by one point from the Australian, Neil Hawke – who played off one!

After the practice round I took my three friends, along with the new Mrs Botham, to a local restaurant which specialised in king-sized meals and challenged anyone to clear a plate of its farmhouse grill. This consisted of steak, lamp chop, pork chop, sausage, ham and eggs, mushrooms, onion-rings, tomatoes – the further one dug down, the more delights were revealed. The chips came in a separate dish. 'Both' not only cleared his plate in the shortest time the proprietor had ever known; he was looking hungrily across the table where Kathy was toying delicately with an egg mayonnaise and asking if she needed any help with that! Here was a young man who was obviously destined to do everything in a big way. After the tournament itself, a snooker match went on long into the night with John Spencer partnering one of the Morecambe members, Jack Ridehalgh (to whom century breaks were not unknown), against F. S. Trueman and Farokh Engineer. The games room was crowded and the conversation which punctuated the snooker provided better cabaret than anything our seaside resort had ever known from professional theatrical entertainers. It was a very happy day for everyone. I have lost count of the times that I have looked back to it over the years when personal relationships with Ian Botham have become less cordial, wishing that we could put the clock back and start all over again. Two years later, when I organised a similar day for the Benefit of David Lloyd, of Lancashire, 'Both' joined us again and was mightily piqued to be pipped for first prize – by Neil Hawke. But once again he was voted a thundering good lad by Morecambe Golf Club members and his cricket career has always been followed with more than passing interest by certain golfers in the north-west of England. By that time he was an established England player but he was still happy to enjoy a round of golf with anyone. As always, he was a natural competitor.

His relationship with his Somerset captain was a close one which became closer when Ian met the young lady who was to become his wife. Brian and Vivienne Close had known Gerry and Jan Waller for ten years when I. T. Botham entered their lives. The Wallers' daughter, Kathryn, idolised 'Uncle Brian', kept a picture of him on her dressing table and acted as a baby sitter after young Lynne Close arrived, followed by their son, Lance. So when the Wallers, together with Kathy and her sister Lindsay, went to watch Brian play for Somerset in a game at Grace Road, Leicester, and Kathy became interested in the burly young all-rounder in the side, Close, you might think, might have shown an avuncular pleasure? Not a bit of it.

In fact Close regarded the burgeoning romance with much the same enthusiasm as Mr Barrett (of Wimpole Street) greeted the suit of Robert Browning. In typically forthright terms he addressed the young couple: 'For a start-off, you [Botham] are not good enough for Kathryn. And you [Kathy] will ruin his career. You're both too young.' Mr Waller was not consulted on the matter – at least not by Closey, who regarded himself firmly as being *in loco parentis*. Ten years later, however, he was happy to express his unqualified pleasure at the way Kathy set out to be a model cricket wife: 'She did everything for him . . . his packing, his correspondence, handled their finances. She's a smashing lass.' And never have I known anyone to disagree with that.

And what of Close's relationship with Botham the player?

> We had to instil a bit of discipline into him at first. In that first season, 1974, he was bowling in a John Player game which was getting a bit tight. A ball was driven back to him.
>
> He stopped it with one hand as the players set off for a daft single and took a pot shot at the stumps, full power. Fortunately it hit the stumps but I gave him hell. 'You've got to use your bloody brains,' I told him. 'If that had missed it could have cost us five

runs. If you get in that situation again, pick the bloody thing up and run to the stumps. Don't take a chance on giving runs away.' I had to keep an eye on him all the time because he could be totally irresponsible. At that time we looked on him as more important to us as a bowler. Tom Cartwright did a tremendous amount for him. Tom was probably one of the greatest bowlers ever to play in first-class cricket and he helped Ian no end. I used to concentrate on trying to help him with his batting. If he got himself out when he was going well I wanted to know what he had been thinking about because he did let his concentration slip. When he got that first century in 1976 I had to keep talking to him, reminding him to keep his mind on what he was doing. It's a hell of a thing, getting your first hundred. It's a great obstacle to get over. He used to answer back a bit. He was a bit cocky at times. But I always had the last word.

And how did Close manage that? 'Oh, easy. I just told him to bloody well shut his mouth.' It is not difficult to see why the two of them got on well together – they spoke the same language!

To this day there is a special bond between the two. Each has got on the other's nerves at times but – certainly with Close – there is a considerable affection for the younger man, a genuine regard: 'He never dreamed about records when he was a lad. They never entered his head. It's reading so much about them that started him thinking on those lines. I know he does some daft things at times but at heart he's a good lad. He would never see you stabbed in the back; he would never see a pal done down.'

If Close's relationship with Botham was built on foundations of physical strength with a certain sentimental attachment, Tom Cartwright's can probably be best described as primarily cerebral with a touch of avuncular affection. He had seen natural gifts and all his instincts as a coach cried out to see them develop. Close, with none of the instincts of a qualified coach, believed that a bellowed rebuke on the field allied to his personal form of leadership by example, was the way to 'bring on' a young player.

Cartwright, with the teacher's eye and philosophy, did not see things in that simplistic way. He remembers that,

> Somerset had finished bottom of everything in 1969. They had no money – I actually worked for them from April to the end of June before I got my first cheque – and the club was low in spirit, in morale, everything. They brought in some players like myself, Derek Taylor and then Closey, and it was a breath of fresh air just afterwards to see this local boy, who wasn't introverted and wasn't a part of this run of 'no success'. I felt, and I have always felt, that he has always needed someone to help him. He needed someone whom he respected to grab him occasionally by the scruff of the neck and say, 'Look, *stop*.' And he hasn't had that for so much of his career. Closey and I left within a year or so, and then it was always going to be like a serpent without a head. It was always going to be a good side because we had got such a good bunch of players together, but no control. Ian was the sort of bloke who needed that. There was all that ability to be channelled but there were the times when you wanted to say 'Stop.'
>
> When he was done for having drugs in his house, it was almost with something like second sight that I thought, 'If they can channel things in the right direction there was something good going to come out of it.' I felt that he, more than anybody, could reverse the present-day trend in young people because he has such a tremendous following. And I felt something good *was* going to come out of it. Now, 'the Walk', no matter how people want to put him down and sneer about the reasons why he did it, was a tremendous effort, you know. That was Ian and I have tremendous admiration that he got together all the people involved and that he actually did it. He needed to be told he had done a good job.

I talked to Ian at some length in a game at Swansea, shortly after he had come back from his tour of the West Indies when he was captain, and he was badly in need of reassurance. In fact I suggested he came off the field with boot trouble so we could talk. There was no boot trouble but he came off just the same and we sat and talked for about twenty minutes, I suppose, and it was really a matter of giving him a boost and getting him to feel that he *could* still go out and do it. Shortly after that Michael [Brearley] came back as England captain and something clicked. He was impressed with the brain of Brearley. If he saw ability, in whatever direction, he would show respect for it. As a kid, he probably thought I could bowl and that was the sort of thing which took on. Closey was a big name and a big personality and although Ian argued with him he still rated Brian. Then when Michael came into his life a little later it was his intelligence which impressed him as much as anything. I think he has been short of people over recent years of that type, people he could look up to a little bit. You can say, 'He's thirty and he ought to be beyond that,' but he's *always* going to need that.

There's one other point which I think may be significant. When he was in that little nucleus of young boys at Somerset there was Roebuck and Slocombe from Millfield and Marks and Lloyds who were at Blundell's School, and people don't realise that it put him in a mix of players from different backgrounds. It wasn't as easy for Ian as people think. He was struggling to get to the top of that particular pile, if you like. He didn't make a fuss about it, didn't let it show, but I have always felt that people didn't really understand how somebody from his background had to push and struggle against the others from different backgrounds. That is not to say that Ian had a *bad* background, but it was a very ordinary one compared with some of the people he was competing with. I am not saying he has got an inferiority complex, because he's completely insensitive (that's one of his problems) but whether it's in his sub-conscious or not, it's always been there, that struggle to get to the top of the pile.

I have tremendous admiration for what he has achieved and a lot of the things he does. He'll exasperate you in the next second, but I found that I could say what I wanted to him – I could bollock him without him wanting to have a go back at me. I can remember being at a meeting at Lord's when Ian was captain of England and he walked into the room where we were having lunch. And he didn't have a tie on. I watched, and no one said anything, but I couldn't stand it any longer. I walked across to him and I really gave him hell. We had that sort of relationship.

One other influence upon his life in Taunton has certainly been Vivian Richards, and it has always been a strange sort of mixed-up relationship – half close personal friendship, half hero-worship – with Ian as the small boy looking with shining eyes at the awe-inspiring ability of the West Indian who is three and a half years older. Richards had to hang around for more than a year before his registration as a Somerset player was approved at Lord's, and he burst thunderously on to the county scene in 1974 with 1223 runs in his first season.

In their entirely different ways, Ian and Vivian Richards became established as stars of the new-look Somerset in the mid-seventies and simultaneously the two of them became firm friends, a friendship which has endured and indeed strengthened during a period when they have become ever fiercer rivals in Test cricket. Botham has been influenced by Richards as a cricketer in a dozen different ways, and even when they play together for Somerset nothing gives Ian greater pleasure than to outdo his friend as a batsman of the most spectacular kind. In the middle of the seventies they were joined, to make the most extraordinary *ménage à trois* in cricket, by a man called Peter McCoombe, soon known universally as 'Jock'. He was a corpulent Scot who had had a previous association with

Manchester United footballers, for whom he carried out an assortment of errands. In Taunton he became established as a sort of aide (some people had a less flattering term for his role) to Botham and Richards, and by the turn of the decade he was very much a part of the Somerset CCC scene, so much so that he was finally taken on the ration-strength of the Club in a role which seemed to other players to be more or less that of a servant-cum-errand-boy to the two stars. He figures in our story on one or two later occasions.

It was not until 1976 that Botham scored his maiden century in county cricket – the key to so many successful first-class careers – and then it was a big one, 167 not out at Trent Bridge; it won the match for Somerset in a race against the clock. Captain Close, a man not given to fulsome compliments, described it as 'worth going miles to see'. Two-thirds of the way through that marvellously sunny summer, England's Selectors gave Ian his first taste of international cricket by picking him for two of the three one-day internationals. At Scarborough he wore England colours for the first time but scored only one run, batting at number seven, and his three overs cost 26 runs for the wicket of Lawrence Rowe. At Edgbaston, the wicket of Michael Holding cost him 31 runs in only three overs and, again at number seven, he scored 20 runs.

England lost both games but in that summer we saw something of the omnipotence of the West Indies which was to extend over so many of the future years. They scored massively in all five Tests, winning three and drawing the other two. Who will readily forget the batting of Richards at Trent Bridge and the Oval, the two centuries of Greenidge at Old Trafford, or Holding's brilliant bowling on a completely unresponsive wicket at the Oval to take eight for 92 and six for 57 in the final Test? In that series they used various permutations of Holding, Roberts, Holder, Daniel and Julien to provide a four-man fast attack, but somehow it was not quite of the white-hot hostility that we were to see in the next few years and it *was* on English wickets. Nevertheless, it was a foretaste of what was to come and, notwithstanding all the threats this presented, the 21-year-old Botham had seen enough of international cricket to give him what was to prove an insatiable appetite for it. He burned with ambition, seethed with impatience and at the end of a season which saw him score 1000 first-class runs for the first time (once Close had moved him up the order) to go with his 66 wickets and 16 catches, he was on his way. He couldn't wait for the 1977 season to start.

In the early weeks of the season, when most cricket journalists like to begin an early speculation about the men who will represent England in the Tests, I began (one amongst several) to mention the name of Ian Terence Botham as a prospect. This brought a rebuke from two close friends, who between them won more than 100 England caps, that I was talking a load of rubbish. Botham, they insisted, was 'not a Test player's backside'. In view of the career which followed I shall spare the blushes of them both by withholding their names, but it might interest Ian himself (in view of his insistence that Test players may only be criticised or chosen by their peers) to know that it was most certainly said in June 1977. A month later, he had been called up and during Australia's first innings, on 28 and 29 July at Trent Bridge, he took five wickets for 74 in his twenty overs – his first Test bowling – and England won by seven wickets. A fortnight after that he took five for 21 at Headingley to play a major role in England's win by an innings and 85 runs. England had regained the Ashes, and when the series ended on 30 August the Post Office's Test scores services had received 22,556,000 calls. This rekindling of interest in international cricket may not have been exclusively due to the presence in the side for two of the Tests of Ian Botham, but his performances over the next ten years were certainly going to give rise to a few million more calls!

4 THE TOURIST

Botham's first tour as an England player was to Pakistan and New Zealand, starting in November 1977. He was *hors de combat* for the first few games because of an accident just before the party assembled in London. It did not take him long to make an impact in another way. On the second night of a sixteen-week tour he exchanged blows with Steve Whiting, cricket correspondent of the *Sun*, in the entrance to the hotel where we were staying, and on the third night he caused what might modestly be described as 'a scene' in the Embassy Staff Club in Islamabad. It was not a promising beginning for a first-time tourist, and the senior member of the press corps thought it might be politic to advise Ken Barrington, the most genial and pleasant of managers, to keep a close if avuncular eye on this explosive young man; possibly as a direct result of this nothing of a similar dramatic nature occurred during the next four months. It is a long time for between thirty and forty players, officials and reporters to be cooped up together, and the friendly spirit which existed throughout the tour was a model for what all tours should be like.

That one, sadly, marked the end of an era. It was the last tour on which we were able to enjoy the close personal friendships which existed between some players and some writers/broadcasters. In 1977–8 we not only travelled in the same aircraft and stayed in the same hotels, but we travelled between airports and hotels in the same bus. If a reporter came down to breakfast and found three players at a table with one vacant place he joined the players, knowing he would be welcome. It was exactly the same in reverse: no player hesitated about joining three journalists. It was a happy relationship which had existed since Jim Swanton and his colleagues had founded the Cricket Writers' Club thirty years earlier on the first tour to Australia after the war. There was rarely, if ever, a case of intrusion. If players wanted to talk of private matters it was immediately understood and one moved on to another table and was quickly joined by other players not, at that moment, needing privacy.

The same sort of thing happened on social occasions. We each had our own friendships with certain players and it was an entirely natural thing to arrange off-duty outings with those friends. It was wholly in the natural order of things for a player to knock on the door of a reporter and ask, 'Do you fancy a game of cards?' Or it might be Scrabble – much in vogue when we were staying in the more remote parts of Pakistan. Or someone might be opening a precious bottle of Scotch, or have been invited out to dinner with the request, 'Bring two or three of the boys.' A case in point: a banker wanted to throw a little dinner party during our stay in Rawalpindi 'for four or five of you'. Chris Old, Bob Taylor and Geoff Miller came along with me without a second's hesitation. In a socially blank week in a pretty desperate hotel in Hyderabad, I was *expected* to make up an evening Scrabble four with Miller, Brian Rose and Graham Roope, and very glad I was to do so. When, in New Zealand, I was invited to take an early-morning flight around Mount Cook and asked to bring along a couple of friends, Steve Whiting and Phil Edmonds were the two who joined me. We all mingled happily together on the best possible terms and touring was a very great pleasure. Even in the direst spots we found solace in mutual laughter. The team-room was the players' personal domain and one did not go there except by invitation (in fact there was no intrusion, no overstepping the mark on either side) but at Christmas in Lahore we not only had a joint party in the team-room but had a golf tournament on the hotel's nine-hole course in which all the players' and journalists' names went into a hat together for the pairings.

If there was a hiccough at all in this entirely pleasant and relaxed situation it occurred in Christchurch, New Zealand, on rest day in the Second Test. A party of us, all harmoniously mixed together, spent the first part of the day jet-boating on the Waimakariri River and the second half being royally entertained in typical New Zealand fashion at the home of (Sir) Alan Wright, uncle of John Wright. Here, Botham – exhilarated no doubt by the activities of the morning – found it necessary for the enhancement of his pleasure to push everyone, preferably when fully clothed, into the swimming pool. Not everyone enjoyed it, but Ian's water fetishism was something one gradually learned to live with. (I remember, three years later, leaving behind watch, wallet, papers – all but the barest essentials – before embarking on an evening cruise off Barbados because it was inevitable that someone would be pushed overboard.) But looking back to 1977–8 in the light of what was to happen in the future to player–press relationships is little short of heart-breaking. What, then, caused that near-Utopian state of affairs to come to an end? Firstly, and most importantly, Kerry Packer happened.

The rewards available for Packer mercenaries, flying around Australia in the winter of 1977–8 and playing matches which owed more to P. T. Barnum (and, perhaps, the emperor Nero) than anyone else, were substantially higher than anything which had been possible for cricketers anywhere else in the world. The time had come for sponsored Test cricket, and it arrived in England in 1978 with the Cornhill Insurance Company. From the first, Cornhill set out to do it right. They gave a contract to a firm of public relations consultants, West Nally, who set up an information service and hospitality facility which was wholly admirable, and remained so when it was taken over by Karen Earl Associates. Tour pay for England players went up from £3000 to £5000, and in home Tests the match fee was increased from £210 to £1000. Umpires, too, benefited from an increase in Test fees from £175 to £750 per match. Now, it was not Cornhill's fault that these sharp increases in pay created a wide gap between the wages of Test players and those of what one might call the bread-and-butter cricketers of the county championship sides. Cornhill were specifically sponsoring the Test series and they were, therefore, concerned with Test players. In some ways the effect was admirable in that it elevated Test cricket to a level of élitism which was what many people wanted to see. But the knock-on effects of the new wage-scale were considerable – and not entirely for the good of the game. *They were to play a vitally important part in the deterioration of player–media relations.* This was no direct fault of Cornhill, by any stretch of imagination, and it would be unfair to claim that it could have been foreseen by their advisers. We all thought cricket was too decent and wholesome a game for it to happen. But it did.

It now became a matter of the greatest financial importance to be selected for Tests and, more important still, to *stay* in the side once selected. There had always been a certain amount of mild and (it was thought) harmless speculation and forecasting when the time for Test selection came around – in newspapers, on radio and, occasionally, on TV. This now began to be seen as not quite so mild and harmless. Rightly or wrongly, players believe that Selectors are influenced by what they read in their newspapers. Selectors deny it but without any great conviction. Cricket-writers, generally speaking, see a lot more cricket than Selectors; they spend longer hours at the matches they attend than most Selectors can afford; and they spend more time talking to players and, in particular, to captains and colleagues and umpires *about* players who might be Test prospects. It would be rather silly of Selectors *not* to read such speculation and, once they have done, it becomes very difficult not to retain the comments which have been read, at least in the subconscious. Players, therefore, have a point in believing that the views of certain critics play a part, no matter how slight, in helping Selectors make up their minds.

It follows, therefore – and most certainly it began to follow from 1978 onwards – that if some doubt is cast upon the current form of one player while attention is drawn to the rise to prominence of another, the player in the first category is going to feel he is being 'written out' of a Test side. While Test fees remained at a relatively modest distance from those enjoyed by county men there was always, it seemed, a generally philosophical acceptance of the influence of critics – real or imagined. Once Test fees had rocketed, however, a far greater significance was placed upon the cricket-writer's comments. In the context of cricket (if not to a comparable degree with pop music, golf and tennis) regular membership of a Test side elevated a player into the superstar class and the fringe benefits began to flow. No one wanted that flow to subside; no one, consequently, wanted to be dropped from a Test side and anyone who wrote or broadcast words which (it might be thought) led to the loss of Test status was now going to be rather less popular than he might have been before. This was an attitude which was not confined to individual players who were, or might be, left out; it spread through whole squads because each player now thought, 'Next time it might be me.'

So what were the cricket journalists to do? Change their whole approach to their job? That was unthinkable. The requirements of the position had not changed because wages had gone up to a startling degree. There were still lots of honest, decent cricketers who accepted the position of the critic, and there were still players who respected the views of individual critics. But the general *bonhomie*, the fundamental goodwill between players and media, began to be eroded from 1978 onwards. And ironically, one of the principal disciples of this new cricketing apartheid, seemed to me (as someone who had got along with him pretty well) to be I. T. Botham. It was ironical, because the one man whose place never seemed to be remotely in jeopardy was 'Both' himself. And that, for at least four years, was fair enough.

Once established as a regular Test player after his return

from Pakistan/New Zealand in 1978, Botham's form was consistently magnificent: his 100th Test wicket *v.* India in two years nine days at the top, his 1000th run little over three weeks later, his 200th wicket in four years thirty-four days and the two great centuries of the 1981 series against Australia, then 2000 runs – on it went. After 1982, however, it has to be asked: would his record as a wicket-taker have been as impressive if Botham had not played so many Tests in such rapid succession? Were there not times in 1982, 1983, 1984, and 1985 when his Test form warranted his being given a rest? It would certainly have been the case with almost any other player who has ever worn England's colours. That is something which we might examine in closer detail later, but in New Zealand, in 1978, the path to glory was just beginning to stretch before him.

His first Test in that country brought the sobering experience of being part of England's first-ever defeat by a New Zealand side. The cross had to be borne principally by Boycott, the unfortunate captain, but the game was interesting in quite another way because it brought into opposition for the first time two men who were destined to be involved in a deep-seated personal rivalry for the next eight years – Ian Botham and Richard Hadlee. They were just about as unlike as any pair can be: Botham, burly and bulky – the gorilla; Hadlee, lean and sinewy – the panther. Botham, loud, flamboyant, a creature of impulse; Hadlee, quiet, intense, thinking about every ball as part of a campaign, much as the great spinners used to do. Botham, needing an evening party of Roman dimensions as earnestly as he needed food and drink; Hadlee, one social beer with the boys, then home to his family. Watching the two of them from the sidelines at the Basin Reserve, Wellington, on 10 February 1978, one could see them sizing each other up, perhaps each seeing potential greatness in the other. It was something we sensed, rather than observed.

The two had met for the first time a week earlier when England played the Canterbury provincial side in Christchurch. It was rain-affected but in the second innings Hadlee had scored a lusty 56, mostly at Botham's expense, and 'Both' has always had a long memory for that sort of thing. He also had a rather patronising attitude towards New Zealand cricketers, regarding them as pretty poor relations, and Hadlee in 1978 could more accurately be described as a bowler who batted a bit than anything like an all-rounder. Two years after the Canterbury game Botham recalled this opening encounter with Hadlee: 'I bowled badly and he smacked me all round the field. I think the feud matured me more than any other experience I've had in cricket. Since then I've curbed myself a little.' That might well have been true in 1980 when the words were uttered; there was no sign of its still applying four years after that when he bowled very much more badly on that same ground of Lancaster Park, but by then, I fear, Ian had gone well over the top and seemed not to regard himself as accountable to anyone for the style and quality of his bowling.

Nevertheless, something rather special in international competition began on that tour and the meeting of Botham and Hadlee has always had a special fascination for me. Both are remarkable characters and great cricketers, but their rivalry is something quite different from Botham's duels with people like Richards, Border, Lillee, Kapil Dev, Imran Khan. He and Hadlee have only had one conversation of any length in their entire overlapping careers, and that was at Taunton when they were thrown together during the end-of-season Silk Cut challenge for all-rounders in 1984. It was entirely a *cricket* chat, the two of them having absolutely nothing in common outside their game, and even then they cannot have found much common ground – the man who will happily plunge into a late-night party during a Test at the drop of a hat and the man who will sit in front of a television screen playing videos to analyse the strengths and weaknesses of the cricketers he is currently engaged in trying to defeat. But all that was in the future as the two squared up to each other at the Basin Reserve, Wellington, in 1978. Hadlee scored 27 not out and 2; he took four wickets for 74 and then six for 26. Botham scored 7 and 19 (top score in

England's wretched 64 all out), took two for 27 and two for 13. The final two days were, of course, entirely New Zealand's, and 15 February 1978 might well be regarded as the day on which modern cricket was born in that country.

With a day and a bit remaining, England needed to score 137 to win – a formality, most of us thought, but with Brian Rose nursing a bruised arm and the first four wickets going down for 18, it suddenly became a little more complicated than that. Enter I. T. Botham. 'He came out looking as though he was going to try to turn the match with an attacking innings,' recalls Hadlee. 'It was an ideal position for a player of his type. A quick 40 would have turned everything round. I felt that he would accept the challenge if I offered it and I bounced him. He tried to hook and was caught at deep square leg.' Botham had doubled England's total but it didn't save the game. The manner of his dismissal was to find many echoes in his own bowling future. The second round went to Botham when he hit a maiden Test century (not without needing a considerable amount of nursing through the later stages by Bob Taylor) in Christchurch and his first-innings five for 75 put him into the record books – only the second England player to take five wickets and score a hundred in the same Test. A remarkable career was taking off.

The two social blemishes in Pakistan apart, 'Both' proved a good, if boisterous, companion on tour. He was in the thick of everything, on the field or off it, but as yet there was nothing unduly obtrusive about his high spirits. He liked to laugh, which is always an asset on tour. He had no great respect for authority, as evidenced by his cold-blooded running-out of Boycott in Christchurch when he felt (and he was not alone in this) that the captain's crawl was jeopardising the team's chance of squaring the series, but, like everyone else, he had the highest regard for Ken Barrington and caused no managerial problems. He came back from Pakistan/New Zealand with his personal standing as a player considerably enhanced and the reputation amongst the media party of being 'a good lad', a good tourist and a tremendously exciting prospect as a player. One minor incident which in fact helped to establish him as a humorist occurred in the early days of the trip. On a Sunday in December 1977, a party of us took the opportunity to visit the Khyber Pass under the leadership of Bernard Thomas, physiotherapist and assistant manager. Once again, it was a mixed bunch of players and media, and on the return journey we stopped in the town of Landi Khotal to explore the bazaar of what must be the smuggling capital of the world. As we rejoined the bus, Botham stopped for a spot of haggling with a seedy-looking local outside a coffee-shop (Pakistan-style, not Kensington). As he climbed on board we asked if he had bought anything. 'No,' he replied airily, 'he had some of the local cannabis but it was poor stuff, poor quality.' Everyone smiled. No one seriously thought that he knew the difference between good and poor quality cannabis. But if he wanted to appear to be a man of the world, why not? It didn't do any harm.

The summer of 1978, at home, brought return fixtures against Pakistan and New Zealand and Botham (who had not played in any of the three winter Tests against them) showed an immediate liking for Pakistan bowling. In the first Test (the first to be sponsored by Cornhill) he earned his £1000 with a score of exactly 100, although it was Chris Old who stole the bowling thunder at Edgbaston with a return of seven for 50. Ian followed this with 108 in the Second Test at Lord's (off only 104 balls) and then put on a brilliant bowling performance which brought him eight wickets for 34 in Pakistan's second innings. He had been in Test cricket for only ten months and the records were already beginning to pile up: now he was the first man to score a century and take eight wickets in an innings of the same Test. The Third Test at Headingley was largely ruined by rain, but not before Botham had added four more wickets to his Test total. The three-match series against New Zealand followed, and while he scored only 51 runs in all he took another 24 wickets including five-in-an-innings three times. At this stage he was beginning to look a little bit like a bowler who could also bat, but few people doubted the quality of his batsmanship. It was just that at number six or seven in the order the opportunities did not arise quite so frequently. He was an automatic choice for the winter tour of Australia under Mike Brearley.

In his first Test innings in Australia Botham was given out caught behind in Brisbane from the bowling of Rodney Hogg, who was to have such a magnificent series (forty-one wickets in six matches) and during the evening's social exchanges 'Both' intimated that Hogg had been a trifle lucky to get the decision in his case. As Hogg had been caught at the wicket off Botham in Australia's first innings, the riposte was immediate and predictable. A bet was struck on a suitably grand scale: a bottle of beer for whichever of them took the other's wicket more times in the series. With the score thus at one-all, it gave Ian more than usual pleasure to bowl Hogg in the second innings, while England's seven-wickets victory deprived the Aussie of a chance to retaliate. In Perth, both of them fell to other bowlers; in Melbourne, Botham made it 3–1; in Sydney, Hogg made it 3–2; in Adelaide, no change; Sydney again no change – and each of them bought the other a beer, several of them in fact, on a tour of King's Cross, Sydney's Soho! There was no repeat of Ian's spectacular success at home during the English summer, but he had done enough to warrant selection for the first Test of 1979 against Venkataraghavan's touring Indians.

In Perth, however, Botham had provided a glimpse of the type of bowling which was to cause much criticism in the future. On the WACA wicket which usually provided the sort of pitch fast bowlers dream about he developed an obsession with bowling the bouncer, and at his pace it brought him no wicket for a hundred runs in the match. Peter Toohey in particular whacked him around while Willis, Hendrick and Lever were reaping the rewards for keeping the ball further up to the bat. Against the Indians, however, he was quickly into his stride with another 'five-for' performance at Edgbaston, followed by yet another at Lord's – the tenth time he had done it in thirty-four Test innings and Gavaskar in the first innings was his 100th victim. At Headingley, and how he must have loved that ground in his early years, he savaged the Indian bowling (by no means the worst in the world since it included Kapil Dev and Bishen Bedi) for 99 before lunch in an innings of 137 and at the Oval he hit his 1000th Test run. It had been quite a season for the statisticians. The 'double' had been accomplished in twenty-one Tests, two matches fewer than Vinoo Mankad, the Indian all-rounder of the 1940s and 50s.

The winter of 1979–80 saw England back in Australia for a three-match series intermingled with a visit from the West Indies, all of which seemed designed primarily to provide camera-fodder for the Packer marketing organisation. Not surprisingly, England declined to regard the Ashes as being at stake, and when they lost all three games antipodean fury towards the whingeing Poms knew no bounds. The game in Perth was notable for much more intelligent bowling by Botham than on his previous visit (six for 78 and five for 98) and for the introduction, short-lived though it was, of the aluminium bat. It was a commercial gimmick, deliberately introduced by Dennis Lillee whose perverse sense of humour was matched by an Australian disregard for convention. In this case, unfortunately for him, he was up against the Laws of Cricket as well ('the blade of the bat shall be made of wood') and, though it took ten minutes to persuade him to change it for a more orthodox piece of equipment, Lillee at least had the satisfaction of going into the record books as scoring three runs with the aluminium blade in the course of four balls from Botham, who enjoyed the experience just as much as the batsman. In Melbourne, where Australia completed their clean sweep, 'Both' made a determined attempt to turn certain defeat into improbable victory by scoring 119 not out from his batting position of number seven.

On their way home, the England party called at Bombay to play in a special golden jubilee Test to mark the fiftieth anniversary of the formation of the BCCI – the Board of Control for Cricket in India – a game which Botham may well remember as a jubilee of his own. It was even marked by an eclipse of the sun! Botham took six wickets for 58 as India were bowled out for 242, then hit 113 which included 17 fours. As India struggled to 149 in the second innings, Botham's bowling figures were seven for 48 and once again the statisticians had a field day. He was the first man to score a century and take ten or more wickets in a Test match, the first to hit a hundred and take five wickets in a Test innings on three occasions. What could we expect from him next? – for, in all truth, we were now expecting as of right some new and startling achievement every time he played. It was a burden which seemed to sit lightly on his shoulders. Everything had gone so right for so long that there seemed no end to the splendours of his career. And yet, amongst the many sage pronouncements of cricket's philosophers is outstandingly the one which decrees that a side's character is best revealed in adversity. How would our hero fare when his personal golden age came to an end? For the moment, few people could foresee an end to it. Botham had become an institution of fabulous success. He had the cricketing Midas touch. One record after another toppled. New targets were envisaged and speedily accomplished. Nothing seemed impossible for Ian Botham and, one suspected, nothing seemed impossible *to* Ian Botham, either.

When the party returned from Australia in February 1980 Mike Brearley, without announcing any retirement from Test cricket, indicated that he did not want to tour again. Indeed, since captains are appointed for individual series or tours (sometimes individual matches) he was actually no longer the Test skipper at that time. His decision to qualify as a psycho-analyst meant that a new leader had to be found for the following winter in the West Indies, so the Selectors had to decide whether to appoint Brearley for the home series that summer or to take the opportunity to 'groom' someone else. It was not going to be an easy ride for anyone, with consecutive series against the West Indies to be faced – home and away. Brearley, in contrast to some other judges, saw Botham as his logical successor in due course. For the moment he would have preferred to lead England in the first two or three games against the Windies at home, with Botham officially recognised as the heir apparent and thus very much involved in discussing tactical and strategic issues. The Selectors, uncertain what course to take and to some extent divided in their ideas, tinkered with the situation by making Botham captain for the two one-day internationals (Prudential Trophy), one of which was won and one lost. On 31 May, Alec Bedser phoned Brearley to say that it had been decided to give the Test captaincy to Botham. By a curious chance, he took the call at Taunton where Middlesex were about to start a game against Somerset and the news, says Brearley, 'was neither unexpected nor entirely unwelcome'. Nevertheless, he felt that Botham, aged twenty-four, was being 'thrown into the deepest of deep ends'. How right that was.

5 THE CAPTAIN

Botham's captaincy of England was doomed to disaster right from the start because he had to take on the West Indies at their most potent – with Clive Lloyd skippering a side who, individually and collectively, would have died for him – while Ian led an England team not really capable of handling the pace attack of Holding, Roberts, Marshall, Croft and Garner. West Indies won the first Test at Trent Bridge by two wickets, and the remaining four were drawn, largely because in a miserable summer so much time was lost to the weather. In none of those games – at Lord's, Old Trafford, the Oval and Headingley – did England get into a position which held out any hope of victory, and it is not unreasonable to feel that whoever had been captain the situation would not have altered a great deal. But before the series even began Brian Close, talking to Botham as a close friend and as his mentor, begged him not to accept the leadership. Close issued a sort of five-point manifesto to indicate why he thought Botham should turn it down:

(1) Your own form will suffer. You are too much of an action man to be able to step back and take an objective view of your players' performances and to give them the help they might need. You'll be driven on by a wish to do it all yourself. (2) Your batting will suffer because your concentration will go when you start thinking about long-term captaincy problems. (3) When you are bowling you will be asking yourself, 'Should I be trying somebody else?' and again you'll lose your concentration. It's just as important when

you are bowling as when you are batting. (4) The results will be bad and you'll have the media on your back and you won't like that. (5) You'll have the most miserable time of your life.

And Close, the man who gave Botham that advice, was an England Selector! As a close friend of the big Yorkshireman, I knew the counsel was genuine and that it was born of a deep concern for a player for whom he had a great regard and personal affection. And how devastatingly right it all turned out to be.

Botham as a captain had come highly recommended by Mike Brearley. His main support within the Selection Committee came from Ken Barrington. The other two members, Alec Bedser (the chairman) and Charlie Elliott, were open to persuasion and were duly persuaded. And at the end of the 1980 season they found themselves in a very difficult position. If they were determined not to give the captaincy to Boycott who was the obvious candidate in terms of experience (and it was now clear that they were adamantly against doing so) there was a distinct shortage of suitable alternatives. Even if an obvious one had presented itself, could they reasonably give him the job of trying to do better in the West Indies that winter than England had been able to do at home against largely the same opposition? Andy Roberts might be beginning to show signs of going just a little over the hill, but there was Colin Croft waiting in the wings and Holding and Garner were just as formidable as ever. So, despite fierce opposition from Close, the Selectors decided to give Botham the captaincy for the winter tour – and that was to prove disastrous for him. It was also to accelerate the downward plunge of player–media relations.

In September 1980 Ian contemplated a season in which England, under his leadership, had played two Prudential Trophy matches against the West Indies, losing by 24 runs at Headingley and winning by three wickets at Lord's, and two against Australia (who had come over for the Centenary Test at Lords – drawn) at Edgbaston and the Oval which were both won by 47 runs and 23 runs respectively. The summer Test series with the West Indies had not brought a win for the new captain, who had scored 169 runs in ten innings (topping 50 only once) and had taken fourteen wickets at 36·21 each. His Somerset form, however, had been good, especially with the bat, and he was in his customary cheerful and buoyant mood when I encountered him playing as a guest celebrity in the Bob Hope Golf Classic at the RAC Club at Epsom.

Along with a BBC colleague, Andy Smith, I spent an entirely pleasant evening with Ian and his father Les over a few beers in the golf clubhouse, and in the course of it I asked if he thought it was wise to take on the captaincy again on a tour where, on the very well-known form of both sides, England had slightly less than no chance at all of winning the series. With terrible but understandable simplicity he replied: 'You don't turn down the England captaincy, do you?' As a basic argument it was, of course, unanswerable. What boy, starting out on the school playing-fields, has not dreamed of leading his country's top players in a Test against the best in the world? What player who had come up through the ranks, so to speak, could even contemplate for a moment saying to the Selectors, 'Thanks very much but . . .'? I believe Botham listened to everything Close had to say – he had always liked and, in his own way, respected his erstwhile Somerset captain. He would not dismiss lightly anything that Brian had to offer about cricket; he would even accept some of the points Closey made. But in the last analysis Ian would believe that somehow (he would not ask himself too closely just *exactly* how) he could overcome all the problems and miraculously – for it would be nothing less – beat the Windies.

The tour, however, did not begin until mid-January, 1981. That left four months for Botham to get himself into the newspapers in an unfortunate context. On a festive season outing to Tiffany's nightclub in Scunthorpe, with his friend Joe Neenan (the United goalkeeper), he encountered one Steven Robert Isbister and the New Year headlines announced that I. T. Botham, captain of England, had been arrested on an assault charge. What had happened was that, in the FA Cup, Scunthorpe had drawn 0–0 in a home tie with non-League club Altrincham, and then lost the replay 0–1 on a penalty awarded against goalkeeper Neenan. There was far more than usual disappointment in Scunthorpe, because the draw for the next round had paired United or Altrincham with Liverpool, where two of the star players were Kevin Keegan and Ray Clemence, both now internationals, but who were both former Scunthorpe United players. It was a dream of a Cup draw for the club and it would now never take place, because in the replay Neenan, reacting to harassment from an Altrincham player, had given away the penalty which decided the match. Now, in Tiffany's, there was a marked absence of seasonal goodwill as Steven Robert Isbister inquired of Joseph Patrick Neenan: 'You're the four-letter-word who cost us the cup-tie with Liverpool, aren't you?' There were later varying reports about what exactly followed that undiplomatic question, but both Neenan and his friend Ian Botham were charged in due course with assault. Neenan pleaded guilty at the local magistrates' court and was fined £100 with £100 costs; Botham denied the charge and elected to go for trial before a jury, which meant that the hearing had to be adjourned because in the week after being charged he was due to join the tour party for the West Indies. There are strong reasons for believing that the matter might never have reached court at all but for an intervention far away from Scunthorpe. When, on 2 January, the press, TV and radio reporters who had descended on the town asked if Botham had in fact been charged with assault, they were told by the police: 'That has not yet been decided. Because of Botham's public importance the decision will have to come from the top.' That led to the West Stirlingshire MP, Mr Dennis Cavanan (after describing the police statement as 'particularly stupid'), announcing: 'It would be very unfortunate if the public was to get the impression that there is one law for England cricketers and another for the rest of us.' On 9 January Botham was charged; the hearing was ordered to be adjourned until the following Wednesday (when the tour team assembled) and his decision to go for trial meant that it was not going to come to court for at least three months. In point of fact, it was not heard until the following September, by which time Botham, for his storybook successes against the touring Australians in England, had become a national hero on a scale almost unprecedented in sporting history. A winter of discontent in the Caribbean had been followed by a summer of miracles against Australia.

When the trial finally took place, at Grimsby Crown Court in September 1981, it began with the usual contradictory broadsides from counsel: prosecution – 'A persistent, cowardly and prolonged attack'; defence – 'Isbister and his friends made up a sensational story in the hope of selling it to a newspaper.' After a three-day hearing the jury of six men and six women failed to agree upon a verdict and the prosecuting counsel, Mr Graham Richards, said the charges would now be dropped because massive media coverage had made it unlikely that an unprejudiced jury could be found anywhere in England. 'It is on humanitarian grounds,' he told the judge, 'that the prosecution can now say they will not seek a further verdict from any jury. Their decision is that they are prepared to offer no further evidence against Mr Botham.'

But all that lay nine months in the future . . . After the events of the 1980 summer not even the most serious and optimistic student of English cricket could expect success from the tour to West Indies which took off from Gatwick in mid-January 1981 under the captaincy of Botham and the managership of Alan Smith, with Ken Barrington as his assistant. There were areas where, in the opinion of some, the party might have been strengthened – Edmonds to bowl in tandem with Emburey, perhaps, and there were arguments in favour of other contestants for one or two of the specialist batting places – but there could be no serious complaint about the party as a whole. With one possible exception, it was as good a job as any group of Selectors could have done in terms of the fifteen players chosen. But

Botham was always going to be on a hiding to nothing against the West Indies in their own conditions, before their own spectators and surrounded by the crackpot hypocrisy which characterises politics in the Caribbean.

The gathering of the cricket correspondents, which takes place alongside that of players and management, is usually a fair barometer to indicate what the cricketing weather is likely to be. On that occasion, nothing but stormclouds appeared in prospect; there was no hint of sunshine. There was a certain amount of cynical anticipation of what was regarded as the inevitable. A sweep was suggested on how long it would be before Bob Willis broke down and had to return home (in the event it happened even earlier than anyone anticipated, posing the pertinent question: if the press could anticipate it so strongly why couldn't the Selectors?) and there was a unanimous acceptance that it was all going to be pretty hard work. Travelling with and living with a side which is consistently unsuccessful can create difficulties all round. With the best will in the world, and exercising all the sympathy that is possible, there has to be an inquest or two in the course of the tour. Some correspondents can imply criticism more charitably than others; some are under more pressure than others from their masters back home to be more punchy in their prose and more devastating in their denunciation. And always there are the sub-editors, the carrion of journalism, who pick the bones of the despatches from overseas for the choicest morsels to provide their headlines.

Thus, an uphill battle against all the odds, no matter how sympathetically described by the man on the spot, can become 'England's Day of Shame' propped up against the teapot on your morning breakfast table. Within a matter of hours, that will be reported to the players themselves via a phone call from a wife or parent at home. Sometimes it can be overdramatised in the translation from the written to the spoken word. And it takes a great deal of understanding from a player to accept that a cricket correspondent is not responsible for the headlines *above* his by-line on a newspaper page and sometimes not for the words below it, either, since it is far from unknown for a correspondent's copy to be re-written in order to provide the 'right' sort of headline.

It is difficult to expect a player to look too closely at such journalistic detail as that, and it is equally difficult to blame the player for feeling resentment when he thinks he is being summarily written off by a man sitting in relative comfort 120 yards or so from the firing line. With Holding, Roberts, Croft and Garner firing their 5½-oz missiles at 120 feet per second from a distance of nineteen or twenty yards, the batsmen had something like one-third of a second in which to pick up the line and length of each delivery and around another one-third for the brain to instruct hands and feet what to do about it. If the ball struck man instead of bat it arrived not with the impact of a 5½-oz projectile *per se*, but with the equivalent force of three tons per square inch! No – criticism from a man on the sidelines was not something to be taken lightly.

It is fair to say that Botham started out as captain of that tour with a great deal of goodwill from the media party, except perhaps for a couple of people with personal axes to grind. A lot of us had a considerable personal liking for the man; all of us had a profound respect for his natural ability as a cricketer. Few, if any of us, felt that he was going to be a successful captain, but then we couldn't think of any alternative candidate who would have any brighter prospects in that role. There are, however, other aspects of captaincy than leading a winning side back to the pavilion, and it was here that some of us found the major cause for concern. To give an entirely personal viewpoint: I did not know Les Botham very well, but I liked immensely what I had seen of him during that evening at the RAC Club just before the tour began, and as the father of a professional sportsman I knew something of how he would feel about his son. I knew Botham's father-in-law, mother-in-law and wife considerably better, and I certainly knew how proud they were of him. I had known the young man himself for the seven years of his first-class career and, with a less dispassionate attitude than ought, professionally, to have been the case, I almost desperately wanted him to do well in every way. But on the second night of the tour he made a complete and utter fool of himself.

The tour had been organised so that the party flew first to the congenial surroundings of Antigua, Vivian Richards's home island, to have a week of acclimatisation and practice before the sterner stuff began. Within forty-eight hours of our arrival Ian had acted with crass idiocy and in full view and earshot of four newspapermen. Even now I am not going to detail the incident because it would cause distress to innocent parties, but in view of the bitterness which was to develop between players and press over the next few years it must be recorded that what happened that evening has never been made public although it was witnessed by three national newspaper cricket correspondents and, more to the point, another pressman who was not connected with cricket-writing in any way. He was there to write a series of articles on Vivvy Richards, whose wedding was due to take place in Antigua in six weeks' time and by pure chance he happened to be an old friend of mine. The following morning he came to see me, described the captain's indiscretion and went on: 'I'm pretty sure I know what the answer is going to be, and of course I shall have to make up my own mind, but I want to hear you say it. What do I do about this story?' I replied: 'If you want to be a hero in your office for about twenty-four hours, you write the story. If you want to wreck relationships for ever more between newspapermen and players on tour, you write the story. If you want to do irreparable harm to the life and career of a foolish fellow who is also our outstanding cricket talent, you write the story.' He acknowledged: 'Thanks. I knew what the answer would be. I won't do the story.' Now that young man was (and is) a very, very good feature-writer. Mercifully for Ian Botham he is also a decent human being. And since the other auditors were equally experienced reporters, though primarily concerned with cricket-writing, they must share the credit for putting the good of the game and the tour before natural journalistic instincts. They didn't write the story, either.

And yet Botham has consistently maintained that 'the bloody press cost him the England captaincy'. It is not true; it was never true. Ian lost the captaincy because he should never have been given it in the first place and the Selectors, rather late in the day, discovered their mistake. He lost it because he was not the right type to hold it. He lost it because he was not capable of doing the job, magnificent *player* though he was. To ignore the generosity of four newspapermen on that occasion in Antigua and to blame 'the bloody press' for his misfortunes has always seemed to me the height of ingratitude and ungraciousness. The 1981 tour party moved south to win a match against the Young West Indies in Pointe-à-Pierre in the south-western corner of Trinidad where they encountered one or two names which were to become better known over the next five years: Richard Austin, Everton Mattis, Thelston Payne, Hartley Alleyne, Jeffrey Dujon (who made a not-out 100 in the game), Roger Harper – and Malcolm Marshall.

In the pleasant island of St Vincent rain ruined the projected four-day match against Windward Islands, but Botham performed heroically in the first of the one-day internationals, scoring 60 of England's 125 runs – which was just 2 short of the West Indies. It was a game of rare excitement with 11,000 islanders, seeing the full might of the West Indies for the first time, packed into a tiny ground sandwiched between the airport runway and the sea. The captain, at least as a player, had started well. Back again to Trinidad, this time for a long stay at the Hilton – built into a rockface with the lifts taking one *down* to one's room – and serenaded by calypsoists and steel bands rehearsing for the approaching carnival, Botham was able to indulge in his favourite activities of pushing people into the swimming pool or bombarding the poolside loungers with fruit and paperbags filled with water from his seventh-floor room. It wasn't *too* unpleasant, nor was it especially dignified conduct in an England captain, but most people shrugged it off as being 'typical Both'. Noticeably, he never included

Peter Willey amongst his targets. The strong silent man from County Durham is a rugged character and the bar gossips had it that he was quite capable of 'filling in' the captain if provoked. Rain again affected the four-day match and although Botham dismissed the Trinidad and Tobago openers he was caught behind without scoring in the drawn game. And so to the first Test.

There was a time when *all* matches on a tour were important as competitive events; indeed, to many people at home, they still are. But not so to the tourists. The Tests are the whole point of going abroad and other matches are regarded quite simply as practice for the big occasion. No one likes to lose a tour game of any kind, of course, but the important thing is to get the batsmen striking well and the bowlers building up their rhythm and getting used to different types of pitches. And now, on 13 February 1981, the big moment had arrived. It did not begin without the demonstrations which were to attract such a large section of the media in 1986, but then they were not drawing attention to such a *cause célèbre* as the inclusion in England's ranks of men who had played in South Africa. On this occasion it was a matter of internal politics: the selection of David Murray as wicket-keeper instead of the local hero, Deryck Murray. This did not arouse the same sort of fervour but it did, along with more showery weather, cut the playing time because of sabotage to a small area of the square. Queen's Park Oval plays lower and slower than the other pitches of the West Indies, not surprisingly since the island produces fewer big fast bowlers and more slim, wiry spinners. The first day's start was three hours late and, because inadequate covering had left damp patches, Botham's decision to field first could not reasonably be faulted. Even if he merely feared the damage which the West Indies fast-bowling quartet might do in those conditions, his first major tactical decision of the tour could not seriously be criticised. Nor was it his fault if the bowling of himself, Dilley, Old and the spinners was not of quite the same penetrative order as that of Holding, Roberts, Garner and Croft.

West Indies declared at 426 for nine on the third morning after Andy Roberts had hit the first five balls of a Botham over for three sixes, a four and a two. The captain's first Test innings of the tour brought the extreme anguish of being out lbw Croft, 0, but it was his batting in the second which brought the dubious shaking of many heads about his attitude. England had followed on, 248 behind, and nearly nine hours of play remained, but after Gooch and Rose had gone cheaply Boycott and Gower staved off potential defeat for another two hours in a partnership of 61. On the final day, there were three interruptions by rain with an ever-present threat of more. It was a day for grafting, for getting the head down and concentrating simply on staying at the wicket. It was, in fact, a perfect situation for Boycott to exercise all his painstaking concentration, but scarcely an ideal one for the Botham we had come to know. Still – he *was* the captain; surely we could now expect the exercising of severe personal discipline? For a time he gave us a glimpse of what so many of us fervently hoped to see.

Now, there are those who have dismissed Clive Lloyd's captaincy of the West Indies, so successful over so many years, as being a relatively simple matter of directing the most potent forces in world cricket: 'You don't have to be a master-tactician with a team like that.' There will even be those who argue that at Port of Spain on 18 February 1981 it did not take a genius to work out what was required, but that, one feels, would be harshly ungenerous. With Boycott as seemingly immovable as ever and Botham showing a sense of responsibility it was hoped could be prolonged, Lloyd now tossed the ball to Vivian Richards, Botham's flatmate in Taunton, his bosom pal and in many ways his idol. It was a tactical move which was pure genius in its simplicity. Would 'Both' be able to resist the challenge? It was impossible to see the expression on Lloyd's face as he made the move, but in the commentary box I felt absolutely certain that it would be done with a smile which would be shared by Richards. With elaborate care, Holding was placed three-quarter-way back on the off side, and obligingly Botham hit the ball straight down his throat. Botham knew exactly what was being offered him, exactly what was in store if he failed and he *should* have known exactly what the consequences of failure would be. Yet he was constitutionally incapable of resisting the challenge. *He* could beat the system. But he didn't. Even *Wisden*, not given to extravagant language, described the stroke as 'ambitious and unnecessary', and so it was, especially at that stage.

It is grossly unfair, of course, to lay the blame for England's defeat entirely at Botham's door. Boycott played a masterly defensive innings for more than five hours and if he hadn't got a ball from Holding which kicked straight at his glove from a good length, who can say that the Yorkshireman might not have found sufficient support from the tail to bat throughout the day? Certainly he was mentally capable of doing so. But Botham *was* the captain. Was it wrong to expect an example from a man of known genius, an example of self-control, of self-sacrifice if you like, knowing what it would mean to him to abandon his naturally aggressive philosophy? Sadly, one had to conclude that such hopes were not wrong and that he had failed one of cricket's many stern tests of character. In my after-match interview with him he was cheerfully mock-regretful – not that he had failed any sort of test but that his attempt to hit his mate out of the ground had not come off. He did not seem to consider for one second the effect his attitude might have on the remainder of his party. It was not captaincy of the highest order.

The cancelled Test in Georgetown, Guyana, has now gone into the pages of political cricket history. The week was spent in the Pegasus Hotel there, virtually in a state of siege, because walking abroad in the streets of the capital was not recommended by anyone, from the British High Commissioner downwards. Bob Willis had flown home from Trinidad for treatment on a damaged knee, and Brian Rose was shortly to follow him because of problems with his eyesight. Robin Jackman, who had taken 121 wickets in the previous English season but who was thirty-five years old, was the nominated replacement for Willis; Bill Athey, the Yorkshire batsman, was to fly from his Australian summer cricket to replace Rose later. Willis's departure meant that a new vice-captain was required, and while Guyana's politicians deliberated upon whether Jackman's associations with South Africa (he had married a South African girl and so, not unnaturally, was a frequent visitor there) made him unacceptable in a country which did not exactly offer the full privileges of democracy to all its people, the England camp was involved in a little political manoeuvring of its own.

The logical successor to Willis as vice-captain was all too clearly Geoffrey Boycott – by far the most experienced Test player in the party and a man of known tactical expertise, if not a Charlemagne or Alexander in terms of leadership of men. When the team meeting broke up the name presented to the waiting media party was that of Geoff Miller. It was an astonishing choice, not because Miller was unsuited to leadership – on the contrary, he later skippered the side wonderfully well, and to a win over the Leeward Islands – but because, although he had played in the Fifth Test, it seemed he was unlikely to be picked in the remaining Tests, given that Emburey was the specialist spinner and Botham the all-rounder. The decision could only be seen as a disinclination by Botham to have a strong right arm on the Test field, a strong character and experienced lieutenant who might seek to curb the extravagance of the captain's approach to Test cricket. There was, as mentioned earlier, an interesting rapport between Botham and Boycott but now it became clear that Botham was unwilling to see it progress beyond a player–player, or captain–player relationship. This was a great pity for, whatever his faults, Boycott knew his cricket, knew the West Indies players, knew the conditions there better than anyone in the party and he knew how to fight. He was, however, not popular with his fellow tourists.

This was illustrated all too clearly by an incident which occurred during the time we spent so many long, weary hours cooped up in the Pegasus. The manager, Harry

Flack, had thoughtfully provided for the players a TV set and video and had somehow collected just about every film cassette in the country, so that at least the players had a reasonably pleasant way of spending their evenings. But they didn't even want Boycott involved with them there. When an action-packed drama was to be shown one evening and Boycott inquired what was on the agenda, he was told *Chitty-Chitty Bang-Bang* so that he stamped off to his room in disgust rather than stay to watch 'that kid-stuff'! But one radio recording I did with Boycott provided such a brilliant analysis of the four West Indian quicks, and the quite distinct problems each of them presented, that I couldn't help feeling it would have been of infinitely more use played at a players' eve-of-Test talk than the captain's 'Come on, we can beat this lot' exhortation. It would certainly have been more practical and realistic. Boycott could have helped Botham, certainly as vice-captain, if Ian had been willing to accept help.

The one game (instead of the original three) to be played in Guyana – the second one-day international – was duly lost, and after the politicians had had a field day of breast-beating we found ourselves in Barbados to be greeted by hundreds of cricket-lovers from home and a number of players' wives and children. Thus I found myself in the Botham family room in the Holiday Inn, reading bedtime stories to young Liam and Sarah while father-in-law Gerry Waller complained that criticism of Ian in the English papers had been grossly unfair. 'But I have offered my share of critical comment, too,' I said. 'Ah, but you're a friend,' replied Gerry – with more generosity than logic, I felt, and wondered how long it could last. Henry Blofeld, in the meantime, had flown in from his usual summer parish of Australia in time for the First Test in Trinidad and fired off a piece to the *Sunday Express* which announced that 'Botham captains the side like a great big baby'. The cutting was duly presented to the captain and he brooded darkly, managing to contain himself until the day the party were flying home via Bermuda, when he finally exploded and manhandled old Blowers in the airport. In strictly human terms he might have felt he had some justification, but as an England captain his gesture was unforgivable. Henry, at the same time, does believe in chancing his arm, and five years later – again jetting in from the Antipodes and again in the context of a Trinidad Test – he had an even bigger go at 'Both' in the *Sunday Express*, as we shall see in due course.

Botham surrounded by his family was, in my book, a 'good lad' and it was always pleasant to get away for an hour or two from the problems he faced on and off the field – and talk golf, or Somerset cricket, or about mutual friends like D. B. Close. But increasingly the professional relationship was becoming more difficult. As a friend and admirer of his immense natural ability I yearned for him to do well; as a professional observer I saw flaws in his leadership in so many ways. His personal form was so disappointing that one interview after another began with my putting to him, as delicately as possible: 'Don't you think your own game is suffering from the constant worries of captaincy?' I didn't blame him for one second for becoming irritated at the repetitiousness of it all, but I did hope that he could see that I was, as most of us were, trying to find excuses for him, to let him escape direct criticism as much as possible. It is important to remember that every reporter had people back in London (with no conception of the problems involved) demanding much more critical pieces than any of us wanted to send. It is one thing to sit behind a desk in Fleet Street or Broadcasting House; it is quite another to be with the players on tour, living with them, eating, drinking, travelling with them; and it is altogether something else to be the man who has to go out into the middle and face ninety-mile-an-hour thunderbolts.

Ian's answers to my professional questions were becoming more and more monosyllabic and grumpy. I didn't – I couldn't – blame him, even if I expected him to understand why, like everyone else, I kept harping on the familiar theme. Finally, after one particularly surly recording, I told him, 'If I send that back to London you will sound a right Charlie.' He snarled, 'I don't care.' This was becoming silly. No one would be particularly interested in the questions I was asking but the listeners would certainly be interested in what the England captain was saying. And it was *his* image which had to suffer. It was distressing to be a part of it, so I tried talking to his father-in-law Gerry. Unfortunately, he could see no wrong in anything Ian did or said so it didn't help.

That first week in Barbados was not the easiest of times. There was a massive relief at being away from Guyana and living in the infinitely more pleasant and hospitable surroundings of Bridgetown, but first we had to have more political posturing to decide whether the remaining games of the tour could be played. When finally it was condescendingly decreed that they could, there was a practice session in the form of a match against a Barbados XI which did not turn out too well for the tourists and Ian followed his first innings of 40 with another duck in the second. And so came the Test match, where he again asked the opposition to bat first and again it was the right decision since the pitch proved to be at its liveliest on the first morning. Greenidge and Haynes, the local lads, totalled only 39 runs between them and there was a certain amount of revenge for the England captain when he caught, quite beautifully, the brilliant Richards at slip for nought. But now we saw the leadership-by-example of Clive Lloyd and the limpet-like qualities of Larry Gomes, who put together 154 for the fifth wicket. Still, 265 was far from a huge total, and now we had another example of Lloyd's shrewd captaincy. He instructed Michael Holding, then the world's fastest bowler, to go absolutely flat out at Boycott from the first ball of the innings – no looseners, no sighters, just sheer blinding pace.

The result was an over which will long be remembered by everyone who saw it. Players who were with Frank Tyson in Australia in 1954 – men like Len Hutton, Johnny Wardle, Bob Appleyard and Trevor Bailey – have told me that the Typhoon's bowling in Melbourne was the fastest from anyone in the history of the game. I didn't see that, and all one can say is that if it was faster than Michael Holding's at the Bridgetown Oval on 14 March 1981, it is possible to feel a rare sympathy for Australian batsmen. Holding delivered to Geoff Boycott an over of such scorching ferocity that the greatest defensive batsman of his day (and many another day) was scarcely able to lay a bat on the ball before his stumps were shattered. Holding bowled four more overs before taking a rest, to be saved for the arrival of Botham, the other England player judged by Lloyd as being capable of swinging the result away from the West Indies. Holding steamed in, all fire and fury, and after the fourth delivery Botham hurled down his bat, walked away to a sort of short gully position and glared down the pitch, plainly nonplussed by it all. Nevertheless, he battled on to be joint top scorer with Gooch on 26, but when Lloyd declared the second innings at lunch on the fourth day the West Indies were 522 ahead. Once again it was merely a matter of whether England could hold out for a draw. A superb 116 by Gooch (out of 224) was really all they had to console themselves with after defeat by 298 runs.

The captain's after-match press conference was a tense affair with journalists showing a certain reluctance to ask that first question! Botham's attitude was one of defiance. He was not unhappy with his own form, he'd got a few runs, he was the leading wicket-taker. Now, this was strictly true but it didn't – measured by his own standards – stand up to a very detailed scrutiny. He had scored 0 and 16 in the First Test, 26 and 1 in the Second. In Trinidad his two wickets had cost 113 from 28 overs, and his victims had been Holding, the number nine batsman, and Garner, number ten. In Barbados he had taken four for 77 (Mattis, number four, playing in his second Test; Roberts, number eight; Garner, number nine; and Holding, number ten) in the first innings. In the second he disposed of Haynes, an opener, Lloyd and Roberts again, and the three wickets had cost 102 runs from 29 overs. It might have come better from the captain to ignore his own achievements and perhaps have offered a little credit to the recently arrived

Jackman, who had taken three first-innings wickets (Greenidge, Haynes and Lloyd) for 67 and Dilley for his three for 51 (Richards, Gomes and Murray).

There was a certain feeling along those lines as the press conference broke up and we went our separate ways to attempt to describe another heavy defeat in terms which were temperate and reasonable. If it seems surprising that the usual relationship of mutual understanding and respect between a tour captain and the accompanying cricket correspondents had deteriorated after only two Tests, then it is necessary to point out that conferences do not take place only at the end of Tests. They are arranged frequently, several times a week, to give the correspondents the 'quotes' which all newspapers demand (or did demand from their representatives before they started buying up their own ghosted columnists from the playing ranks) and to give captain and manager the opportunity to make points of their own. At none of these did Botham ever show a realistic attitude to his problems. No one expects a captain to say, 'We've no bloody chance. We shall just have to go out and go through the motions.' But what seemed rather stupid – particularly in view of the previous summer's results, the forces at his disposal, the quality of the opposition, and the way both teams had played in the first two Tests – was Ian's continued insistence that all was well in every possible way. It made it rather more difficult to sustain our inherent sympathy with him in all his difficulties in our reports back home. That in turn confirmed his belief that those who were not for him were automatically against him and that generally we were just a 'gang of bloody knockers'. We were all on a dreadful downhill spiral.

Matters were not helped by the arrival in the West Indies of the egregious 'Jock' McCoombe, taking up the role he filled back in Taunton. Now he took it upon himself to arrange any meetings or interviews the media party required with the captain! This really was outrageous. Such meetings take place by arrangement with the manager and no cricket reporter on tour seeks to bypass the system. If any correspondent happens by chance upon a worthwhile 'quote' while, for instance, waiting at an airport or having a social drink with a player, then he knows whether it is on or off the record. In short, everyone knows the ropes. When a third party (and one very much outside the tour group as far as the media are concerned) starts volunteering to 'fix' meetings with the captain, and in some cases actually doing so, then there is bound to be trouble.

From the moment McCoombe arrived on the scene he spent a certain part of each evening in the company of some newspaper representatives and being ignored by others. Those of us who shunned him could not help being concerned, nevertheless, that he might 'fix' something for the others or drop a hint of a story. Even those who joined the McCoombe circle were uncertain whether some tasty morsel might be vouchsafed to a rival on some *other* occasion. It was an uneasy sort of situation and one which Botham should most certainly not have allowed to happen. Overall, it played its part in diminishing Ian as a captain in the eyes of many of those who reported the 1981 tour.

We had our share of news reporters on that tour, too. First there was the political situation involving the governments of Barbados, Jamaica, Antigua and Montserrat (where later games were due to be played), which caused most branches of the media to fly in additional staff. Then came the bizarre 'kidnapping' of the train-robber Ronald Biggs in Brazil and his projected arrival in Barbados, but by and large the newsmen did not interfere with the cricket personnel involved in the tour, as was to happen five years later. 'Jock' McCoombe, though, was up to his neck in the cricket side of things from the moment he arrived in 1981. The trouble was that McCoombe was 'a mate', and as far as Ian was concerned you stuck by your mates; 'Jock' was doing nothing wrong as far as he was concerned. There was just one further problem: amongst the cricket-lovers who had come to Barbados for a holiday were many with lurid tales of critical headlines appearing in newspapers back home. They fed Ian's ego with 'you-are-not-going-to-stand-for-that-are-you?' incendiarism, which duly started more fires. As England's captain he ought to have been able to stand aloof. Sadly, he didn't.

The death of Kenny Barrington, the much-loved assistant manager of the tour, cast the deepest pall of gloom over that fortnight in Barbados, but the win over Leeward Islands (led by Geoff Miller) in the delightful island of Montserrat was accomplished while the captain was taking a rest to attend Vivvy Richards's wedding in neighbouring Antigua, and morale improved a little – as it did when the first-ever Test to be played in that island was drawn, largely due to a battling century by Willey, going in at number seven with a scoreboard which read 138–5. But with nothing more certain than a Richards century before his own supporters, West Indies again piled up a big total in their only innings – 468 for nine declared – and Botham's four victims this time (he had scored only one run) were Haynes, Mattis, Gomes and Murray. They cost 127 runs but they included three frontline batsmen. He had two wickets in the final Test in Kingston, Jamaica, for 73 runs – Holding and Croft, numbers 10 and 11. Gooch and Gower batted brilliantly and the Test was drawn.

West Indies had not been bowled out twice in any of the four Tests. Botham had scored 73 runs in seven Test innings and had taken 15 of the 38 wickets which fell. Of these his victims had been Haynes (twice), Mattis (twice), Lloyd (once), Gomes (once), Murray (once), Holding (three times), Garner (twice), Roberts (twice) and Croft (once). He still insisted that captaincy had not affected his own game. What, then, had?

Certainly the opposition was tougher than that offered by any other international side, and I think it is fair to say that we all – writers and broadcasters – acknowledged this regularly. Perhaps if we had been watching it all happen for a second time, as the media representatives did in 1986, we might have made even more allowances. It is true that there were some highly inflammatory headlines and introductions appearing in England, but they were not the work of the journalists accompanying the tour. The deterioration in relations between players and reporters was by no means the exclusive work of one party. By his steadfast refusal to accept that he might be guilty of any personal faults, by his eagerness (illogical though it was) to attribute so many of his misfortunes to 'the press', Ian Botham, it has to be said, played a major part in destroying that relationship. It had been a threat ever since the rewards for Test cricket had soared and the loss of them represented a major blow. Anyone who wrote a word which might conceivably cause the Selectors to think in terms of dropping a Test player was quickly marked down as 'an enemy'.

6 THE FLAWS

Let us pause for a moment at this point in our story to examine the whole issue of captaincy – Ian Botham's concept of captaincy and his attitude to the leadership of others, not only on the cricket field but outside it. Going back to his schooldays, I find myself interested in the fact that he would rather have had six of the best from his headmaster than have his transgressions reported to his parents. That makes it clear that from the first Ian had been brought up to have a proper respect for authority in what has become known as the 'old-fashioned' way. If he had been seen to have kicked over the traces at school he would be in a proportionate amount of trouble at home for doing so. That makes pleasant reading in an age when so many parents seem all too willing to plunge into litigation against schoolteachers at the first hint of a complaint about little Johnny. Nevertheless, on the Lord's staff, we have seen, a liking for discipline was not near the top of Ian's list of priorities, but once he had graduated to Somerset's first eleven there was little chance of the young man getting out of hand during his first four years in top-class cricket because Close was in control.

During the whole of his twenty-eight years in the county game, 'Closey' was the most formidable figure in the game in terms of his physical presence. He was a very tough man indeed, and universally respected as such by everyone who played with him or against him. Even though he was twenty-three years older than Ian he would have thought nothing of picking up the young giant by the scruff of his neck and boxing his ears if he had felt it necessary. 'Closey' led from the front. He fielded in all the suicide positions close to the wicket, and even invented a few as well. In addition, he had an encyclopaedic knowledge of the strengths and weaknesses of everyone playing first-class cricket and he tended to concentrate on the weaknesses, as he saw them, and to ignore the strengths – if in fact he allowed himself to think of them as having any relevance. The Close type of leadership was that seen in the young First World War subalterns who led suicide charges on the enemy trenches armed only with a swagger-stick. Those subalterns who survived learned better sense as they grew older; Close never did, as we saw at Lord's in 1963 when he walked down the pitch to meet the bowling of Wes Hall, then the most feared quickie in the world. He was an intensely subjective leader and always believed implicitly in the rightness of what he was doing. Has enough been said for us to recognise the influence of *that* style of captaincy upon the young Botham?

There is one further aspect of Close's leadership which must be mentioned: he *cared* for his players in his own highly individual fashion. At Middlesbrough in 1963 (when, of course, he was still with Yorkshire) John Hampshire was felled by a thunderbolt from Charlie Griffith, who was widely regarded as a chucker when he bowled a really fast one. After he had been dissuaded from going out and strangling Griffith, Close hovered anxiously above the unconscious form of Hampshire, lying prone on the dressing-room table. When the batsman's eyelids fluttered, his first sight was of the lined and furrowed brow of D. B. Close who asked, with deep concern, 'Are you all right, Jackie lad?'

'I think so, captain,' replied Hampshire, feebly. 'Right,' said Close. 'Now I want to tell you something, lad. If you ever get hit again, try to fall *inside* the crease, otherwise they can run you out.' Close's priorities were simple and absolute: first make sure you are not out, then worry about the knock.

Botham did not play for England under Tony Greig but he played alongside him and saw a lot of Greig around the

English circuit when he *was* captain of England and there are unmistakable signs that Ian was influenced by the Greig style of seeking to intimidate the opposition in verbal exchanges. Since nine of Botham's matches as captain were against the West Indies there was not much opportunity to seek a psychological advantage in this way, but in his bowling we have often seen the technique applied – often in moments of ridiculous futility! Batting success against him has always brought out the worst in Ian, as we saw against Sri Lanka at Lord's in 1984 when Mendis and Wettimuny batted so brilliantly, and at Madras against India in 1982. Here Viswanath, with a record 222, and Yashpal Sharma (140) batted together through a whole day in which not a wicket fell, to make a third-wicket partnership of 316. Botham seemed to think that Viswanath's seniority, experience and distinguished record entitled him to a certain amount of respect, but the century of Yashpal roused him to great heights of fury. Even above the normal hubbub of a cricket Test in India his frenzied shouts of abuse could be heard and, lest Yashpal should have any problems of translation from the idiomatic English, the six-letter noun was accompanied by gestures of an unambiguous nature.

When Botham entered England's ranks at Trent Bridge in 1977 the captaincy was in the hands of Mike Brearley, a leader of a very different type from Greig. How could Botham, an academically undistinguished scholar of Buckler's Mead, Yeovil, cope with John Michael Brearley, scholarship winner from the City of London School to St John's College, Cambridge, where his brilliance won him not only his Master of Arts degree but a lectureship in philosophy at Newcastle-on-Tyne University? Brearley was perfectly capable of talking to his teams in terms which indicated that he could be 'one of the boys', and indeed generally did so. He was a profound thinker about the game, and analysed the strengths and weaknesses of players in a way which was no less expert than Close's. His conclusions were simply reached via a different route. But for all that he was closely identified with his players in many ways, he was still a man apart by the very nature of his academic distinction. It gave an entirely new, and quite separate, dimension to the status of his captaincy. Whether they knew it or not, the players were in awe of a man whose cricket thinking was often carried out in (or at least related to) philosophical terms, who concentrated on his batting by humming classical music to himself and whose conversation might include a *bon mot* from classical literature in the next phrase to a bit of basic Anglo-Saxon terseness. In his admirable book, *The Art of Captaincy*, he tells us that he often got a better performance from Botham by offering jibes, usually about his bowling, which, to some minds, will contrast rather strangely with appointing a very young Botham to the tour committee on the 1979–80 trip to Australia. The sort of mentality which requires an obvious and crude insult to spur it to greater efforts does not, at first glance, seem to indicate the ideal mind to bring sagacity and responsibility to an important committee. Other people, no doubt, look at these things in a different way.

When the premature return of Willis from the West Indies in 1981 robbed him of his chief adviser, Botham was doubly dismayed because it deprived him, too, of his closest friend. As England captain, he was in the curious position of skippering his own *county* captain, but he did not turn to Rose for advice or companionship. Willis's departure meant that the two remaining players with experience of touring in the West Indies were the Yorkshiremen, Geoffrey Boycott and Chris Old, but he did not turn to them for advice either (although he enjoyed the company of Old as a drinking companion from time to time).

On the field he preferred to go it alone; off it, he ended up with his social life largely undertaken in the company of another Yorkshireman, Graham Stevenson, who was not likely to burden him with conversation of a deeply intellectual nature. His *attitude* in the England dressing-room did not change overmuch as the captain. He was, as he always has been, noisy, rumbustious and elephantine in his humour which usually involves someone being soaked in water at some stage. He liked to demonstrate his strength and, when they were picked together, found a willing contestant in Phil Edmonds, who had had a useful career at Cambridge as a Number Eight forward. One such battle of the Titans ended with Chris Old's suitcase being crushed as thirty stones of wrestling humanity fell upon it. Another exchange involving the same three individuals was of a strictly verbal nature. At Lord's in 1978 Botham was approaching his third Test century, his second in successive innings and, of course, his first at Headquarters. But with seven wickets down as Old joined him, Botham was in danger of running out of partners. Old delivered a message from Brearley: 'If the century comes, it comes. Don't feel you have to go mad and try to get it in double-quick time.' Having said that, Old chipped the next ball from the Pakistani quick bowler Sikander Bakht straight to mid-wicket. The number ten batsman was Edmonds, who strolled across to Botham with a smile and told him, 'Believe it or not, I bring the same message!' Old, who got on well with Botham, feels that as a captain he was a victim of his own strong-mindedness: 'He has clear-cut views of what he thinks should happen and they don't always fit in with the circumstances of a game. If something went wrong he would get very angry and that often made matters worse.'

On the other hand, making 'Both' angry could have the reverse effect. Brian Rose, his captain for six years at Somerset, was always aware of the big man with the big reputation and big presence in his dressing-room, and this often created its own problems. But Rose managed to avoid any open breach with Botham except on one occasion: 'We were playing Warwickshire and getting whacked around. "Both" was bowling and didn't want to be taken off but finally I insisted that he *should* be taken off. He was livid and when he went out to bat he was still in such a temper that in no time at all he had scored 100 to give us a win. I count myself lucky to have had only the one major disagreement with him in six seasons. It was certainly not easy controlling his exuberance at times.'

Brearley, whose view on any aspect of cricket has to be respected, regarded Botham as his logical successor and was pleased by his appointment as captain in 1980. That in turn pleased Botham, so that it is more than a pity that he could not accept Brearley's verdict after one home season and one tour as skipper: 'His own performance declined and he became highly sensitive to criticism' (*The Art of Captaincy*). If Ian would not accept these findings from professional critics, surely he could see their value when expressed by the man who had, in effect, recommended him for the captaincy? If only he had been able to do that his entire career and, indeed, his life, might well have taken a different course. It would certainly have been a happier life not only for him but for everyone else because – difficult though he might find it to believe – no one enjoyed his failure as captain, no one enjoyed seeing it affect his own game and no one took any pleasure in calling for his removal. Sadly, the brooding resentment which he felt was so obviously manifested in his play under the captains who followed him. If he could not be the boss himself he was certainly going to be the power behind the throne – often rather ostentatiously *in front of* the throne.

Brearley feels that both Willis and Gower allowed themselves to be 'bulldozed' by Botham, and from 1982 onwards that was all too painfully obvious. How often since then have we seen him bowling badly and then angrily (and openly) complaining about the field-placing? How often have we seen him demanding that a fieldsman be placed in the position where he has just been struck for four when the boundary has simply been the result of a bad ball? That is childish capriciousness carried to absurd lengths when it happens in the middle of a Test match. How often have we seen him being allowed to go on bowling when he has so clearly lost control of line, length, his temper and any conception of the field which has been set? Yet he *was* allowed to go on bowling badly and he *was* selected automatically in Test after Test. Is there any wonder, then, that he became fixed in his idea that there was one set of rules for him and another one for everyone else? When he was guilty of outrageously bad behaviour on the field he was either given a gentle tap on the knuckles or not called to account at all. If anyone at Lord's had been capable of the wisdom shown by his headmaster it might have been another story altogether. Or would it? As we shall see, he didn't really understand what had been said to him on that occasion, but at least Mr Morgan knew that Ian respected *some* form of authority. From 1982 onwards, once Brearley had given up the captaincy again, Botham became his own worst enemy and, even though the records continued to pile up, he was a flawed hero.

7 THE HERO

There is always only a short interval between the end of a tour to the West Indies and the start of the English domestic season, and there was only time for the briefest of rests for the players who had been so severely mauled. That summer's tourists were Kim Hughes' Australians, far from the most potent force from that country ever to tour England but, as ever, a series against the Aussies was something special to English players, no less than to cricket-lovers. This is something the West Indies, incidentally, have never quite been able to understand during their recent years of dominance in international cricket. Indeed, in 1981, one very experienced West Indian official went so far as to tell me that 'as the world champions we must be allowed to call the tune in everything about the game'. It is perhaps as well for our national cricketing sanity, after experiencing two home series and two tours to West Indies in the 1980s, that we are able to revert to that hundred-year-old love-hate relationship with our antipodean cousins from time to time.

The 1981 Aussies brought Dennis Lillee, still a truly magnificent fast bowler, and if he was not now at his fastest he had enriched his repertoire with a series of subtle variations in the Lindwall tradition. The support in terms of pace came from Geoff Lawson, Rodney Hogg and the relatively unknown (in this country) Terry Alderman. It was a formidable attack when considered in terms of the traditional qualities of quicker bowling – pace allied to swing and movement off the seam. In short, it did not rely mainly on sheer pace; it was bowling which could be faced with a proper respect for the possibilities of losing one's wicket rather than one's life. The batting, on paper, looked a long way short of the quality of some of the line-ups which had preceded it. It did not, for example, compare for one second with an order which read: Morris, Barnes, Bradman, Hassett, Harvey, Miller, Loxton, and there had been others since that Debrett assembly of 1948 which had presented more problems to an English attack than Kim Hughes' forces seemed likely to do in 1981. So, given that England were not too demoralised after their winter tour, an interesting and evenly contested series seemed in prospect.

There remained the problem of the captaincy. John Edrich had joined the Selectors after the sad loss of Ken Barrington, thus bringing him alongside Brian Close for the first time since the two of them had gone down fighting in Test cricket for the last time in that torrid evening session at Old Trafford in 1976, when they were so severely battered by Holding, Roberts and Daniel. Both were grim, steely characters not much given to sentiment.

Close, it should be remembered, was a personal friend of Botham as well as a man who had nurtured Ian through the early stages of his career, but he had been against making Botham captain in the first place. Alec Bedser and Charlie Elliott tended towards the view that, after the torments of his first two series as skipper, Botham was entitled a fair crack of the whip by leading the side against manageable opposition (and most assuredly Barrington would have taken that view had he lived). Finally, it was decided to give Botham the captaincy on a limited basis, and the First Test at Trent Bridge was lost in something under four days by four wickets. The pitch was unsatisfactory, not so much from any negligence on the part of that conscientious and genial groundsman Ron Allsop, but more probably because of a commendable zealousness in trying to get a pacey wicket which would encourage stroke play. In the event, England's first-innings 185 was the highest total achieved in the match, but their second-innings 125 was the lowest. Botham's scores were 1 and 33 (the highest in the second innings); his bowling figures two for 34 and one for 34. More than anything else apart from the pitch it was the batting of Alan Border (60 and 20) and the bowling of Lillee and Alderman (eight for 80 and nine for 130 respectively) which won the game for Australia, and yet it is difficult to think about the game without recalling a missed catch to Paul Downton off Mike Hendrick's bowling.

It is possible to make out a case for Hendrick as the unluckiest bowler ever to play Test cricket, and here we had a classic example of his misfortune which, it can be argued, was very much Botham's misfortune (as the captain) as well. Hendrick bowled in the Brian Statham style, aiming to pitch the ball on a fullish length on the nine-inch width represented by the stumps, moving the ball either way off the seam, which made him equally effective against right- and left-handers. He thus looked for the difference between a player middling the ball and the ball finding the edge of the bat. He found the edge of Border's when the future Australian captain was 10, and Downton put down a straightforward chance which, nine times out of ten, he would have taken. On such fractional margins have reputations teetered over the years. Downton lost his place for the series, Hendrick lost a wicket (and *his* place in the next four Tests), England lost the Test and Botham's reputation as a captain was no nearer salvation. The last act was played out in the Second Test at Lord's.

The details of the drawn game are not important enough to our story to dwell upon in detail. The one point of major significance was that Botham, still protesting that captaincy was not affecting his own performances, bagged a pair and took three wickets for 83 in the match. The Selectors, meanwhile, had been having a busy final day of consultation and there had been some mildly surprising changes in attitude. Close now wanted to give Botham one more chance as captain providing 'he was told what to do'. Edrich wanted him replaced at once. The other two were less emphatic about dismissal but were nevertheless thinking on those lines. Discussion ranged over the possible alternatives – Keith Fletcher of Essex and the recall of Mike Brearley. Close was adamantly against Brearley, arguing that (a) his record of success as a captain had been against sides which were under strength in the Packer era; (b) he had always questioned Brearley's qualifications for England simply on his batting ability; and (c) it was Brearley's advocacy of Botham as his successor which had landed them in their current mess. (It is, incidentally, interesting that Brearley has written with considerable generosity of Close as an England and county captain.)

The argument against Fletcher from the Selection panel as a whole – which might sound a little odd to some people – hinged on the fact that the Third Test was to be played at Headingley, which was not likely to be one of the Essex man's favourite grounds. It was there, in 1968, that Fletcher had made his first Test appearance and joined that distinguished line of players who have failed to score on their international débuts. But as he had also put down a couple of slip catches a section of misguidedly patriotic Yorkshiremen who felt the place ought to have gone to Philip Sharpe (then in fine batting form and a specialist slip-catcher of the highest pedigree) gave Fletcher a very rough ride indeed. It was a demonstration, albeit largely emanating from a section of the crowd who had clearly spent too much of the afternoon in the beer tents, which reflected no credit at all on Yorkshire's reputation for knowing its cricket, and in fact it shocked Tom Graveney who skippered England in the absence of the injured Colin Cowdrey. Yet it seems just a little strange that, nearly thirteen years later, England's Selectors should allow this incident to influence them in rejecting the claims to the England captaincy of a man who had established himself as a skipper of proven quality and was immensely popular with his players and widely respected throughout the game.

The discussion ranged on throughout the day, and by tea-time there were two formal propositions before the Selectors: Close – that Botham be given one more Test; Edrich – that he be replaced. One thing had been clearly resolved, at least: that Botham was not going to be appointed for the remainder of the series and this enabled him to salvage something personally from the ruins. As he walked into the Lord's pavilion at the end of the match he asked Alec Bedser: 'Are you going to make me captain for the rest of the series?' Bedser replied, 'No.' Botham then told him, 'Right – I resign.'

Mike Brearley had, in fact, been 'sounded out' through a third party a fortnight earlier with an inquiry as to whether he would be willing to take over the captaincy if offered it, and he had agreed that he would. However, he heard nothing more of this until eight o'clock in the evening after the Second Test had ended. Then came a phone call from the *Daily Express* to ask if he 'had heard anything'. Brearley was able to say that he hadn't because it was not until half an hour later that the chairman of the Selectors telephoned him (on a transferred-charge call because of trouble with a public telephone) to offer him the captaincy for the remaining four Tests. Brearley accepted and the scene was set for Botham to give the lie to himself in claiming that his personal form had not been affected by the captaincy, *or* for Ian simply to prove a point to his own satisfaction: that everyone had been talking and writing a load of nonsense. He *still* insists that his form wasn't affected by skippering England, dismissing his lack of personal success in that period as 'just one of those things'.

This is the sort of vague protestation which can mean anything one wants it to mean and Ian, conveniently, has used it to mean that his lack of success during his captaincy was mere coincidence – the sort of loss-of-form which happens to most players at some stage of their careers. It is a view which really cannot be justified. Nevertheless, tragic though the loss of the captaincy undoubtedly was to him, it resulted in a summer of such splendour, such drama, such incredible heroics that those of us who watched it all must feel a certain curious gratitude to the Selectors. It began in the very next Test at Headingley, and the result was that in a way we had not seen since the immediate post-war years the whole country was talking and thinking cricket. People stopped each other in the street to ask: 'Have you heard what's happening at Headingley [or Edgbaston or Old Trafford]?' Those television shops with demonstration sets in their windows had huge crowds congregated outside, blocking pavements and spilling over on to the roads. Motorists who had car radios stopped to pass on the glad tidings to those who hadn't. It was a golden summer of English cricket and most of it centred round one man: Ian Terence Botham. And yet it started almost by accident.

The captains 'read' the pitch in rather different ways, or so it seemed from the final selections. England opted for a four-man pace attack of Willis, Dilley, Old and Botham (with Gooch and Gatting as supplementary seamers if required), leaving out the off-spinner, Emburey. Australia omitted Hogg in favour of the slow left-armer, Ray Bright. Australia won the toss, decided to bat and at the end of the first day were 210 for three on a pitch where, Brearley recalls with a wry smile, he said to David Evans, one of the umpires, 'If all went well you could bowl a side out for 90.' Botham, who bowled 236 deliveries in the innings, took six wickets for 95 while Willis and Dilley (the two fastest bowlers) and Old (the best line-and-length man in the side) collected two between the three of them. Australia declared at 401 for nine. It is particularly interesting to note, especially in view of some of the fierce criticism of Botham's short-pitched bowling in subsequent seasons, that Brearley thought he had been too sparing in his employment of the bouncer!

By Saturday evening England were in disarray and when Botham went out to bat at number seven the score read 87–5. It was a situation which, under captains like Hutton, Close, Illingworth (all Yorkshiremen? Well, the match *was* being played at Headingley!) would have brought the instruction: 'Get your head down and graft. It could rain all through the weekend and we might have a chance of saving the game.' In contrast, Brearley, in his book *Phoenix from the Ashes* recalls: 'He [Botham] commented before he left the dressing-room that he did not intend to hang about and immediately played with abandon. Early on, he tried to smash a ball on the off side and missed it; he looked up to the balcony where I was sitting. I grinned and indicated that he should have tried to hit it even harder.' Strange are the differing ways of captains. And Close was sitting beside Brearley on the pavilion balcony at the time! England were all out for 174 (Botham 50 from fifty-four balls) and with one session of the day remaining, followed by the Sunday rest-day, Hughes was well placed to enforce the follow-on. England lost Gooch before bad light came to their rescue, but as the crowd filed soberly away they saw Ladbroke's odds flashed up on the scoreboard near the Kirkstall Lane entrance to the ground: 'England: 500–1.' That seemed about right.

It is now a matter of history that a couple of the Australians, to most of whom a wager is as natural as breathing, could not resist a bet when such odds were offered in a cricket match. I was indirectly involved in this aspect of it myself when playing, on the Sunday, in the immensely enjoyable annual golf match between Moortown and the Forty Club. One of my four-ball was Albert Geoffrey Parker, something of a legendary figure in both Bradford League cricket and Yorkshire Rugby Union circles, and as we established the stakes for our match he grinned: 'If I lose I can pay you out of my winnings from Ladbroke's.'

'You didn't back England?' I asked incredulously. 'Of course,' Albert replied. 'Five hundred to one in a cricket match? I wasn't going to miss that. I've got a fiver on the lads.' He missed Tuesday's play at Headingley, though keeping in touch with developments from radio and TV, because as a worldly wise Yorkshireman he knew well enough that winnings of £2500 would inevitably involve him in buying £2501 worth of drinks. But he's always had a soft spot for Ian Botham.

The wicket on Monday played in a more unpredictable way than it had during England's first innings with uneven bounce causing the main problems. The brilliant defensive technique of Boycott and the sheer guts and determination of Willey took the score from 41–4 to 105 before Willey was caught in the odd position of third-man-very-square-and-two-thirds-of-the-way-back, which Hughes, shrewdly observing the misbehaviour of the pitch and Willey's approach to combating it, had sent Dyson to patrol: 115–5. Boycott, after three and a half hours' resolute defence, was lbw to Alderman: 133–6. Bob Taylor came and went, it seemed, in what the Germans graphically call an *Augenblick*: 135–7. England, following on, were still 92 runs adrift when Graham Dilley joined Botham. Both had booked out of their hotel that morning in common with most of the England side. It was not yet half past three on the fourth afternoon when they came together. It was a quarter to five before they were separated, and by that time the pair had put on 117 runs with Dilley, it seemed, the senior partner in the early stages. Botham at first played soberly, scoring 39 in nearly an hour and a half up to the tea interval – an unprecedentedly sedate rate for him. Dilley, who is by no means a novice with the bat, began to show us some front-foot drives and one could sense the reaction in Botham, even from 100 yards away. He visibly bristled. In the midst of trying to make victory for Australia as difficult as possible, soberly and with dignity keeping them in the field as long as he was able, he was being upstaged by the young man from Kent.

In the England dressing-room wild hopes began to rise of seeing the Aussies have to go out to bat again, if only for a modest number of runs, as Botham at first hesitantly, then with relish, began to join in an orgy of exotic stroke-making. And perish the thought that one is taking anything away from the grandeur of the occasion but things started to go England's way. It was a position which called for every bit of luck to be on their side, and Fortune indeed favoured the brave in those last two hours of the day. Despite their Sunday rest, the Australian bowlers now began to feel the effects of Saturday's long stints as well as the sustained spells of bowling they had to undertake throughout Monday. Hughes felt that Bright was not going to be effective on the pitch as it was now playing (he bowled only four overs in the innings) and Australia had no Gooch or Gatting to 'spell' the quicker men. Lillee began to feel his thirty-two years; Alderman and Lawson dragged their aching legs to the wicket willingly enough, only to see a Divine Providence hovering over Botham's bat (it was Gooch's actually, borrowed for the occasion on the premise that as its owner had scored only 2 and 0, it ought to have a few runs in it). Often the ball screamed through the slips or over their heads – once for six! – but with equal frequency it hurtled off the middle of the bat through mid-off, extra cover and square on the offside. It was batting of ferocious magnificence.

Word spread through the city centre, I learned later, as so often it had done in the past on great occasions at Headingley, and people rushed into the homes and offices of friends with television sets or radios. Dilley had made a 56 he will remember all his life when he played on to the near-exhausted Alderman and Chris Old went out before his own crowd. He was, in fact, captain of Yorkshire at the time, but fear of failure in front of his own kinsmen was as nothing compared with the retribution which awaited him, he was told (notably by the formidable Peter Willey), in the dressing-room if he didn't stay there with Botham. He stayed. He stayed while another 67 historic runs were scored against an attack which had now been cut to ribbons. Hughes just did not know how to set a field to check the runs; as he strove to cut down the flow the bowlers increasingly lost their grip on what *line* to bowl. In desperation, Lawson – never the sweetest-tempered bowler when things are not going well – let go two beamers in an over at Botham, who sneered contempt at him. By the time Old was out for 29 of the bravest and certainly the most valuable runs of his entire career, England were 319–8, and now we saw yet another touch of greatness from Botham. During the last twenty minutes of play, he farmed the bowling so effectively that last man Willis had to face only five balls (to which he stoically applied that huge forward lunge) while the score advanced by another 31 runs. At close of play, England were 124 runs ahead and, while no one felt it could last on the morrow, most of us went home and prayed fervently that somehow it would.

Botham refused to speak to reporters that evening, and while it is wholly understandable in the context of the game – he must have been desperately tired, and finding the right words to utter as a hero is not the easiest of tasks – that has to be seen as a mistake in the overall picture of the love–hate relationship which has marked his relationship with the media. If he was soured by the criticism of his captaincy and felt he was only 'wanted' when he had done well, then he was refusing to accept a harsh but obvious fact of life. It is indeed tough at the top. But the players were undoubtedly in his corner when he took his stand against meeting the media, and from their point of view that was understandable too. Yet not *all* the media are interested merely in heroics; not all its representatives are quick to knock idols from their pedestals; not all rejoice when the mighty are fallen. And amongst those who were disappointed that Ian did not want to talk that evening not all were angered – some were merely saddened.

Half the England team staged a modest celebration of the day's events by going for a fish and chip supper in Headingley, where the four-year-old Liam Botham had the misfortune to get a bone stuck in his throat. The party should have chosen the alternative establishment of Charlie Brett, a little closer to the ground. They would probably have run into the press, but they wouldn't have found bones in their fish!

On the morning of 21 July it is fair to say that the mood in the English camp was more wistful than optimistic – 'if only we had another 50 runs to play with we might be in with a chance'. But enough miracles had been accomplished the previous day; more could not be expected from the last wicket pair, or the bowlers. And after 5 runs had been added Willis fell to Alderman, leaving Botham 149 not out. Few of us had ever seen an innings like his. There have been Test centuries which have lingered long in the mind and which will always be a part of cricket history: Hutton's 364 at the Oval in 1938, McCabe's 232 at Trent Bridge in the same series, Compton at Old Trafford and Trent Bridge in 1948 . . . one can go back to Bradman's 300 in a day (Headingley, 1930), to Herbert Sutcliffe, to Hammond, to so many great names and so much great batting. But can anyone ever remember a game which was swung so completely by one innings, and such a spectacular innings? It was an unbelievable turnabout brought about by an incredible piece of striking. But it needed an awful lot of luck. Botham's innings two Tests later was much, much better, as we shall see.

For the moment we are concerned with Australia's needing 130 to win with most of a fair, pleasant day to get them. Brearley immediately put himself in the position of the opposition. '*They* will be nervous now,' he told his men as, ever the psychologist, he gave the new ball and the Kirkstall Lane downslope to Botham in the hope that, charged up as he must be, another miracle could be wrought. His first two balls were hit for 4, but in his second over he took the wicket of Graeme Wood. At the other end Dilley conceded 11 runs from his first two overs and *didn't* take a wicket. Willis took over at the Rugby Stand end, striving for as much pace as possible for five overs and then asking to be switched. Brearley at first declined, but after consultation with Taylor and Botham decided to give it a go. It was a calculated risk because Willis was frequently plagued by no-balling troubles, and the considerable slope down to the plateau on which the Headingley square is sited often disturbs the rhythm of bowlers not accustomed to operating there regularly. But England were in a position in which they had nothing to lose and everything to gain from all-out attack. If Willis's bull-like charge to the stumps represented a risk of his being 'called', it had to be taken. And another miracle occurred.

Bowling with a fire few had seen from him, Willis took all the remaining wickets except that of Border (bowled by Old) and his eight for 43 was, and remained, the best bowling performance of his career. Australia were all out early in the afternoon for 111, with all that figure's mystical significance for English players, and England had won by

18 runs – their first Test victory since the Jubilee match in Bombay in February 1980. It was a wonderful day for English cricket which even the most hardened cynics were happy to share, and on the balcony of the pavilion the hero of the hour, Bob Willis, gave a singularly graceless interview to BBC TV in which he saw an attack on the media as more suitable to the occasion than joining in the general rejoicing. It had not, it seemed, been appropriate for cricket-writers (and broadcasters) to offer any word of criticism on the first two days of the game. England's cricket in the early stages of the Test had, we were given to understand, been immaculate. We were left to assume, therefore, that Botham's century and Willis's own bowling were commonplace occurrences – performances which we all saw regularly.

It was a particularly stupid piece of PR which might have got a cheap laugh or two at the media's expense, but it reflected no credit whatever on the man who was shortly to become England's captain. He was Botham's pal and we can give him a few marks for loyalty if (as he plainly was) he was attacking those who Ian claimed had cost him the captaincy. But the marks would be for loyalty only, not for common sense, or for the accuracy of his assumptions. The gulf between players and media was becoming an abyss. The Cricket Writers' Club members in particular were aghast at Willis's attack, and before Brearley left Headingley he was approached by Peter Smith, on behalf of the CWC, who made three important points: (1) that writers are not responsible for the headlines which appear above their copy; (2) that while he and his members are at Tests to write about the cricket, almost every newspaper (together with radio and TV) has a second-string journalist present whose job it is to get 'quotes' and to write about 'fringe' topics ancillary to the game itself; (3) there was something illogical about certain players accepting large sums of money for articles they didn't write and then turning round and biting the hand that fed them.

It is interesting, therefore, to learn from Brearley (in *Phoenix from the Ashes*) that on the eve of the Fourth Test at Edgbaston he was asked by Peter Lush, marketing manager of the Test and County Cricket Board who also acts as its public relations officer, to persuade the players to co-operate with the press 'in the interests of the general coverage of the game'. It should, perhaps, be mentioned here that Brearley's handling of press conferences (and radio and TV interviews) was never less than interesting. He did not suffer fools gladly and pounced like a tiger if someone asked a stupid or provocative question. But in a sensible exchange of views he was courteous and, on the occasion when a questioner showed a little naïvety (which was not uncommon) he was helpful without being overtly patronising. He was staunch in his defence of his own players in the face of queries which he thought were not strictly relevant, but he could accept that some things were open to criticism. Only once did I personally cross swords with him, and the exchange was brief and to the point. It happened in the wilds of Pakistan at a place called Bahawalpur where conditions were not entirely comfortable and the media party were quartered some distance away from the players in a billet which would have been awarded something less than one star. I had called on professional duties at the players' accommodation and had been offered a piece of marmite toast by Bernard Thomas, the physiotherapist, which represented the best meal I had during the whole five days in Bahawalpur. Between munching pieces of toast I was telling Bernard about something which had happened back home and referred to a man we both knew as 'a creep'. Brearley, who was close at hand but not involved in the conversation, intervened to say, 'I do not think he is a creep.' I replied, 'I do,' and that was the extent of the exchange. But like most cricket-writers and broadcasters I had a wholesome respect for Brearley.

It was no more than one would have expected that at the players' dinner before the Edgbaston Test he canvassed the views of all his men on the subject of the dispute with the media and learned that 'Botham was still simmering over the injustices he felt he had suffered while captain'. He had, presumably, conveniently forgotten the incident in Antigua when newspapermen covered up for him but, that apart, Botham really could not complain of unfair criticism of his cricket or captaincy on that tour. He could not point to any instances of 'personal' knocks for which cricket-writers or broadcasters were responsible, and it was difficult to recall any instance of critical comment on his cricket which was not justified by the events. On that eve-of-Test occasion in Birmingham, however, he cited two cases of intrusion into his private life which he was most certainly entitled to resent, one involving a party at his home and one relating to his small son, Liam. 'He now reacted to all this,' says Brearley, 'by refusing to talk to the press during the Edgbaston match. When I went round the table, however, everyone else was prepared to co-operate provided the requests were not too frequent. And three days later Ian had a talk with Smith, after which he, too, agreed to go along with these little interviews.' Peter Smith, it should be said, has long had a tightrope to walk, balancing between what his paper has felt he *should* write on occasions and preserving a good relationship with the biggest personality in the game. We have all faced that problem at one time or another but no one, perhaps, quite to the same extent as Smithie!

And so to the game at Edgbaston. Brearley won the toss and decided to bat in a festival-like atmosphere (apart from the euphoria of the Headingley win, the wedding of Prince Charles and Lady Diana Spencer had taken place the previous day). In contrast, events out in the middle took an acrimonious turn because of one or two decisions resented by the Australians but England, just the same, ended with a disappointing total of 189, largely due to some superb bowling by Terry Alderman, whose five for 43 were remarkable figures on an Edgbaston wicket. He had now taken twenty-five wickets in the series so far. Australia gained a lead of 69, bowled out England again for 219, leaving themselves needing 151 to win. Before play ended on Saturday night they lost Wood for 2 and resumed at 9–1 at noon on Sunday (there was no rest day in that match).

There was beautiful weather for the whole of that Test and it was good to see a huge crowd in a ground which is not usually the best for support on such occasions. But this was now a very special series and those who turned up, perhaps for the first time, were not disappointed. On a pitch with no life, Willis bowled magnificently though with scant luck, and for his dramatic breakthrough which won the game Botham clearly owes a great deal to his friend. Yet for all the drama of that Sunday afternoon, for all the way Botham again pulled out a miraculous performance (this time with the ball) for me the vital wicket was taken by Emburey, the wicket which changed the whole course of the game. After Dyson and Hughes had gone the total was still only 29 and Border, going in at number three, was batting with rare skill. He gave a chance to Brearley at slip, off Willis, which was not taken and that, we could not help feeling, was going to be a costly miss – perhaps like Downton's at Trent Bridge. Yallop finally went at 87–4 and Martin Kent, who had batted beautifully in the first innings, joined Border, suffering acutely from stomach trouble. At 105, Embury produced a ball which bounced astonishingly; Border could not get his glove out of the way and he was caught by Gatting.

He had scored 40 of Australia's runs and all the recognised batting had now gone, except for Kent who was playing in his first Test match and could reasonably be expected to feel the pressure; 46 were needed from the last five wickets. On paper, Australia still looked favourites, but to those watching they were clearly apprehensive and struggling. England had, in fact, been firmly on top except for one brief period during the stand between Border and Yallop when runs suddenly but inexplicably began to flow at an unacceptable rate. Brearley (through Willis and Emburey) had put the stopper in that bottle and now the Aussies were plainly up against it. But it only needed a few profitable edges, a few fortunate flails, to change the picture.

Brearley, in fact, felt that Emburey would be the man to win the game and was toying with the idea of pairing

Willey with him in an all-off-spin partnership, but when Border was out he turned to Botham. Now, it would be more than interesting to know if Brearley would have done the same thing three or four seasons later when Botham, while still ploughing steadily on through a sea of Test wickets, was nevertheless proving increasingly expensive, the more so in limited-overs games where 'tightness' is essential. But here, at Edgbaston in 1981, Brearley felt Botham was capable of heeding the instruction to 'keep it tight'. Not only that, with the inspirational touch which stamped him as a leader of distinction, he felt that Botham was the man with the golden arm who could produce exactly what was required in the circumstances. Botham, in fact, did not particularly want to bowl at that stage, and in view of the man's belief in himself – which is not suggested as a criticism in this context – that is surprising. But even *he* must have been surprised by what happened next.

In the space of twenty-eight deliveries Botham now dismissed Marsh, Bright, Lillee, Kent and Alderman for just 1 run. He had been asked by his captain simply to keep it tight. He had done that with a vengeance, and England were now one up in the series. Whether the players believe it or not, cricket journalists are no less patriotic than the rest of the country (even if professional codes do not allow them to address themselves to the sentiment with special eloquence) and there was much rejoicing in certain areas. It is good to have something fine and heroic and successful to talk and write about. And then I looked at some of my Australian colleagues, addressing themselves to microphones and typewriters already swimming in vitriol. It was impossible to resist a slightly cynical smile: if Botham and Willis thought they had a hard time from the British media, how could they ever be capable of facing the sort of denunciation which now awaited the Aussies?

During the past twenty years or so the Old Trafford pitch has undergone some remarkable changes of character. Contrast, for instance, the match against Australia there in 1964 with the one against West Indies in 1976. In the former, Bobby Simpson and Bill Lawry put on 201 for the first wicket, Simpson went on to score 311 in an innings of twelve hours forty-two minutes. For more than two days the men involved in bowling to him included, notably, Tom Cartwright (77 overs) and Fred Rumsey (35.5 overs) who were both playing in their first Test! When England batted, Ken Barrington got 256 and Ted Dexter 174, and Tom Veivers had to bowl 95.1 overs – but at least, unlike Rumsey and Cartwright, he was a *slow* bowler. Twelve years later, Mike Selvey played in *his* first Test at Old Trafford, took a wicket against the majestic Windies with his sixth ball and three for 6 in his first twenty. The top came off the wicket almost from the start and a marvellous innings by Gordon Greenidge gave him 134 out of his side's first-innings total of 211 before England were dismissed for 71. Since then, no one has been entirely sure how the pitch was likely to play from one season to another, and in 1981 there was the additional complexity caused by torrential rains which swept the country just before the Fifth Test.

England reckoned they might need two spinners but had to consider to what extent this might weaken the batting, which generally had not been too secure against the Australian attack in previous Tests. Willey was left out to give Chris Tavaré the chance to play as a specialist number three batsman, and in another change (which was enforced) Paul Allott came into the opening attack on his 'home' ground because Old was injured. But the decision to call up an extra spinner into the Test party of twelve meant that somehow the batting had to be strengthened. This was achieved by bringing in Alan Knott as the wicket-keeper in place of Bob Taylor. They were outstandingly the two best 'keepers in the country and, although contrasting in their styles and personalities, there was little if anything to choose between them behind the stumps. As a batsman, however, Knott's great gifts as an improviser – as well as considerable technical accomplishment – gave him the edge and so, with a Selectorial explanation to Taylor which was sincere in its regret, the change was made. The calling up of Knott as well as Underwood was widely interpreted as a move of double specialisation – the Kent wicket-keeper to take the Kent left-arm spinner – so that when Underwood was made twelfth man on the morning of 13 August, the Selectors left themselves open to a certain critical fire.

Indeed, it caused some quizzical comment in the Australian dressing-room, but the explanation was that England were, in fact, thinking defensively, reasoning that a draw would be satisfactory to them if they couldn't force a win (being one up in the series) and thus it was safer to go in with an extra batsman rather than two spinners. With Botham at number seven the batting certainly looked safe. The Australians had a problem of a more serious nature since an all-out attempt to win was the obvious course for them. Instead, they found themselves without Lawson, who had a back injury, and late in the day Hogg withdrew as well. From a fair sprinkling of Australian pace bowlers scattered around England who were engaged in some level of professional cricket the tourists chose Mike Whitney, who had originally come over to play in the Northern League (which has clubs in mid and north Lancashire plus two in Cumbria) but who was doing a certain amount of deputising for the injured Mike Procter as a Gloucs player. He was a left-armer of no violent pace and not a lot of variation, so he did not appear likely to trouble England in anything like the same way as Lawson or Hogg might have done. But there were still Alderman and Lillee to be reckoned with and, with Whitney weighing in with the two worthy wickets of Tavaré and Gower, they were the pair who bowled out England for 231, only to be dismissed for 130 themselves.

At close of play England were 70 for one on their second innings, and a big Saturday crowd prepared to watch a spell of consolidation. With Tavaré, for the second time in the match, looking very much the answer to England's number three problems but not exactly delighting the crowd, Gower, Gatting and Brearley went cheaply at the other end. I have always found it difficult to commentate on radio when Chris Tavaré is batting in Tests. That gentle inching forward as the bowler reaches his delivery stride seems to commit him irrevocably to the forward defensive push, and his eccentric grip on the handle emphasises a defensive attitude. It is not easy to see where a scoring shot is likely to come from, let alone one of grandeur, and the one thing a radio commentator hates above everything else is a situation which drives him into a corner of repetitious description. Yet Chris is a delightful man, if a trifle shy and withdrawn amongst strange company. He is intelligent, well-mannered, unfailingly pleasant and a good man to tour with. (I once amused myself along a dreary motorway trek with the theory that 'Tav' spent so long at the wicket to avoid having to sit in the same dressing-room for any length of time with Botham who, if he cannot be persuaded to sleep, rampages around the place more like a rogue elephant than a caged lion.)

Although in a perfect world it shouldn't happen, I have often found myself searching twice as hard as usual for something different to say about his defence rather than allowing myself to lapse into something approaching exasperation. This was particularly the case once in Madras in 1981–2. When commentating from India and Pakistan there is a consciousness that hundreds of thousands of people are getting up on a cold winter's morning eager to hear about some cricket and my view, rightly or wrongly, has always been that they deserve something a little more colourful than the straightforward 'Kapil Dev bowls, Tavaré plays forwards defensively, the ball runs out on the off side and there is no run.' On that occasion in Madras, Chris (having taken over as opener from the departed Geoffrey Boycott) batted for five and a half hours (239 balls) for just 36 runs and I felt rather strongly at the end of the innings that there was a limit, even in a beautiful and flexible language like English, to the number of ways one could describe the forward defensive stroke! When I mentioned this to him later in the day he smiled a smile which told me far more eloquently than words that he understood. Would that there were more Chris Tavarés in the game, even if more than one in the same *team* might tax spectators' patience just a little more than commentators' vocabularies!

And so, on the afternoon of 15 August 1981, Botham joined Tavaré at the crease – not for long, but long enough to provide a most marvellous contrast in styles. And then most of the rest of the day belonged to Botham alone. His was an innings of such rare magnificence that in the course of nearly 150 Tests which I have been privileged to see there has been nothing like it. When he was 28, Australia took the new ball and Lillee allowed himself the luxury of two long legs, an indulgence which one cannot really see that fine bowler applying to any other batsman in the game. He invited the hook, and Botham – this was a challenge he was utterly incapable of resisting – obliged. Twice in the over he hit Lillee for six, over the heads of the two fieldsmen and far back into the rows of spectators around the Old Trafford scoreboard. Both were incredible shots because both came from *good*, deliberate bouncers, delivered straight at the throat. Botham got his feet quickly into position, watched the ball until the last possible moment, then tucked his chin into his left shoulder and went through with the hook shot with the ball played from somewhere perilously close to his right ear.

Much has been written about the weight of Botham's bats and they have become favourite subject-matter for modern cartoonists, who picture his weapons as ranging somewhere between a Samoan war-club and the mace habitually carried into battle by that redoubtable fourteenth-century Bishop of Durham, Antony Bek. In point of fact, Botham's bats weigh less than 3 lbs, considerably lighter than Clive Lloyd's, for instance. Duncan Fearnley, who makes the bats in Worcester, tells us:

> The bats Ian used when he first came to me were about 2 lbs 8 oz. He then moved on to about 2 lbs 11 oz and started having a thicker grip, which obviously helps the pick-up and balance. Nowadays I go through piles of willow to select one or two pieces which I think will be suitable – where I can leave a lot of

timber in the back of the bat but get a lighter pick-up – so that he ends with a bat weighing just under 3 lbs with three rubber grips round the handle.

It is interesting to note, in passing, that Len Hutton scored most of his 40,140 first-class runs (6971 in seventy-nine Tests) using a bat which weighed 2 lbs 2 oz. Today, very few top-class batsmen use anything weighing less than 2½ lbs. Let no one be amazed at the near-disappearance of the late cut from the batting repertoire!

It is probable that those tremendous strokes of Botham at Old Trafford owed as much to the sheer strength and power of the man as to the weight of his bat. And he hit another six to the same area in Lillee's next over. He gave two half-chances, one to third man (!) and the other which caused the débutant Whitney to reflect that there is more to playing Test cricket than honour and glory. He found himself under a dreadful swirling skier at a deepish mid-off position and suffered all kinds of muscular contortions before missing it. No one in the crowd blamed him, not merely because it was a shot which soared to an immense height and hung, but also because no one of English birth wanted the innings to end. Botham went on to pull Alderman into the crowd to the left of the pavilion for six and hit Bright straight for another to show a fine impartiality. But it was the assault upon Lillee which gave him most pleasure, because he had long respected the West Australian for the great bowler he was, and which caused those of us watching to catch our breath. One wished Cardus could have been there to describe it.

In a truly memorable innings of 118, Botham received only 102 balls (and the first 30 of those produced only three singles as he carefully, if uncharacteristically, played himself in) so in fact 115 runs actually came from 72 deliveries. He hit one six and three fours off Alderman, two sixes and two fours off Bright, three sixes and four fours off Lillee and just four fours off Whitney – no sixes, as Mike delights in telling them back home in Sydney. Lillee, it should be recorded, was as generous as any Australian as Botham was applauded all the way back to the dressing-room. The Aussies may be the world's worst losers but they know quality when they see it. By lunchtime on Sunday, they needed 506 to win and Hughes wryly reflected that the target, on their record that season, could not be regarded as much more difficult than 130! The openers, however, had other ideas. Wood, who over a number of years had established himself as a judge of a single in the kamikaze mould, turned his attention this time to his partner and left Dyson high and dry with just seven runs scored. Understandably rattled, Wood then played a bad shot to a bad ball and was caught behind, but with Hughes offering sterner resistance to score 43 and Yallop looking very sound, Australia had reached 210 for three inside the last hour of the day. Emburey then dismissed Yallop for 114 and Kent for 2 – his first real failure of a short career. But Border was still there and Marsh settled in with him to see Australia 210–5 at seven o'clock.

At close of play I drove to Manchester Airport to pick up two professional golfers who were flying in from Carroll's Irish Open Championship to see the final day of the Test. One was Graham Marsh, to whom I was able to report that his brother was not out; the other was my elder son with whom I was looking forward immensely to spending a day at a Test match for the first time. They did not see a momentous day's play, but for a time it was tense as Border farmed the bowling and the score mounted slowly. It was – it had to be – Botham who finally put it out of reach for the Aussies by flinging himself through the air to hold a brilliant catch; this accounted for Lillee, who had scored 28 of a partnership of 53 with Border. Even so, Whitney marked his Test début by staying an hour without scoring, and when he was finally out Border was unbeaten on 123. The Aussies had lost the Ashes, but they had certainly made a fight of it at Old Trafford and Allan Border had given us an indication of what was to come from him in 1985. But it was Botham's series. The man who had started the summer as a surly and disgruntled misanthrope ended it as Britain's national sporting hero.

8 THE HEAVYWEIGHT

The choice of Keith Fletcher to lead the tour to India (with the inaugural Test in Sri Lanka at the end of it) through the winter of 1981–2 was a logical and generally popular one. 'Fletch' was a highly respected county captain who had led Essex into the most successful period in their history; he was as knowledgeable as anyone available about conditions on the sub-continent; he was a good player of spin bowling, which was likely to be encountered in most matches even though the wizardry of Bedi, Prasanna, Venkataraghavan and Chandrasekhar had now passed into the record books. If Botham was disappointed at not being recalled as the England captain he could scarcely have any serious complaints about the selection of Fletcher. Some of the other choices found less favour. The party included two spinners – Underwood and Emburey – and was otherwise packed with fast and medium-fast bowlers on the premise that Indian batsmen were not always comfortable against anything above medium pace. Someone at Lord's, it seemed, had not really kept up to date with developments in Indian cricket.

Gone were the days when, as Freddie Trueman has delightedly described, as he ran in to bowl he could see Tony Lock (fielding at leg slip) clearly visible in the gap between the stumps and the retreating batsman. Gavaskar had proved on grounds all over the world that *he* didn't get out of the way; so had Vengsarkar and the hugely talented little man from the south, Viswanath. Sandip Patel was a middle-order bat who actually had the effrontery to *attack* fast-medium bowling, and now we saw for the first time a player who went even further than that. The multi-syllabic Madrassi, Krishnamachari Srikkanth, skippered the Indian Under–22 side in Poona on three blazing hot days and led from the front by blasting 87 and 74 in, by Indian batting standards, no time at all. His bat looked like a treasured relic from childhood and his kit generally would have brought disapproving glances if he had been appearing for a Public Schools' XI, but there was no doubting the quality of his stroke play. If Botham tried short-pitching to him, Srikkanth hooked, and hooked well. Few people had seen Indian batsmanship of this type and he looked likely to prove a difficult customer in the one-day internationals, at least. Botham, however, had had enough of the young upstart in Poona and in the first limited-overs international in Ahmedabad he produced something special to remove Srikkanth for a duck. He bowled well, and batted well too, as England won handsomely by six wickets to reach Bombay, and the First Test, with four wins and a draw from their first five matches.

And there, all illusions about a successful tour were rudely shattered. It is fair to say that England had got themselves into a right old state about umpiring mistakes before the game even began. Gooch, in particular, had suffered in the earlier games, and once the seeds of doubt are sown amongst a touring party the damage is done. Almost every conversation involving the players in their off-duty moments hinged on umpiring decisions, and we were all well aware of it. With a pleasant and approachable captain and an excellent manager (Raman Subba Row) well acquainted with all aspects of public relations, the media problems of the previous winter (and, to some extent, the summer) were behind us, and if personal relationships were not quite in the 1977–8 mould it was still a sound and well-integrated party who mixed well with the reporters. Indeed, I found myself in trouble back home with a handful of readers of the *Guardian* for voicing the doubts and fears of players who were not permitted to speak for themselves on such matters. I have always believed, rightly or wrongly, that unless a correspondent accompanying a tour party writes or speaks of the conditions under which the games are being played he is failing in his duty as a reporter.

Conditions in India – and some other countries as well – are *not* like playing at Chelmsford, Chesterfield or Cheltenham. There *are* rats in some hotels, and in some dressing-rooms as well. The food is *not* what one is accustomed to at home. The water, and particularly the ice, *can* cause all kinds of illnesses. Pitches, by and large, *are* slow and low and umpiring mistakes *do* occur. Where I did not entirely subscribe to the players' morbid fears was in believing that some decisions were prompted by patriotic instincts. I spent a lot of time chatting to Indian umpires and in almost every case found them great enthusiasts for the game and decent, basically honest men. However, they were not former players who had spent years intimately involved in cricket at its highest level and thus had not the advantage of the experience gained by umpires in England. It has to be said, though, that I was startled by the views of one Indian umpire on the laws relating to balls pitching outside the leg stump, especially as the dapper Bengali, Dilip Doshi, liked to exploit the bowler's rough with his slow left-arm spinners. And Doshi, much to the chagrin of at least three English batsmen, took five for 39 in England's first Test innings of the tour. He was not the man, however, who ultimately bowled England to defeat by 138 runs in a game in which the highest individual score was 55. That was Sharma Madan Lal, a little chap with good shoulders who skidded through his medium-fast seamers on a pitch quite unlike anything most of us had ever seen in India to take five second-innings wickets for 23, while his infinitely more renowned partner, Kapil Dev, was taking five for 70 at the other end. Madan Lal had toured England in 1974 and after that had gained lots of experience in the Leagues of the North without ever looking the bowler he did now. Indeed, in a broadcast at the end of the Test I said, 'Five for 23 against England. They'll never believe that in the Huddersfield League.'

In talking about conditions in India being 'different', there is another important point to consider. Word now went round that at Bangalore, New Delhi, Calcutta, Madras and Kanpur, where the remaining five Tests were to be played, the wickets from now on must be very low and very slow. Officials smilingly acknowledged that it would indeed be so, even when talking about a game three months in the future. If it sounds incredible to English ears it is a matter of no great remark in India. One Test had been won; if the remaining five were drawn, that would do very nicely, thank you, to give the home side the series. Coming on top of their suspicions about umpiring standards, the players could have been forgiven for being depressed as they contemplated the remaining long weeks of the tour. It is a great tribute to Fletcher and Subba Row that morale never deteriorated. The smiles might have become a little rueful, and there was a certain degree of exasperation at times, but despair and misery never took over. The party soldiered on, doing their individual and collective duties with professional application and Botham, with an odd lapse here and there, was a good member of a good tour.

At some stage he acquired one of those tape-and-cassette players, so prized by West Indians. It was about the size of a Welsh dresser and apart from the deafening sound it emitted it looked to be a needlessly heavy burden to lug around between hotels and airports and grounds as well. His team-mates were not spared the cacophony at any stage, and when I asked him why he had bought such a huge instrument Ian replied, with a grin of pure delight, 'It's bigger than Viv's.' The competition with his Taunton mate penetrated into the most remote areas.

During the Delhi Test I went to the dressing-room one morning to fix up my close-of-play interview with Geoff Boycott after he had passed Gary Sobers's record of 8032 Test runs and found half the side – the intrepid Botham amongst them – standing on the table because a rat had joined them, foraging for rations. 'Get it out of here,' roared Ian. 'How do you suggest I do that?' I inquired. 'Belt it with a bloody bat,' was the advice. The nearest available bat was Mike Gatting's, but he was not disposed to have it used as a rat-remover. As the investigative reporters of the Sunday papers used to say, I made an excuse and left. If evasive action was good enough for The Gorilla it was good enough for me.

His exploits of the previous summer had been devoured by the Indian cricket public, which is immense and wildly enthusiastic, and everyone was looking forward in the series to comparing him with Kapil Dev. Interestingly, Kapil was known as 'India's Ian Botham', and not the other way round, which I thought was as nice a compliment as could have been conferred. They had to wait until the final, rain-affected, Test in Kanpur before direct comparison could be made, however, and then, in terms of entertainment value, it was Kapil Dev who came out on top with a brilliant 116 which included two sixes and sixteen fours. But if one takes that century and then considers Botham's 142 strictly in context, the Englishman's was the more valuable. At that stage we did not know how much play was going to be lost. Ian's hundred was a vital and responsible innings which established England's position; Kapil's came when a draw was a foregone conclusion and he had nothing to lose by a display of fireworks. It was in Indore, a week before that last Test, that Botham added to his personal legend, with a hundred off forty-eight deliveries in fifty minutes with seven sixes and sixteen fours. He has never struck the ball better. He topped the Test batting averages with 440 runs at 55 and took seventeen wickets, more than anyone else, at 38.82. He could still bowl his outswinger, even in bright sunlight. The saddest legacy of that tour was that Gavaskar, determined to draw the Tests after his initial success in Bombay, managed to slow the over-rate down to nine an hour – with the two slow left-armers, Doshi and Shastri, bowling! To anyone who has experienced that, eleven an hour by the West Indian quicks seems like greased lightning.

Before the party returned home there was a short but extremely pleasant visit to Sri Lanka, where the first one-day international was narrowly won by 5 runs and the second even more narrowly lost by 3 runs before the first

Test match to be played in that attractive island. It was won by England, not because of the three-man quick attack of Willis, Allott and Botham but by the spinners: Underwood (five for 28 in the first innings) and Emburey (six for 33 in the second). However, the three games were enough to show that there was a fair amount of useful talent in Sri Lanka to follow in the footsteps of men who had played in English county cricket like Stan Jayasinghe, Clive Inman and Gamini Gooneseena. In fact, since then the Sri Lankans have shown that their ability to produce good players is out of all proportion to the relatively small numbers who have a chance to learn the game at school. Their batsmen are well coached and thus play in a beautifully stylish way; their spinners are wily and they have unearthed one or two useful quick men like De Mel, John and Ratnayeke. They were to show a Lord's crowd some pretty good cricket at the end of 1984.

In the summer ahead, however, there was, first, the return bout with India – a three-Test series in which the second was Ian Botham's fiftieth Test in less than five years. He celebrated with a century, his tenth in Tests, at Old Trafford, 60 and five for 47 at Lord's, then struck 208 runs at the Oval from only 226 balls. The second half of the season was occupied by three Tests against Pakistan, and since this book is much concerned with relations between players and media one incident at Lord's is worth recalling. Mohsin Khan, who got a double hundred when he opened the Pakistan first innings, was on 199 when rain stopped play. It was a lengthy stoppage and during the course of it I noticed Mohsin outside the dressing-room and wondered idly if it might be possible to carry out an interview with him. I knew him as a pleasant young man who had played as a professional in the Lancashire League with Todmorden, a club for which I have a certain affection. Not many people have been interviewed on 199 in the middle of a Test match, I thought, so I put my request to the manager, Intikhab Alam, without any real hope that he would agree. 'Why not?' he replied, smilingly, and with the greatest delight I whistled the young opener up one flight of stairs to the commentary box where he did a really first-class bit of chat. When play finally resumed I whispered a completely unpatriotic prayer that the break had not unsettled him. He reached the 200 – only just, but he did it.

Pakistan won that Test too, by ten wickets, but once again it was Botham to the rescue with four for 70 and five for 74 in the deciding test at Headingley. During the winter the tour party went to Australia once again, where the Ashes were lost by two Tests to one with two drawn. In Adelaide, Botham clocked up his 1000th run against Australia and in Perth he reached 3000 Test runs and 250 wickets, but by now he was beginning to pay dearly for his victims. His eighteen wickets in the five-Test series cost 40.5 runs apiece and there was no 'five-for' performance in any of them. The view of experienced and fast bowlers of a previous generation was that he was carrying too much weight around the middle which affected the way he delivered the ball. In consequence, gone was the late outswinger which was his most potent weapon and it is a fact that he got a remarkable proportion of those eighteen wickets from bad balls.

On his return, he angrily denied that he was overweight. He resented any suggestion that he was and the Australian wag who had introduced in Sydney a large pig with 'Botham' painted on its flank was lucky 'Both' was not in a position to get hold of him. He insisted at the start of the 1983 season, 'I am exactly the same weight as I was two years ago.' It might well have been the case but, if so, the avoirdupois had been redistributed. It was World Cup year and competition for the Prudential Cup was given a tantalising start by Zimbabwe's defeat of Australia by 13 runs at Trent Bridge and India's victory over West Indies at Old Trafford by 34 runs in a wonderful match spread over two days. On his home ground of Taunton, Ian missed out badly in England's defeat of Sri Lanka when he was run out without scoring and did not take a wicket while conceding 60 runs from his twelve overs. Despite this, he still couldn't be persuaded to rate the Sri Lankans very highly even after they had scored 286 from an attack of himself, Willis, Allott, Dilley and Marks. England came unstuck at Edgbaston, where New Zealand beat them by two wickets after Botham had been pushed up the order to number three, where Gower had hitherto played in masterly fashion. The theory was that he could demolish the gentle swingers of Jeremy Coney and the off-spin of John Bracewell who, because of their all-round talents, had to be employed to do a certain amount of bowling. That plan came to grief when Bracewell hung on to a hot return catch and Botham was gone for 12. With the ball he fared no better – one for 47 in twelve overs. The man with the ability to turn round completely a five-day Test was so rarely a match-winner in the knockabout stuff.

In seven World Cup matches Ian scored only 40 runs and took eight wickets, for 288 runs in eighty overs. And so to the four-Test series with New Zealand and a renewal of that personal duel with Richard Hadlee which has never been openly discussed, but which both men know well enough exists. Indeed, the two have never conversed much at all. Probably their most extensive exchange of views came during one of those comic-opera events at the end of the season when the two of them were pitted against each other and other notable all-round players like Imran Khan, Clive Rice and Kapil Dev which really could not prove much at all but provided a certain diversion. The conversation during that match was entirely on cricketing topics; outside that subject they have little in common.

In the First Test Hadlee bowled Botham for 15 and Botham caught and bowled Hadlee for 84 (out of a total of 196), but England won the match by 189 runs. Hadlee, however, was the Cornhill man of the match. In the second (which provided an historic first win for New Zealand in England), Botham scored a total of 42 runs and took no wickets at all for 85 runs. Hadlee, too, failed to get a wicket and hit 81 runs for once out. Neither took the other's wicket and it was the same story in the Third Test, where Botham totalled 69 runs against Hadlee's 30 but the New Zealander took eight wickets for 135 against Botham's five for 70. Between the Third and Fourth Tests, Ian played what was described as 'one of the most disciplined innings of his career' to take Somerset to the final of the Natwest Trophy – a brilliant 96 not out occupying fifty of the sixty overs, and thus controlling the Somerset chase for 223 to win. They actually finished on 222, but for eight wickets against Middlesex's nine, and so they won by virtue of having lost fewer wickets. It was Botham who played out the final over without attempting to score a run, a personal achievement of rare distinction. He celebrated with a century in the final Test (103) to which Hadlee replied with 92 not out in a hopeless situation. Botham's innings 'of massive authority' (*Benson and Hedges Cricket Year*) saw him reach 100 off 99 balls with three sixes and fourteen fours. Hadlee, who reached 200 Test wickets in the course of the game, was man of the series. They went their separate ways to do battle another day, but in between to reach new personal heights of greatness.

Before the season was over. Botham had the pleasure of skippering Somerset to victory over Kent in the Natwest Final at Lord's. It had not been an outstanding year for him as a player in World Cup, Test or even county cricket, but he had had his moments – a first-class batting average of 40.57 (but only twenty-two wickets at 33.09), a brilliant 152 at Leicester and, of course, that Natwest semi-final innings. He now faced another long winter tour which was to see his name in the headlines once again – but more spectacularly on the front page rather than the back.

The 1983–4 tour broke new ground by starting in Fiji, and it was a happy choice as the place for the players to acclimatise themselves after setting out from the depths of an English winter. A champagne reception at 5 a.m. was followed closely by a splendid New Year's Eve party and two one-day games against a remarkable assortment of local players. All in all, it was an extremely pleasant first week and as it was to be followed by seven weeks in New Zealand before we moved on to Pakistan a few of us wondered how we might feel during the last part of the tour. Pakistan is not everyone's idea of the perfect place to spend a month and it was going to be just a little hard to enjoy ourselves in the meantime, knowing what lay ahead. (In 1977–8 the hard slog of nine weeks in Pakistan was made very much more bearable by the thought that at the end of it we would move on to New Zealand's green and pleasant land. It didn't look so good in reverse.)

There were those amongst us, however, who were not going to concern themselves too much with the future while the present could be enjoyed, and the first week in New Zealand brought the first hint of possible problems ahead. A certain Saturday night liveliness in the Sheraton Hotel, Auckland, prompted an English businessman to fire off a telex to, of all papers, the *Daily Express* denouncing drunken horseplay. It was all a trifle exaggerated and the complainant's case was not helped, at least in the eyes of those of us living in the hotel, by his including in a list of culprits the name of Chris Tavaré! It would have been impossible to find in New Zealand that evening a more reserved, respectable and civilised individual than Christopher James Tavaré (Sevenoaks School and St John's College, Oxford). True, he *had* been in the bar during the evening – for his one glass of fruit-juice before retiring to his room to write letters. But in the message to the *Daily Express* he was mentioned along with the rest. Consequently, any credibility the complaint *might* have found in managerial eyes was immediately destroyed. There had been fun and games, certainly, and it had had at its centre the inevitable duo of Botham and Lamb, but it was rated as nothing more serious than a hyped-up edition of the usual Saturday-night high jinks on any tour. Newspapers, however, have long memories and good filing systems. The incident was not forgotten either by the *Daily Express* or by other national newspapers, at least in their London headquarters.

For the moment, those of us covering the tour were more immediately concerned with the antics of an extremely lively young lady who was engaged to one of the cricket correspondents; much to the surprise of everyone else, he had brought her along for the tour. By the time we reached Hamilton for the third game of the tour she had made her mark in a variety of ways, and each morning there was usually a new adventure to be retailed. On the day before the Northern Districts match a couple of police officers arrived at the hotel asking to see either the girl or her fiancé. They wanted some help about a taxi fare which had not been paid, they said, the previous night. At the same time, the hotel manager was somewhat less than happy about a window in one of his rooms which had been broken by the Botham–Lamb combination in circumstances unknown. As the players and management were at practice, and most of the media party had departed on an outing while I waited for a call from London, I was asked about both incidents. With a sense of relief I was able to say I hadn't a clue about either since I had spent the previous evening with friends at the other end of town. But it was beginning to look as though this tour might be a little different from others.

The First Test, in Wellington, resulted in a high-scoring draw in which Botham (dropped before he had scored, again when he was 19 and for a third time at 75) rode his luck to hit 138 – his thirteenth Test hundred, including two sixes and twenty-two fours. The end of it was as spectacular as anything during its course. Ian aimed a huge drive off the bowling of Lance Cairns, miscued and the ball soared to an enormous height, quite the greatest altitude I can ever recall seeing a ball rise. Such catches are by general consent always the wicket-keeper's, but for some reason or other Ian Smith made no move as the ball swirled around at its astonishing height somewhere above a shortish cover position. It was left to poor Jeff Crowe to advance, quaking, from an orthodox cover position, and somehow he held on to the catch as he sank to his knees. Catches which live in the memory come in an assortment of guises but never have I seen one quite like that. As Botham had taken five wickets in New Zealand's first innings (his twenty-fifth five-wicket haul) it was something of a match of records – Willis overtook Fred Trueman's 307 in Tests, Gatting took his first Test wicket and Jeremy Coney and Lance Cairns achieved career-best Test scores. But the Second Test in Christchurch was to prove the starkest of contrasts.

Long before the party reached 'the most English city' in New Zealand, doubts had been expressed about the fitness of the Lancaster Park pitch to stage a Test match. Auckland had been bowled out there for 94 in a Shell Trophy match in December, and Northern Districts (skippered by Geoff Howarth, the New Zealand captain) for 104 in January. McLean Park, in Napier, was put on stand-by to host the Second Test against England if Lancaster Park was judged to be sub-standard. However, during the Wellington Test the news came that it had passed Board of Control scrutiny and the Second Test would start there as planned on 20 January. There are few things quite so effective as planting the seeds of suspicion in players' minds, and for two days before the match started a succession of them doubtfully inspected the strip prepared for the Test. Anxious questions were asked of the groundsman, of members of the Canterbury Cricket Association, of anyone who happened to be passing. Those New Zealand newspaper reports of a sub-standard wicket had done their work well. Given that the rumours and the season's case-history of the pitch were all well-founded, it was going to be tough for the batsmen and so there was a gleam of anticipation in more than one bowler's eyes when Howarth won the toss and decided to bat.

England were without Neil Foster, who had broken a toe in the nets the previous Sunday, and so Tony Pigott, the Sussex fast bowler who was wintering in Wellington, was called up for the Test which started on Friday. He had arranged to be married the following Monday, but postponed the nuptials when the Test call came. As things turned out, he need not have bothered . . . Bob Willis's second ball of the match took off, climbed over John Wright's head, over Bob Taylor's as well and dropped, first bounce, just short of the boundary rope. It was a horribly dismaying start for all watching batsmen. It is extremely important, therefore, to emphasise that that was the only delivery which misbehaved seriously in the whole game. It was a pitch for line-and-length bowling from men who could be accurate and content to let the turf do the rest; it was a pitch for grafting batsmen willing to curb natural desires for stroke-making until the right moment (or the right delivery) arrived. In short, it was a pitch which called for a thoroughly professional approach to all aspects of cricket, and England were the professionals. New Zealand, with the exception of the three who played in England (Wright, Howarth and Hadlee), were literally the amateurs. Yet they were the ones who played like the truest of professionals while England performed like the rawest amateur recruits. And none, sadly, more so than I. T. Botham. He dropped a catch in the morning session at the end of which New Zealand were 87 for four and England reckoned they would be 130 or 140 all out. In fact they scored 307.

This happened primarily because of an absolutely appalling exhibition of bowling by Botham and some extraordinary direction in the field by Willis, the captain. Cowans had looked the most penetrative of the bowlers, had taken two of the first three wickets to fall and with any luck at all might have had a couple more. Willis was economical and Pigott, flogging himself into the wind in three spells, did more than could have been expected in his first Test match. Meanwhile, Botham was serving up the juiciest diet of long hops, varied by the occasional half-volley, to Jeff Crowe, to Coney and to (of all people) Richard Hadlee, who must have thought it was his birthday. Hadlee recalls,

> He couldn't get anywhere near the right place. It was 'that contest' all over again. He just tried to bowl short at me, then he'd toss one up. He never tried to bowl straight at me. He gave me too much room, too much width to play the sort of game that I am used to playing. Pigott was left on far too long and I hardly saw anything of Cowans. Willis bowled a few overs off the short run; he never charged in at me at all. But 'Both' and Pigott were used far too long and it allowed me to get going. Once I was in, well, it was one of those days and you take advantage of them. But I was

> very surprised at 'Both'. It was the sort of pitch on which you bowl line and length, which the English pros generally do so well, but they seemed to ignore the whole of the basics, the practical issues of bowling on that type of wicket.

That was the view of the man on the receiving end of the attack. Watching from the sidelines, it was sheer horror to English eyes (and there were a few parties of supporters, even 12,000 miles from home). Throughout it all, Cowans languished on the boundary edge – he bowled just four deliveries while Hadlee scored 99 – and Willis watched Botham's extraordinary performance from mid-off as if mesmerised: one wicket for 88 from seventeen overs on a seamer's wicket! In his ghosted column in the *Sun*, back home, readers later learned that Ian had 'bowled like a drain'. But was anyone else allowed to observe that? Not on your life. Rain hit the game on Saturday and Sunday, but not hard enough to save England from utter humiliation. They were given an object lesson in line-and-length bowling, not only by the immaculate Hadlee but by his supporting cast of Cairns and Chatfield plus the slow left-armer, Boock; England were all out 82, on the Saturday morning, and all out 93 on the Sunday afternoon. New Zealand won in fractionally over twelve hours' playing time.

And did England's professionals follow the lead of New Zealand's amateurs by getting their heads down and grafting on a pitch which, while not of Test match excellence, was far from impossible? They did not. And did they retire to their team-room to dwell upon the shortcomings of their performance? They did not, at least not all of them. There were those for whom I had, and still have, the highest possible personal and professional respect, who brooded upon a crushing defeat and an abysmal performance. Of the others . . . one, late that Sunday night, drove a car when he was in a condition which would have made him dangerous in charge of a tricycle; another was to be seen with eyes glazed and vacant, wheeling round and round a room with arms outstretched, apparently under the impression that he was an aeroplane; yet another spent most of the still watches of the night crashing up and down a corridor on one of those trolleys normally used to take meals to hotel rooms, making such a deafening noise in his enjoyment that the cricket correspondent of one of our 'quality' newspapers vowed to take literary revenge if it took the rest of his career.

Such matters are passed on to newspaper (and broadcasting) offices back home in the course of phone calls, not as stories for publication but as part of the general 'chat' in the correspondent's links with England. There are those there who wish they were out on tour and are naturally anxious to hear about all sides of a tour. And as these anecdotes are passed round London offices ears are pricked up by those less concerned with cricketing matters than others. When, therefore, an England team is seen to perform badly there will always be those in every branch of the media who say: 'Shouldn't we be asking why this has happened? Is there something more to it than loss of form?' In addition, there were a lot of disappointed English supporters at Lancaster Park, many of them in two groups led by former England players John Snow and John Jameson. They had gatherings in the hotel where the England team were staying. Some of *them* returned home with stories that all was not quite as decorous as it might have been. That message from Auckland to the *Daily Express* was now recalled, and soon the stormclouds were gathering. As news went around Fleet Street, that one newspaper had despatched investigative reporters to New Zealand, others followed suit. While the last Test, in Auckland, was drawn and three one-day internationals were played (2–1 to England), the newsmen were seeking out those who claimed to have been present on festive occasions when certain England players were alleged to have been less than discreet.

As a moment of light relief, perhaps I might at this point tell a story against myself which, quite by coincidence has slight overtones of the personal duel between Botham and

Hadlee. On every match during a tour John Thicknesse, cricket correspondent of the (London) *Standard*, makes a book on just about every aspect of the game – not merely the result, but individual performances with bat and ball, the margin of the victory or defeat, concession of runs-per-over, and scoring rates. It's good fun for everyone, including players, who regard the odds he gives in any particular context as an indication of his cricket expertise and are never slow to give 'Thickers' a bit of good-natured stick if he comes a cropper. On the Saturday morning of the Second Test the two of us had breakfast together and were musing over the possibilities in the day's play. John, who never loses an opportunity to drum up custom for his 'book', was tossing out bait-balls about whether England could avoid the follow-on from a position of being 53 for seven against a New Zealand total of 307.

He was not thinking in terms of offering generous odds by any stretch of imagination, but when I suggested they might find it difficult to avoid an innings defeat, let alone the follow-on, he leapt in: 'Ten to one New Zealand don't win by an innings.'

'You're on,' I replied with equal promptness. 'Ten dollars to a hundred.' It is, of course, a well-known fact that Yorkshiremen (D. B. Close apart) only bet on certainties. They look after their brass too carefully for anything else. So on the Sunday evening, while the BBC's cricket correspondent was dismayed by the result, the Yorkshireman was gleefully counting his 100 NZ dollars. Thickers does not take reverses of that sort lightly, and during the next week he tempted me with all sorts of odds in all sorts of situations, none of which, however, appealed to me.

Then, during the second one-day international in Wellington, he tried again. John had begun to sound like some sort of oriental pedlar as he reeled off the financial delights in store for me if only I would try his wares. Finally, with New Zealand all out for 135 in 47.1 overs, I grudgingly drew a ten-dollar bill from my wallet and said: 'England to win by seven wickets.' Done! The odds were, I think, four to one against. With England at 135 for three I called across to John from the commentary box: 'How about it? England by seven wickets.' Thickers is not a Yorkshireman, but at that moment he could have passed for one.

'Don't be in such a hurry,' he cautioned. 'You haven't won yet.' Randall was on 21, Botham 15, and I grinned contentedly. It was going to break the bookie's heart to have to pay me out twice in such quick succession. Botham faced up to Hadlee from the pavilion end. And the lunatic tried to play a reverse sweep! To Hadlee! It was the most terrible moment of my life as Botham's leg stump duly went cartwheeling out of the ground. To make matters worse, it was the last ball of the over. Gatting came in merely to watch Randall hit the first ball of Cairns's next over for four to give England the match – by *six* wickets. It quite made the tour for John Thicknesse.

But it was the visit to Christchurch which interested the investigative reporters when they arrived. Elton John, the English pop singer, was staging a concert (I believe it was called) in a park there and a number of players from both England and New Zealand teams went to it. With a group of friends I got as far away as possible by having dinner in a hilltop restaurant which, I was told, was ten kilometres distant from the E. John jamboree. We could hear the noise, nevertheless, as we dined, so it was not surprising to learn that the local constabulary had been bombarded with complaints from people living rather closer to the epicentre of sound. But what interested the *Mail on Sunday* team when they arrived was the circulation of stories about pot-smoking amongst some of the players. A New Zealand player at the concert had said to me afterwards, 'What's with the tequila?' The Mexican fire-water was that year's 'in' drink amongst a certain fraternity within the England side, so that was easy enough to answer. Not so easy was the next question: 'What were they smoking? It smelled like a Turkish brothel.' I couldn't answer that one. Against that, let it be said that Bob Taylor, the England wicket-keeper and a man of integrity, went to the concert and saw no evidence of his team-mates smoking 'pot'. He added in his autobiography, *Standing Up, Standing Back*: 'Of course, the air was full of the stuff. It always is at such gatherings, but to my knowledge it had nothing to do with us.'

'Sex' and 'drugs' are short but evocative words which fit snugly into newspaper headlines, especially the tabloids, and they carry a dramatic impact. If they can be coupled with the name of England's star player they are guaranteed to catch any eye, and by the time we reached Pakistan rumours were flying thick and fast round the hotel. Substance was given to the possibility of at least one English newspaper making serious allegations by the arrival of two *Mail on Sunday* reporters who camped out in the team's (and cricket correspondents') hotel in Lahore. It was a tense and miserable time for everyone. And before we moved to Faisalabad from Lahore, the *Mail on Sunday* broke its story of 'booze, birds and pot-smoking', coupled with the names of Botham and Lamb. Botham denied it and his solicitor instituted legal action against the *Mail on Sunday* which called a halt to further allegations the newspaper had planned for the following week. Lamb, without instituting legal proceedings against the paper, described the story to those of us accompanying the tour as a load of rubbish. Meanwhile the tour manager, Alan Smith, had announced that Botham was to return home for an operation on an injured knee. In his best managerial manner, 'A.C.' firmly asserted that this had nothing whatsoever to do with the newspaper story. Even to the sceptics it was an obvious relief to have 'Both' out of the way. The whole atmosphere of the tour was now quite awful, and even the sanest and most responsible player hesitated to be seen talking to a reporter – *any* reporter.

In hospital in England for treatment, Botham was interviewed by my colleague, Pat Murphy, who, naturally enough, had established the terms of reference beforehand as far as subject matter was concerned. The chat ranged over general tour topics and Ian, in a clumsy but entirely understandable attempt at a humorous remark, said that 'Pakistan was a place every mother-in-law should be sent for a month.' It was a remark which might be regarded as offensive only at the most pompous levels of officialdom but it was to bring down the laughable wrath of Lord's upon his head. When the TCCB came to inquire, a couple of months later, into the *Mail on Sunday* allegations and the 'insult' to Pakistan, it was the latter which brought him a reprimand. The inquiry did not even bother to ask the newspaper what evidence it had about the other matters!

But in all truth, a tour which had started so pleasantly and promisingly degenerated into a sad and unhappy mess. The likeable Taylor became increasingly withdrawn from the main group of players and, while he cheerfully and charitably explained this as due to the generation gap, it is nevertheless a fact that he felt he had less and less in common with many of his fellow tourists as far as cricket, and life in general, was concerned. Taylor believed that the team-room was the place to meet and exchange views and to do any social drinking (after all, there is always unlimited *free* hooch available for tour teams) that anyone felt necessary. In particular Taylor could not find much common ground between himself and the Botham–Lamb partnership in terms of off-duty activities. He was one of those stunned and shocked by the performance in Christchurch: 'We were awful. It didn't seem to hurt enough when we lost.' And that, as I saw it, was exactly right. Significantly, when Botham had returned home, followed by Willis (after recurring illness), the team-room in the hotel was always full in the evenings.

Immediately after the publication of the *Mail on Sunday* article, Botham's solicitor flew into Lahore, collecting affidavits from members of the tour party stating that they had seen nothing irregular happening during the time which had been spent in New Zealand. Two men refused to sign: Bob Taylor (because of something he *had* seen) and Bernard Thomas, who more than anyone else was responsible for the health and well-being of all the party. Bernard also submitted a report on the tour as a whole to the TCCB on his return. That has never been made public but I would not mind a bet that it caused a few flutterings in the Lord's dovecote when it arrived there. It certainly caused a whole flood of newspaper inquiries to Bernard when events took their more dramatic turn in April 1986.

To all outward appearances, Botham had spent the entire regime of Bob Willis's captaincy doing exactly as he liked, bowling or batting. David Gower on the other hand had impressed with his quietly authoritative handling of the side during Willis's illness in Pakistan and he took over as captain for the 1984 home series against the West Indies. It was always going to be difficult because there was currently no side in the world capable of beating the Windies, and few who looked likely to hold them to a draw. In English conditions, and with the best available side pulling strongly together and playing with a high degree of dedication, it should have been possible to do at least a little better than England fared that summer. No one was readily going to hold Gower responsible if things went wrong. There was an acceptance on all sides that he had the most difficult of tasks, and it is fair to say that as Botham had done four years earlier he took over the captaincy with the greatest possible goodwill from all cricket correspondents. We all *wanted* him to make a success of the job.

The summer started depressingly. The opening match having been lost by an innings and 180 runs, the scene switched to Lord's, where Clive Lloyd put England in to bat and we feared the worst. However, Fowler and the resolute Chris Broad put together an opening partnership of 107 with the Lancastrian going on to make 106. It was the happiest of starts to the game, and when Fowler was out I let an hour pass to give him time to shower and rest before going down from the commentary box to the England dressing-room. There, I requested the attendant to ask Fowler if he would come out for a word with me. Graeme duly appeared and I put it to him: 'Well done. Will you come up to the box so I can record an interview?' It was the sort of request which is made by one or other of us in 'Test Match Special' on every day of every Test and every tour. Very occasionally it's tricky when things have not gone too well, but rarely is there any serious problem in the end. Now, to my surprise, the extremely pleasant and friendly Fowler appeared ill at ease. 'What's the matter?' I asked. He seemed refreshed and, one would have expected, a very happy young man after scoring a century at Lord's, and we had always got on very well during the previous winter's tour where we had the coincidental bond of being the only two north-countrymen in the party. Now he positively squirmed with embarrassment as he said, finally, 'The captain doesn't want me to do it.'

This really was intriguing. One tries always to be reasonable about these things – not to ask for interviews immediately after a player has come back from a long innings or soon after a tiring, even though successful, bowling spell. We certainly don't ask just before a side is going out into the field or a batsman is going to start an innings. None of these criteria applied at this moment. I could not understand it, and the obvious discomfort of the normally frank and open Fowler made things all the more puzzling. We stood, neither of us knowing quite what to say. At that moment the door of the dressing-room was flung open and Botham rampaged out, thrust a piece of paper into my hand and roared: 'That's bloody charming. The lads loved that. Bloody charming!' And as I tried to ask what he was talking about, 'Both' stormed back, followed, after a sheepish grin which seemed more a plea for understanding than anything else, by Fowler. I then unfolded the paper which Ian had pushed into my hand. It was a cutting from the *Morecambe Visitor*, the weekly paper in the town where I live.

We now move back five months to that hammering in the Second Test in Christchurch. In common with everyone else reporting the tour I had been severely critical of England's performance in that game. On my return the assistant editor of the *Visitor* had asked to do an interview with me about the tour (this was a customary procedure when I returned from tour, anyway) and in it I had repeated my criticisms already voiced on BBC Radio. They would be heard by hundreds of thousands of listeners and, through relatives, the players would not be unaware of them; the article in the *Visitor* would be read by perhaps 20,000 people. So what had moved Ian to such transports of fury? I still don't know and I have never felt a burning desire to inquire.

But the reason for Graeme Fowler's discomfiture was now quite obvious. 'Both' had been on one of his rampages in the dressing-room and decreed that anybody who talked to me was beyond the pale. I did not like to think, at that stage, that he had browbeaten his captain into instructing Fowler to say that he would not be interviewed. Later, however, as it became increasingly clear that Ian regarded himself as a law unto himself, it seemed not beyond the bounds of possibility. I have never embarrassed Fowler by asking for the answer to that question. Some day, perhaps, I may do so. With Botham taking eight for 103 to leave the West Indies trailing in the first innings by 41 runs, it all now created something of a problem since the Radio Sports Unit, across the West End in Broadcasting House, now wanted an interview with the man himself. 'Not me,' I said firmly. 'Under no circumstances whatsoever am I going cap in hand to that loud-mouthed hooligan to ask for an interview.' So my colleague Pat Murphy – on the strength of his amicable meeting in hospital with Botham and conveniently dismissing from his mind the consequences of that for Ian! – volunteered.

Back he came a quarter of an hour later with the news that 'he [Botham] and Lambie had made a pact not to talk to the press for the rest of the season'. It was not, of course, just a matter of an article in a Lancashire weekly paper. He could not be expected to like the recollection of a performance in which, to use his own words, he had bowled like a drain, but it wasn't just that. It couldn't be. It obviously recalled the unwelcome attentions of news reporters in New Zealand and Pakistan; there had been one or two mildly critical views expressed about his bowling at Edgbaston in the current series; and his mind had gone back to 1981 when 'the press cost him the England captaincy'. We were dealing with a petulant child. The 'good lad' of earlier years had long since become a less engaging character; he was now beginning to act and sound like the most temperamental of prima donnas. He still had the golden touch as a player. He was still the man to empty bars and to fill grounds, still the man to destroy attacks and mow down batsmen. But as a personality he had become, in my book, almost a complete mess.

The following year Ian was talking on a Radio 2 late night programme to Stuart Hall, whose interviewing of sporting personalities owes more to Uriah Heep than Sir Robin Day and, when asked about his media critics, replied: 'How can they talk about me when they haven't done it themselves at this level?' We shall examine, shortly, his reaction to criticism by men who most certainly *have* done it at his level.

But to return to the man's cricket, at Lord's in 1984 he ran in with all his old fire and at times seemed to have recaptured his ability to swing the ball late. It was a splendid piece of bowling for which, perhaps, the media might claim a little of the credit since we have the evidence of two of his captains that he performs better when something has geed him up. It could not, nevertheless, prevent another West Indian win by nine wickets as Gordon Greenidge gave us an innings to remember of 214 not out. At Headingley we saw a second successive century by Lamb, some fine bowling by Paul Allott, and the end of Willis's Test career (he had already announced his retirement from first-class cricket at the end of the season) as his bowling was utterly mutilated by Michael Holding in a tail-end thrash. There was an ironic twist to the day for Willis. From most grounds it has become the habit in recent years for a hard core of the Test side to sort out one particular pub in which to spend varying lengths of time in revelry after close of play. At Old Trafford, it is an establishment in Wilmslow; from Headingley, they go to one in Otley. It is a particularly stupid custom because if the day has not gone well and some of the most prominent players can be seen publicly and noisily getting themselves well and truly oiled, what are the public to think? Some think more quickly than others, like the young lady in the

Otley pub who was wearing a bandeau when the heavy mob of the England team arrived. Willis, whose figures of two for 123 off eighteen overs made sad reading, looked at the girl and said with mock solicitude, 'I hope your head gets better soon.' Like a flash came the retort: 'I hope your bowling does.'

Headingley was lost by eight wickets, Old Trafford by an innings and 64 runs and, at the Oval, West Indies won by 172 runs. Botham took more wickets in the series than anyone else – nineteen at 35.1 – and was second in the batting averages with 347 runs at 34.7. He held five catches. Gower averaged a modest 19 from nine completed innings. Was captaincy affecting *his* batting? Better not ask that one.

9 THE STAR

Having declined the 1984–5 tour to India, Botham remained in England seeing something of his family, playing football occasionally with Scunthorpe United Reserves and then moving to Yeovil Town to get more regular involvement. His first game was against Northwich Victoria and, though Yeovil lost 0–1, the gate was up by 1000. Maidstone's gate improved, too, when the cricket star went there for a Bob Lord Trophy match, but although Ian scored a goal his team lost 1–3.

At the start of 1985 I was listening anxiously to the one o'clock news from the BBC to see how the pound was faring against the dollar; as my wife and I were due to spend the month of February in the USA it was a matter of some importance to us! The pound was faring badly, as it happened – 1.04 – but that was only the *second* item in the news. The first was that 'Ian Botham and his wife Kathryn had been arrested after police had visited their home and taken away a certain substance'. Our reaction was one of stark horror that Kathy had been involved. No charge was made against her, happily, and it was Ian alone who was fined £100 for possession of cannabis, the chairman of the bench questioning whether 'in this case he had set the best example to his impressionable young admirers'. It was a question which was echoed in a *Daily Telegraph* leader and one which, indeed, would be asked by parents all over the country.

Cedric Rhoades, then Lancashire CCC chairman, called for a policy decision from the Test and County Cricket Board: 'Cricket should distance itself from any connection with drug-taking – it is one of the worst aspects of society today. I certainly do not want cricket connected with drugs and I hope we can do something about it.' On 14 March, a sub-committee of the TCCB interviewed Botham and afterwards issued this statement:

> Following the court action involving I. T. Botham when the England player was found guilty of being in possession of a small quantity of cannabis at his home the executive committee reaffirmed their abhorrence of the possession of illegal drugs by anyone in cricket. The committee agreed that retrospective action should not be taken against I. T. Botham and that he will be available for selection against Australia this summer. The committee do intend, in consultation with the Board's lawyers, to propose that the Board, in future, should penalise severely any player found guilty of possessing or using illegal drugs and thus bringing the game into disrepute.

One wondered, idly, why the words 'a small quantity' had been used. Would it have influenced the Committee if there had been a hundredweight?

Meanwhile, if England's winter tour to India was not without its dramas (and what could have been more dramatic than the start being delayed because of national unrest following the assassination of Mrs Gandhi?) the results were more satisfactory than on England's previous visit. The First Test was lost by eight wickets, the Second was won by eight wickets, the Third drawn, the Fourth won by nine wickets and the Fifth drawn. Of the five one-day internationals, the first, third and fifth were won, the fourth was lost and the second was won on a superior scoring-rate when the England innings was curtailed. It was a good and successful tour, started in circumstances which were difficult in the extreme and continuing through distractions caused by the internal political feuding of the dominant Indian cricket factions of Bombay and Delhi. At any given moment one of these two authorities inevitably has the upper hand and this is usually reflected by the national team's captaincy: Gavaskar if Bombay are running the show, Kapil Dev if Delhi are in command. It has always seemed mildly amusing to me that in recent years Calcutta and Madras never seem to get control, though they contribute so many talented cricketers to the Test side!

It was obviously a settled and noticeably happy touring side, led by Gower and managed for the first time by Tony Brown, a former Gloucs captain and secretary, more recently the chief executive at Somerset. Before the tour began there was much speculation in the newspapers upon how the party would fare without Botham, and significantly the major aspect of this conjecture centred not upon how much his all-round talents would be missed but upon how Gower would enjoy freedom with the removal from his neck of this albatross of talent, personality and temperament. When the party returned, *hints* about this side of things had changed to outright assertions: there was doubt in very few minds that Gower had had an easier ride, that he had enjoyed captaincy a good deal more, that the side had performed better as a direct consequence. It is worth pausing for a moment here to consider what was cause and what was effect in this situation. Botham rightly or wrongly blamed 'the press' (he lumped together newspapers, radio and TV under the one generic head) for his downfall as captain in 1981; 'the press' uniformly disagreed with him. In the season which followed, 'the press' were only too happy to applaud his magnificent achievements, but he responded with an ungraciousness best illustrated at Headingley and Edgbaston that year.

At that time he had the qualified support of most of his colleagues, in particular Bob Willis. Since then, three years had gone by in which Ian had continued to make personal history – his first double century in Tests, the double of 2000 Test runs and 200 wickets, then 3000 Test runs – but it had not been a period of unqualified success for the teams in which he played. The series in India (1981–2) had been lost, India at home in 1982 had been beaten 1–0 with two drawn, Pakistan in the same season had been beaten 2–1, the Ashes had been lost in Australia the following winter and in 1983 England had been removed from the World Cup (by the eventual winners, India) at the semi-final stage and had lost a Test to New Zealand in England for the first time, although they won the four-match series 3–1. The Botham path to glory had now become a gradual ascent rather than a lightning uphill dash, and yet while lesser mortals found themselves selected from time to time and judged on their actual performances, Ian was selected automatically and judged on his potential. It was Graeme Fowler who once reflected whimsically, 'The Selectors should just put Ian's name down then invite eleven other players to join him.' And while the amiable Fowler intended no malice in his remark it nevertheless reflected an attitude shared to some extent by other players.

Keith Fletcher had been churlishly and illogically discarded after his 1981–2 tour as captain in India, and Willis was his successor. This could not be seen as a good move by any stretch of imagination. As the number one strike bowler Willis would rarely be in a position to look at a situation objectively in the field; he experienced all the problems Brian Close had forecast for Botham against the West Indies, and to a greater extent. Because Willis was such a big man he needed to use his periods of rest from bowling to restore and build up his reserves of energy for the next burst; it was always going to be difficult for him to concentrate on those subtle touches of changes in field-placing, lines of attack and analyses of batting vulnerability which are essential in the field. To make matters worse, Willis was very much a Botham man and the players out in the middle were not the only ones to notice that Ian was allowed to go on bowling when he had lost control of line and length (and sometimes his temper as well), to set his own fields (some of them absurd) and to do as he liked in terms of net practice. The critics of this era were by no means confined to the press or broadcasting boxes.

Consequently, it was an entirely legitimate function for 'the press' to point to the difference in atmosphere and attitude which had been present during a Botham-less tour. Relationships between players and touring journalists had been very much easier than they had been for years, and there was both relief and gratitude in the way this was reflected. It did not pass unnoticed by ITB, resting at home for the winter, nor was it likely to be viewed with any particular enthusiasm by David Gower, despite his temporary respite. David knew that, come next summer, Botham would be back in the dressing-room as sure as night followed day, with all that that entailed, and he knew that for all his smiling and urbane protestations to press conferences and in television interviews the Botham presence *was* more than he could cope with. The man was just a bit larger than life in every way. But there was still one additional burden to bear – the managerial influence of Tim Hudson.

George Timothy Hudson first came to the notice of the English cricket world to any marked degree early in 1984. His personally issued biography claimed that he had been a wicket-keeper in the Lancs and Surrey Second XIs, and it is true that Peter Lever, the former Lancs and England fast bowler and coach at Old Trafford, remembers him there – but only as 'a big windbag'. There seems to be no record of him at the Oval. He was born into a Cheshire family, educated at a Scottish public school (Strathallan) and went to California where he briefly managed the pop group Moody Blues, fronted a radio programme and married a wealthy divorcee called Maxi Bilber. Hudson started coming back to England in 1981 and then bought Birtles Old Hall in one of the prime residential areas of Cheshire, where he created his own cricket ground. In no time at all he had upset the rather sedate neighbourhood by creating an estate which was gimmickry gone mad. A statuette of a cowgirl was posted near the entrance; a flagpole flew his personal emblem in the flower power (a phrase he claimed to have invented) colours of black, yellow, red and green. His Jack Russell terrier, Henry, had a collar in the colours and when Botham, the following season, began to play wearing sweatbands in the same colours there were those who labelled him now 'the pet poodle' (though not to his face!).

Hudson really announced himself to the world of first-class cricket in early 1984 by promoting a match for the joint benefits of Botham and Geoffrey Boycott to be staged on his private ground 'for a purse of £10,000'. Despite acres of publicity in newspapers and the elaborate staging of the game, however, it attracted only 500 spectators. Cheshire, it seemed, was not yet ready for the Hudson brand of cricket. But there is no doubt that he captured the imagination of I. T. Botham who, by the end of the year, was utterly mesmerised by the way-out life-style and vivid imagination of his new mentor. Hudson talked of making Botham into a Hollywood star and of transforming the whole structure of cricket. He asked for meetings with the Selectors to discuss his ideas for changing the face of the game and received no encouragement whatsoever. But he certainly sold himself to Ian Botham.

Since 1978, Reg Hayter, a highly respected Fleet Street figure, had been Botham's agent and had guided him through a county and Test career until his earnings reached six figures from cricket itself and fringe benefits. More importantly, he had taught Ian a great deal about newspaper publicity and how to handle it. When Botham resented an article and announced, 'I'm not going to talk to that bastard again,' it was Reg Hayter who would point out that when you are big news you remain big news twenty-four hours a day and *everything* you do has some news value to someone. It was Hayter who headed off full-scale denunciations of 'the press' by pointing out that the Fourth Estate was not just the *Sun* and the *Daily Mirror*, but the *Financial Times* and the *Yorkshire Post* and the *Northern Echo* and 'all those papers who would never turn anybody over'. It was Hayter who explained that no matter how big a personality one becomes, it is futile to expect sycophancy every minute of the day and night. And Hayter, there is no doubt, had a genuine affection for the young man he had seen grow from a youngster of promise (recommended to him by Basil D'Oliveira) to the game's biggest attraction.

He was unhappy when Botham approached him in April 1985, and asked him to join in a 'Hayter/Hudson venture scheme'. Having been in journalism, publicity and promotion all his working life, the Fleet Street veteran was bound to look rather sceptically at the far-fetched and grandiose schemes of a man with Hudson's background. He declined to join the venture and Botham then gave him six months' notice of the ending of their contract. This is what hurt the most. When Botham had first talked of his new-found guru he had assured Hayter, 'You are my agent and always will be. The situation with Tim Hudson does not affect that.' Now it was *all* changed. Sadly, Hayter said his professional good-byes to the young man whose career had been an important part of his life for nearly seven years.

For some time it had been apparent to many of us that Botham was beginning to regard himself as a special case as a Test cricketer, a player to whom the usual restraints did not apply. Since the appointment of Gower as captain at the start of the difficult 1984 season against the West Indies, everyone had seen his ostentatious disapproval of the captain's field-placings – angry and contemptuous gestures which he made no attempt to disguise on the field. In the single Test against Sri Lanka at the end of that season, when the experienced Wettimuny and Mendis and the youngsters Ranatunga and Silva gave Lord's a beautiful exhibition of classically correct batting, Botham roundly abused them on the field and was reprimanded for it not by the captain or chairman of the Selectors but by one of the umpires! It seemed that every time he was hit for four he wanted a fieldsman covering the area in which the boundary had been struck. It was childlike and impractical, but it went on and on.

In 1985, things got worse. By now his new 'minder' – Andy Withers, a former lock-forward with Wiveliscombe Rugby Club – was a regular visitor to the England dressing-room to get his instructions; the now seven-year-old Liam took his place in England's knock-ups before the day's play began (causing a few hearts-in-mouths lest the little fellow should be hit by a ball struck or thrown by one of the players); when the team turned to the routine of physical exercises to start the day, there was usually one member of the side missing – I. T. Botham. He strutted about pavilions, or posed for photographs, not in his England blazer but in the gaudy livery of the Hudson empire; his hair was grown long and tinted with golden streaks to fit the image created by Hudson's imagination. Ian was incapable of seeing what an absolute idiot he was making of himself, and woe betide anyone who offered even the mildest criticism of his new mentor. In a match at Taunton where he appeared on the ground before the game in his garish garb, Barry Dudlestone, one of the umpires, innocently inquired: 'How many times do you have to wear it before you win your bet?' No pressman, however intimate, would have dared such a comment. But Botham, the national hero, spent most of the 1985 season making himself into an object of ridicule.

Yet it was not all dross. For Somerset at Edgbaston in July he made a dazzling 138 not out from only 65 balls, with thirteen fours and twelve sixes, and this on one of the biggest grounds in the country. His hundred came in just fifty deliveries, the fastest century of the season, beating his own record against Hampshire at Taunton in May by twenty-six deliveries. It was his golden season of six-hitting. At Weston-super-Mare, in August, he smote ten of them in what was described as 'another breath-taking hundred', taking his total for the season to seventy-four and thus surpassing the long-cherished record of a revered former Somerset player, Arthur Wellard, for sixes in a season. If he had not missed the last five championship games through injury, it is a matter of conjecture what the total might have been.

Further Test glamour, however, still eluded him in a season in which Australia sent to England a party in which only Border with the bat and McDermott, the least experienced of their bowlers, acquitted themselves creditably. Indeed, it seemed incredible to those of us who had seen

Australian tour parties going back to pre-war days that so many players could play consistently so badly. Botham started with a top score of 72 in the first one-day international, 29 in the second and did not bat in the third. Now, with no pretensions as a swing bowler but trying to be an out-and-out fast man with the bouncer (quite often it was no more than a short-pitched ball) as his main weapon, he took one for 41 from eleven overs, two for 38 from ten and one for 27 from eight. Then came the Tests. At Headingley Botham scored 60 and 12 and took three for 86 followed by four for 107 in England's win by five wickets. At Lord's he hit 5 and 85, had another five-wicket haul in Australia's first innings but once again conceded more than 100 runs in twenty-four overs, taking two for 49 in the second innings as Australia levelled the series at 1–1 with a five-wickets victory.

By this time Ian was largely uncommunicative towards the media (apart from his column in the *Sun*, of course) but manager Hudson more than compensated for this silence with a series of increasingly improbable forecasts of the glamorous future in store. Pressmen generally were something more than sceptical about these announcements, but if one sought any sort of comment from the Botham camp it was necessary to take with it a massive dose of Hudsonian 'bull' at the same time. The cricket-writers were able to indulge themselves in the luxury of largely ignoring it, but the newsmen, not without a certain tongue-in-cheek reservation, found themselves able to sprinkle their column inches with eye-catching references to James Bond, Errol Flynn, films in Australia and careers in Hollywood. BBC TV went one better by screening an extended interview (filmed on the Sunday rest day of the Fourth Test at Old Trafford) with Tim Hudson at Birtles Old Hall, which largely reduced those viewers who were not squirming with embarrassment to hysterical laughter. What was happening to cricket?

Unfortunately, there was nothing even remotely humorous about Ian's next excursion into the cricketing headlines, and this time he needed no managerial assistance in taking it. On the Saturday afternoon of the Third Test, at Trent Bridge, Alan Border was given 'out' to a slip catch by Botham which the batsman plainly thought had come from the pad rather than the bat. The incident created a certain atmosphere out in the middle, and Wood and Ritchie settled into a sixth-wicket partnership which was not only necessary for Australian salvation, it was all-too-clearly motivated by a desire to compensate for what was felt in the opposition camp to have been a miscarriage of justice. Botham hurled himself into the fray with more enthusiasm than subtlety, and his figures began to suffer in inverse ratio to the improvement in Australia's position in the game.

Then came an lbw appeal by Botham against Ritchie, which umpire Whitehead turned down, believing that the batsman had got a fine edge on to the ball before it hit the pad; Botham expressed his furious disappointment by hurling down a whole barrage of short-pitched deliveries, mainly directed at Ritchie. One of these was top-edged outside the off-stump and flew down towards deep third man where Edmonds was stationed. His attention firmly focused on the flight of the ball through the air, Edmonds was in no position to see Mr Whitehead standing with one arm outstretched to indicate a no ball and almost certainly he had not heard the umpire's shout because the buzz around the ground resulting from the highly charged atmosphere in the middle of the field had grown to a crescendo as Botham released the bouncer. Edmonds ran in, saw the ball dropping agonisingly in front of him, projected himself forward another yard and took a magnificent catch inches from the ground as he plunged on to the turf. It was a superb 'take' by any standards, and it was natural enough for the whole crowd to voice its collective admiration. But those who had heard the shout or seen the signal knew, nevertheless, that it wasn't a wicket. Certainly Botham could not have failed to hear the shout, which came as he was literally within a yard of the shouter. Nevertheless, his reaction was that of a petulant child who has had a favourite toy suddenly and *unexpectedly* – this is where he damned himself: he had to know it was a no ball – snatched from his grasp.

He reacted by sending down from the Radcliffe Road end a flurry of fast, short-pitched deliveries which clearly constituted a breach of Law 42 (8), and it was the unfortunate Alan Whitehead who once again became the focus of attention. He had to speak to Botham about his bowling (would that West Indian umpires had been as meticulous in their application of the regulations about intimidatory bowling in Jamaica in 1986). Botham responded with a series of theatrical gestures which indicated to the furthermost areas of the ground that he was not happy. Invoking section 13 of Law 42, Whitehead had no alternative to addressing himself to the fielding captain, who in turn spoke to Botham. Anyone with only a rudimentary knowledge of the temperament and character of the two who now held centre stage knew that no expression of remorse or regret was even remotely likely to result. One felt sorry for Gower, but it was an episode which did no credit to the game of cricket at all.

Another, more technical, aspect of the situation now presented itself. Botham was using a relatively new ball and, so obviously having lost his temper, he was using it with no glimmering of intelligence at all. For the past half-dozen overs we had seen very little except one short-pitched delivery after another, and while Botham was bowling very fast indeed he was, at his fastest, no Malcolm Marshall, no Michael Holding, no Patrick Patterson. The only danger to the batsman was if he failed to avoid the ball, or failed in an attempt to hook – in short, it was danger to his personal safety. To his stumps there was no danger at all. It was a complete waste of the new ball.

The following day Denis Compton in the *Sunday Express* and Freddie Trueman in the *Sunday People* – quite understandably appalled at (a) childish misbehaviour on the field of play and (b) profligate waste of precious ammunition – voiced their opinions. Compton: 'Botham had an lbw appeal turned down, and thousands of TV viewers then saw a close-up of the England star standing at the end of the pitch mouthing expletives. This traumatic outburst by Botham was quite disgraceful. He must not regard himself as bigger than the game.' Trueman: 'Botham then wasted the new ball, bowling so badly that his frustrations led to the clash with umpire Whitehead.' And sitting beside me in the Radio 3 commentary box as I tried to describe the unsavoury scene of Saturday afternoon, Ray Illingworth, providing the expert between-the-overs comments, had said much the same thing. 'This isn't what might be described as the most intelligent use of the new ball,' he said, with a slightly cynical smile. So there we had three former Test players of the highest pedigree – men who *had* played Test cricket at the same level and, if one wanted to rub a little salt in the wound by saying, in the light of the opposition in their day, a somewhat *higher* level – criticising Botham's bowling and behaviour in a pretty reasoned and not intemperate way.

Was this acceptable to the man at whom it was directed? Not on your life. In his ghost-written column in the *Sun* the following Thursday (for which he was at that time paid more than £25,000 a year) Botham allowed the debate to descend to gutter level: 'Fred Trueman managed to put down his pint and his pipe for a few minutes to hammer me for wasting the second new ball. Compton was another golden oldie who couldn't resist having a pop. He thought my behaviour was disgraceful, but then I'd love to know exactly where he was watching the action from for most of the day.'

It was the shabbiest, cheapest sort of riposte that one could expect from a man who had no case. Moreover it was a piece either dictated by Botham or dreamed up (with Bothamian approval) by his 'ghost', Alasdair Ross, based on hoary and inaccurate folklore and without either of them taking the elementary precaution of checking the few – the pitifully few – *facts* in the column. Denis Compton watched the day's play from the press box, as a simple call to the *Sun*'s own cricket correspondent would have established. Fred Trueman hasn't had a pint in his hand for more years than I can remember. It might conform to the image dreamed up in some quarters of the horny-handed northcountryman permanently attached to his pint of bitter, but in Fred's case that would be totally wrong. But of course the whole idea of the innuendo was to suggest that both F.S. and Compo had spent the day in the bar and then decided on a spectacular line of attack when they came to dictate their articles at close of play. And by a major journalistic misjudgment, Botham and his 'ghost' decided on an intro to that infamous column which read: 'I knew exactly how John McEnroe usually feels as the critics gathered at Trent Bridge.' Either Botham was singularly unfortunate in the choice of words by his 'ghost' or he was guilty of crass idiocy himself in deciding to identify with a man whose talent as a tennis-player was shortly to be submerged in a sea of bad publicity based on gross discourtesy and bad manners.

The *Sun*, which seems to have a nice line in sadism when dealing with its own staff, then directed its cricket correspondent, Steve Whiting, to ask Denis Compton what he thought of the Botham column on the day after it appeared. 'Pathetic, isn't it?' replied Compton. 'I suppose he was implying I was in the bar, but I was in the press box all day. I wrote what I thought and I've no regrets. I'd do the same again. Botham's not a nice chap. He doesn't play it straight down the line. They didn't play it like that in my day but I suppose this is the new generation. His example to the young is awful. I can't understand what Peter May and David Gower are doing. They have a word with him . . . and he carries on as he likes.'

Botham made much of his personal friendship with Alan Border and frequently referred to their going off for a drink together at the end of the day's play. Fine. Everyone was glad to hear about it and it was good to know that sort of relationship was still in the game. 'Still?' Oh yes. The Botham–Border relationship was hardly something new in the game. In the forties and fifties the duels between Compton and Keith Miller – arguably the greatest Australian all-rounder of all time – were colourful, spectacular and in deadly earnest. They provided absolutely marvellous cricket, games which still linger vividly in the minds of those lucky enough to see them. And scarcely an evening passed in those series, in England or Australia, without Compton and Miller being in each other's company. And they are still close friends today. They played it hard – very hard – out in the middle, but not with unpleasant histrionics or inflammatory journalism off the field.

Three days after Botham's column appeared, Compton and Trueman took up the attack once again in their respective Sunday newspapers, and it was left to the *Daily Mail*'s Ian Wooldridge, outstandingly Britain's best sporting columnist and a man with as deep a disapproval of ghost-written journalism as had one of his principal mentors, the late J. L. Manning. On 25 July Wooldridge wrote:

> If I were a professional cricketer I would be deeply concerned at being attacked simultaneously in three Sunday newspapers by former Test players of the stature of Denis Compton, Ted Dexter (who had addressed an open letter to Botham in the *Sunday Mirror*) and Fred Trueman. I wonder if Ian Botham feels the same. Or whether he believes himself so secure in the public affection that he can dismiss their strictures with a yobbish, contemptuous V-sign?
>
> Certainly he seems as impervious to advice as he is sensitive to criticism – curious fallibilities in one who receives the bulk of his income either directly or indirectly from the media. The biggest disaster in which he is currently involved is his column in the *Sun* newspaper for which he reportedly receives more than £25,000 a year for not writing a word of it. Last Thursday's column, the one which drew the fire of Compton, Dexter and Trueman, was actually written by a journalist, Alasdair Ross, and it was coarse, crude and rude. In these circumstances it was important to establish whether it accurately represented Mr Botham's considered views. A senior *Sun* executive assures me it did. In which case cricket's disciplinary

committee meeting at Lord's today may well decide to expand their agenda to discuss a matter which assuredly is bringing the game into disrepute – the peddling of gratuitous abuse for profit. Cricket's latest uncivil war broke out because Trueman and Compton in particular dared to suggest that Botham had bowled less than magnificently in the Third Test. Botham's riposte under the headline 'Get Lost – You're Talking a lot of Twaddle' implied that neither man knew what he was talking about.

Since Compton was a better Test batsman than Botham and Trueman a better Test bowler than Botham, the Somerset captain – since we know it wasn't the work of Alasdair Ross – was at best conferring on himself a stature normally left to the judgment of others. No one questions Botham's gargantuan talent as an instinctive cricketer. Few would see his 34.7 batting average and nineteen wickets at 35.10 apiece against West Indies in a truly world-class series last summer as the statistics of immortality.

After recalling some of the choicer quotes in the articles by Compton, Dexter and Trueman, Wooldridge went on:

All provocative ammunition in the tabloid circulation war, perhaps, but desperately damaging to the increasingly tarnished image of cricket. It is not an easy matter for the Test and County Cricket Board to tackle. Botham, in his worst excesses, has a following as loyal as McEnroe's. Regrettably, his power to influence a susceptible generation is just as great. For reasons far removed from cricket, this might have been the season when Botham decided to maintain a low profile. Alas, such professional advice as he has received does not appear to have considered it. If he is enraged at further criticism he should take to reading the drama critics. It would be a good practice, anyway, for his projected career in Hollywood.

If Ian Wooldridge's words were reported to him – the *Daily Mail* is not Botham's selected reading except when someone sends him a cutting which suggests that all is not well with his cricket, or fitness, or weight, or public image – he showed no signs of taking some very sound advice. The profile became higher than ever, even though in six Tests he scored only 250 runs from eight innings. He did take thirty-one Australian wickets at 27.58 and he held eight catches, the same number as Phil Edmonds who played in five Tests. He bowled more overs than any other Englishman, but after the Second Test at Lord's, where he had five for 109, he did not take five wickets in an innings again during the series. And his bowling thunder was rather stolen in the final two Tests by Richard Ellison who returned – a very much more complete bowler than he had been in 1984 – to take seventeen wickets in 75.5 overs, a remarkable striking rate, and the wickets cost 10.88 each. Somerset finished second from bottom of their Benson and Hedges Regional Group table, eleventh in the John Player Special League, bottom of the Britannic Assurance County Championship, and departed from the Natwest Trophy at the quarter-final stage, crushed by Hampshire.

In August, the incidents at Trent Bridge resulted in Ian's appearance before the TCCB Disciplinary Committee, who admonished him for his conduct. This brought a broadside from the formidable John Junor when his *Sunday Express* column thunderously proclaimed:

> With his dyed-blond permed hair long enough to be tied in a bun, Ian Botham was whistling as he climbed into his new Jaguar after his so-called disciplinary hearing by the Test and County Cricket Board. Can you blame him? Here is a man who set an appalling example to the young by his disgraceful conduct in front of a capacity crowd and millions watching on TV. Nor is it the first time he has shown character flaws. His drug offence on its own should have precluded him from being chosen for England. Yet all the committee members administer as punishment is

> a tickle on the wrist. Are we to count it as a mercy that at least they did not queue up for his autograph? Or do you suppose the contemptible creeps did that too?

I imagine they already had the autograph.

Botham's great following amongst the cricket public were not yet, however, willing to take the word of the critics, no matter how experienced or distinguished, for an alleged decline in their hero's personal standards. When the 'Test Match Special' commentary team gathered at Old Trafford for the Fourth Test, the postbag included a letter to Fred Trueman ticking him off in the most forthright terms for his criticism of Ian during the Third Test. It came from Canon Leslie Ward (from whom we have already heard), who had seen that Botham innings against Hampshire at Taunton, eleven years earlier, and had been an admirer ever since. Did Trueman, he asked, regard himself as a greater bowler than Botham? There is a very short answer to that, of course, and the affirmative would be echoed by just about everyone who has followed their respective careers closely.

Fred took his 307 Test wickets at a time, and in circumstances, entirely different from Botham's, and few people ever expected the record to be overtaken because few people ever expected to see the enormous increase in the number of Tests which were going to be played in rapid succession. Fred took his wickets in 67 Tests which (through the much fiercer competition for places in his day – Statham, Tyson, Loader, White, Moss, Price, Rumsey were all his contemporaries and no one had then thought of bowling four fast bowlers all day in savage spells of short-pitching – and through Selectorial displeasure at odd displays of temperament) covered a period of thirteen years. In parenthesis, it is interesting to recall that Fred missed whole tours for transgressions far less ostentatious than those which became commonplace in the Botham era. When he wasn't playing in Tests during an English summer he was required to bowl in *every* championship game for

Yorkshire. In 1960, for instance, Trueman played in all five Tests against a good South African side (Waite, McLean, Goddard, McGlew, Carlstein, O'Linn) and took 25 wickets at 20.32. In the same season he took 132 county championship wickets at 12.79. In 1963, he played in all five Tests against a very good West Indies side (Hunte, Kanhai, Butcher, Sobers, Worrell, Solomon) and took 34 wickets at 17.47, while in the same season he took 76 county championship wickets for Yorkshire at 12.84. Take any season at the peak of his career and you will come up with a comparable set of imposing Test statistics while Fred was doing his usual overtime stint for Yorkshire as well. Oh yes – he was incomparably a greater bowler, to answer Canon Ward's rhetorical question. But he wasn't, like Ian, an all-rounder. The canon's attack upon Fred was sincerely, if misguidedly (in my view) based.

I sought further enlightenment from Canon Ward, and this is what he wrote to me:

> Already in 1986 some are forecasting the decline and retirement of Botham [this was written *before* the tour to the West Indies]. He has broken most records for all-rounders at international level and will surely surpass the very best before he says farewell to the world's cricket arena. In twelve years he has given an immeasurable amount of pleasure to millions of cricket fans – the bustling, bouncing, thinking bowler; the incredible diving, sure-fingered fielder (despite the hands-on-knees critics) and above all the most exciting middle-order batsman I could ever hope to see. Ian can be exhilarating and defiant with bat and ball, giving more joy in thirty minutes than many give in three full days. He can also appear careless and indifferent, especially on lesser occasions. I am not unaware of other aspects of this very public man. He does have a habit of writing the wrong headlines for himself. Who was it who wrote, 'Creative people are notoriously more wayward, more temperamental, less disciplined and less organised than others. Volatility,

tantrums are included in the price that must be paid for creativity'? Applied to quite a few – certainly Botham – these phrases are very illuminating. Most of us only know of him what the media makes known, and it is true that we can be puzzled and sad. But to judge by all appearances he seems a very fortunate husband and father and I believe in marriage enough to trust that Kathryn and the children will hold fast to this shooting star . . . for all our sakes.

'Is he an example to youth?' they ask in *The Times* correspondence columns. He certainly bears an image of brashness and matches the aggressiveness of the age. Yet I still reckon that his followers and fans in their thousands remember most, and envy most, his indisputable and massive cricket skills. And the recent revelation of his gentle, caring concern for sick children seemed, quite unintentionally, a most powerful answer to many of his critics. Well done, Ian. Thank you for being so keen and enthusiastic as well as gifted to bring us so much pleasure – and for being so wise as to heed such good friends to the game as Brian Close and Mike Brearley – and for being so confident as to help you ignore many others.

That is a remarkable, and indeed moving, tribute from a man with no personal knowledge of Ian Botham but one who, from his background, his intelligence and his obvious love of cricket, might well be held to be a typical supporter of the game. At about the same time I received a letter from Ampleforth College, the great Roman Catholic public school in North Yorkshire, demanding to know why the British so readily found fault with their own heroes.

Notwithstanding a conviction for being in possession of drugs, the childish and childlike displays of bad temper and bad manners on the field, and the roistering life-style off it on so many occasions, the public at large was not yet ready to feel that its idol had feet of clay. But as we have heard one voice of Somerset support raised in Hosannas, let us harken to another at the end of 1985 (for the sake of a chance of peace and prosperity it is necessary to preserve his anonymity):

> Botham seems to have no comprehension of the tide of discontent that has been swirling around Somerset. He has been so busy counting his sixes and the money he might be going to make outside cricket that he hasn't really had time to tot up the mere two dozen wickets he has taken for Somerset this season or to realise he led the side to the bottom of the county championship – a competition he had prophesied in a television interview a year earlier that they would *win*. Equally, the huge Benefit has left some people feeling uneasy about the spectacle of an already wealthy man rattling his tin to get tanners out of schoolboys and less well-off supporters. The walk-off against Hampshire [we shall come to that shortly] in the famous dazzling window game infuriated some supporters; and in a strange way, the older spirit of Somerset didn't really want to see Arthur Wellard's six-hit record smashed in so ruthless and obsessional a way. Things don't really change so fast down here. Despite the heady last decade, Sammy Woods, Robinson Crusoe [R.C. Robertson-Glasgow], 'Farmer' White, Harold Gimblett, Bill Alley and 'Dasher' Denning are the people Somerset is made of. Old men, and the sons of old men, still live on the tales of Bill Andrews and Arthur Wellard and talk of how, in the long shadows of a summer's evening in Taunton, people would leave their shops and offices with an excuse of errands to carry out if word went round that the tail-end pair were batting. Also, it is being said that Botham's swaggering presence in the dressing-room reduces conversation to the level of a Highland Light Infantry barrack-room on a bad day.

Autre temps, autre moeurs.

In this account of a 1985 season which saw Botham (in the eyes of many people closely involved in the game day in, day out) plunging headlong to disaster in one way or another, it is worth recalling the 'dazzling window' incident which shows our subject in his two starkly contrasting images. It happened at Taunton on 7 August in a Natwest Trophy quarter-final against (who else?) Hampshire, who were to bat first. (Ironically, once again I had driven there from an Old Trafford Test to report the game; I should have known something out-of-the-ordinary was inevitable.) There had been overnight rain but, with mopping-up operations starting early in the morning, the announcement came that play would start at the scheduled time. Although the wicket had been prepared and rolled, however, the ground staff were putting a few finishing touches to their operations in the outfield when the umpires should have been standing in the middle and the fieldsmen taking up position. Not, I suspect, without an impish delight (though carefully disguised) as well as tactical satisfaction, Hampshire's captain, Mark Nicholas, gravely asked for a second application of the roller. Botham was outraged and demanded to know what he was talking about. Solemnly, Nicholas pointed out Law 10: 'If, after the toss, and before the first innings of the match, the start is delayed, the captain of the batting side shall have the right to have the pitch rolled for not more than seven minutes.' Botham demanded that the umpires check with Lord's before he allowed it to happen, but the pitch *was* rolled again and it was nearly half an hour after the scheduled start when the Somerset captain, in a fearful temper, led his side on to the field.

He was no happier when Hampshire scored 299 for five in their sixty overs, with Robin Smith making a brilliant century and Paul Terry a less sumptuous but equally valuable hundred. It was virtually a lost cause for Somerset but with Botham, we mused, all things are possible. However, when Somerset found themselves at 43 for five, it was going to need another Headingley '81 miracle from their captain to save them. It was then that we saw Botham in heated discussion with the umpires amidst much waving of arms; the reason for the delay was not clear to the spectators (or the reporters). Then we saw Botham walk to the pavilion, followed hesitantly by one or two fieldsmen and – even more uncertainly – by one umpire. The other, and most of the fieldsmen, stayed on the field in apparent bewilderment until it became obvious that the Somerset skipper was not going to return. Then everyone left the field, leaving a capacity crowd mystified until the announcement came over the public address system: 'The reflection of the setting sun from a window outside the ground was dazzling the batsmen and the captains had therefore agreed to suspend play.' Nicholas, a charming and courteous captain, did not publicly dissent from the announcement. The umpires – the sole judges of the fitness of the ground, weather and light for play, according to Law 3 (8) – declined, with rueful smiles, to comment.

Botham, to those able and brave enough to fight their way through the crush for a comment, tersely snapped that he couldn't bloody well see. By this time, needless to say – and in fact within two minutes of his walk-off – the sun had moved round to a point where the offending window no longer provided an offending reflection! No one felt it would be diplomatic to point this out, though. It all meant that the usual capacity crowd were left with an anti-climactic end to their day, and many of them would not be able to return the following day to see the finish. There would certainly be those who hoped, and even some who believed, that with Ian not out a Somerset win could somehow be contrived. If that happened, they would be unable to see it. The crowd filed miserably home. Botham obviously felt he had won a debating point and that provided the balm he needed for being hopelessly outflanked in the morning, but his committee were in a state of the most acute embarrassment. At 10.30 a.m. on 8 August out came Botham again to hit 64 in Somerset's total of 150, before even he had to admit defeat.

10 THE BENEFICIARY

Quite apart from the off-the-field considerations referred to in the Ian Wooldridge column, Botham's second year as the Somerset captain in 1985 had brought results which equally suggested that a low profile might be advisable. But that is not the Botham way, and in any case his career was now to a very large extent in the hands of the colourful Mr Hudson. To be absolutely fair to Ian it is necessary to relate Somerset's poor showing under his official captaincy to the relatively short time he was available because six Tests and three one-day internationals took an enormous slice out of the season. So did the weather. But by the late end of the season, well into the second half of September, the Somerset Committee were clearly worried about a wretched series of results, the apparently inexhaustible capacity of their captain to get himself into widely publicised situations which were too often of an unfortunate nature and the increasingly frequent appearances of Tim Hudson at Taunton, where he seemed to expect the very highest VIP treatment as of right. 'At times, I began to think very seriously that perhaps he had organised a secret takeover of the Club and the rest of us were only there on sufferance,' confessed one Committee man.

In thirteen first-class matches, Botham entertained regally with the bat, establishing his record number of eighty six-hits, scoring 1530 mightily entertaining runs and averaging a healthy 69.54. But as a bowler it was a different story – only thirteen wickets at 40.07 each. Was Close's prophecy coming true to a calamitous degree? It was difficult not to sympathise to some extent with a man who scored runs in such abundance and with such magnificent panache, but he *was* the outstanding all-rounder of his age and, as Trevor Bailey pointed out in his Foreword, that is a terribly difficult role to sustain. Five years earlier a book had been published entitled *Botham, the Great All-rounder* – not 'a' great all-rounder but '*the*'. To some extent he was being hoist with his own petard. Somerset CCC, founded 110 years ago and 're-organised' ten years later, had languished as a county noted for its rustic good fellowship and very little else for a hundred years. Heady success had come late in life, harnessed to the two most exciting cricketers in the world, and a new generation of supporters had been recruited on the strength of it. The handsome new pavilion in Taunton was the monument to so many great victories and so much spectacular cricket. It could not all be allowed to slip away.

Botham was still a heroic figure to most of his public, but he never grew to realise that the great anonymous mass 'out there' was made up of individuals who just occasionally found themselves in closer contact with him. Or, if he did realise it, he didn't seem to care. He had offended many of them in his Benefit year and astonished quite a few more, notably in Blackpool – far removed from the green hills of Somerset – where a match was arranged jointly for his and Geoff Boycott's Benefits. Before Ian was due to bat there, Andy the Minder appeared in the bar with a peremptory demand for a bottle of tequila. The bar did not stock it. Then they must send out for a bottle, it was recommended. And so emissaries were despatched to the nearest bottle-shop (it wouldn't be *very* near if one takes into account the geographical location of Blackpool's ground) for the tequila which Botham regarded as necessary before he batted. This was, of course, a bit of light relief in a season where helpers were angered in other centres by Ian's late arrival, sometimes non-arrival, and short stays when considerable effort had been put in to raise money for him.

And in one case at least he had given offence in his own county two years earlier with that same flamboyant disregard for what others might think. Before the start of the 1982 season the Somerset County Club had arranged a wine and cheese evening at which guests were invited to meet the players, the hope being that some could be persuaded to become county members or vice-presidents. It was a public relations exercise aimed at strengthening the Club's future, but it turned out to be counterproductive as far as at least one individual was concerned. Far from becoming a vice-president, as he had intended, he wrote to the Committee to complain that Ian Botham appeared, by his demeanour and dress, to be totally uninterested in the evening's proceedings:

> During most of the event, he was seated at a table with his back to the general function area and remained in conversation with a small group of his friends. Together with a number of other players he ignored the formal introduction of the team members to the assembled persons, remaining in the bar for the period of the presentation. His dress of dirty jeans and sports shirt, in my opinion, was out of keeping with that expected of an ex-England captain and the type of function being presented. I accept that Mr Botham is an important member of the playing staff and that his presence in the team is economically desirable. He is, however, only one member of a team and as such needs the other members of the playing staff and the Club officials to assist him in reaping the benefits of his undoubted skill. The overall impression conveyed by Mr Botham's conduct left me feeling very disappointed having regard to the elevated position in which he is held at the Club and in the country. When Mr McCoombe (who I believe is, or was, a Club official) arrived at the function the tone of the event was immediately lowered. He was dressed in such a manner that had he been a member of the public presenting himself at the function he would have been refused admission. Mr McCoombe was invited by Mr Botham to join him at his table and as he did so Mr Botham

It's tough at the top. Botham, aged eighteen, is hit by Andy Roberts at Taunton, 1974. Solicitude from Peter Sainsbury

1000 Test runs and 100 wickets in 21 Tests. A medal and champagne is presented by Alec Bedser at the Oval, 1979

Aggression – the bowler

Aggression – the batsman

The greatest prize of all –
the wicket of his friend Vivian Richards, Old Trafford, 1980

A yard ahead of first slip, but this one sticks.
Exit Larry Gomes, the Oval, 1984

Oh dear, how sad, never mind – one that got away. Trent Bridge, 1985

Fast bowlers have long memories.
Geoff Lawson to Botham, Headingley, 1981 . . .

. . . and Botham to Lawson, Headingley, 1985

'No, captaincy is *not* affecting my cricket.' Trinidad, 1981

'This is what we think of the press' – Botham and Lamb help the *Daily Mirror*'s Chris Lander to an early bath, Melbourne, 1982

Yeovil Town's new striker makes his debut, January 1985

'Will the real 007 step forward?' Botham, with partner Sean Connery, drives off in the Bob Hope Classic, 1980

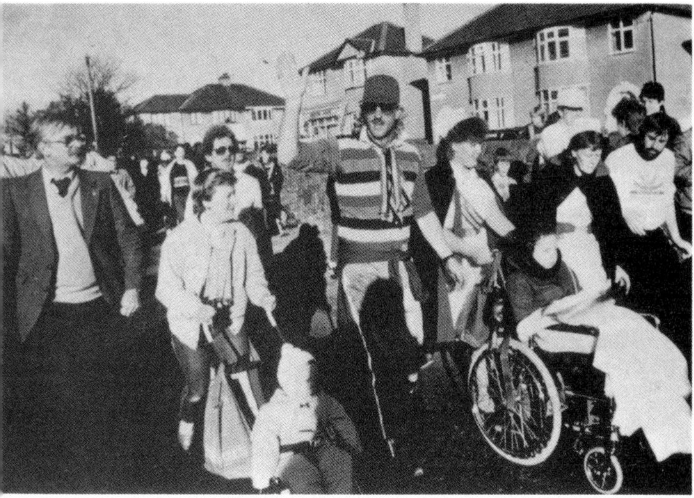

Passing through Lancaster on The Walk, November 1985

Kathy (with Rebecca) joins her husband

It's over, after 874 miles.
Well done, indeed

There's simply nothing like messing about in boats,
whether it's white water rafting in New Zealand, 1984 . . .

. . . or sailing gently in the Caribbean (no nets today), 1986

> pulled the tee-shirt that was being worn by Mr McCoombe up to his chin. This exposed Mr McCoombe's large stomach for all the assembled persons, including the ladies, in the bar area to see. Mr McCoombe reciprocated by placing his cupped hands between Mr Botham's thighs. The whole incident was a very unsavoury exhibition of two supposedly responsible and professional members of your Club.

This was by no means the only occasion when the Club's permanent administrative staff had problems with the most glamorous player. The previous season (1981), when Ian was in the middle of a bad trot for the county, his return to the pavilion after making a small score was the signal for some abusive comment by a spectator sitting on the River Tone side of the ground. Grimly, he unbuckled his pads and set off in search of the barracker – pursued, in turn, by the Club's chief executive who, for all his sympathy with the target of a bit of cheap and ignorant abuse, feared the worst if Botham, in the heat of the moment, got his hands on his critic. It was not long before David Seward began to feel his sympathy was misplaced for when, in 1982, he sought to move McCoombe sideways from what appeared to be a sinecure position in charge of the Club's lotteries to one where Somerset might be seen to get a little more for the salary they paid him, McCoombe resisted the course of action strenuously. There was an open confrontation in which Botham and his friend Richards ranged themselves staunchly beside McCoombe. Someone had to go. Incredibly, it was the Club's chief executive who went! This was player-power gone berserk; the tail was wagging the dog with a vengeance, and it could only be seen as the Club storing up an awful lot of trouble for itself.

One example which provides an illustration of bad manners in his Benefit year was provided by the visit of the Old England XI, sponsored by the Courage Brewery Group, to Taunton, in September. This side of former Test players raised a great deal of money for charity but did not normally turn out in Benefit matches. When the players learned that part of the proceeds of their match in Taunton were to go to Botham's Benefit there was a great deal of reluctance by many of the former internationals to play. Not many of them approved either of Botham or his attitude towards cricket and Reg Hayter, who managed the XI as well as being Botham's agent, needed all his powers of persuasion to coax his veterans into turning out. It was respect for Hayter which finally swung the balance and the caravan of stars of the sixties – Trueman, Edrich, D'Oliveira, Titmus, Murray, Wilson, Close and Co – travelled down to the West Country. Half the proceeds were to go to local charities, half to the Botham Benefit. At the end of the match the Old England XI eased their creaking joints on to the dressing-room seats, enjoyed a beer and waited for Botham to call with a simple 'thank you'.

He did not appear. After showering and changing, the players trooped downstairs to the main bar where the Beneficiary was standing with a group of his cronies. He ignored the men who represented collectively more than 200 Test caps and who had just done duty at least 50 per cent on his behalf, never invited them to have a beer or even offered a simple word of thanks. 'Right,' said captain F. S. Trueman. 'Sod him. Let's get back to the hotel.' Botham had stored up yet more ill-will for himself for want of the simplest gesture of courtesy. Exactly one year later the Somerset Club itself found some of its chickens coming home to roost. 'Jock' McCoombe had gone, but Tim Hudson was on the scene in all his multi-coloured glory.

It was in their new pavilion that the Committee met to discuss a situation which was alarming in the extreme. Only one Britannic Championship match had been won all season – against Lancashire at Bath in June, and that while Botham was on Test duty at Headingley. Three had been lost under his captaincy in a demoralising start to the season against Notts (by nine wickets), Glamorgan (nine wickets) and Hampshire (five wickets) in addition to the not-unexpected mauling from the Australian tourists (233 runs). In the Benson and Hedges, Somerset had managed to beat Minor Counties but no one else, and in the Natwest, after a win over Buckinghamshire and another against Yorkshire (where Botham had somehow got himself involved in a race-relations row), they had put up only the most modest of resistance to Hampshire in a quarter-final.

On 17 July, Somerset went to Headingley to play Yorkshire in the second round of the Natwest Cup and Viv Richards had been given not out by the umpire, John Jameson, in response to an appeal for a catch at the wicket. It was not the sort of decision on which even the most extremely partisan supporter can normally feel qualified to offer a view, but Richards *had* turned towards the pavilion when the appeal went up and he *had* started to take off his gloves. He went on to make 87 not out and Yorkshire lost the game. Richards's explanation, in the light of the row which followed, that his actions represented simply a nervous mannerism of his after a near escape did nothing to placate those sections of the crowd who thought Yorkshire had suffered from a wrong decision. Nor can Richards's actions – nervous mannerism or not – be seen as doing much to help the umpire. It led to shouted criticism of a racist nature directed at Richards from a number of hotheads in the crowd and this, in turn, led to Botham giving (for reasons best known to himself) an exclusive interview to a local commercial radio station in which he said: 'I think you will find Viv was probably extracting the Michael from the Yorkshire crowd. They think because he is black they can give him stick and I have no time for racist idiots. I have got to the stage where I do not want to come back and play at Headingley and most of the Somerset side probably feel the same way.' There was, naturally, an immediate outcry in Yorkshire. Their Committee, Boycott-dominated at that time, was chaired by Reg Kirk, a man who liked nothing better than to see himself on TV or his name in the newspapers. He blasted back: 'Yorkshire cricket followers are very tolerant of ethnic communities and we should all be delighted in Yorkshire when the first coloured player arrives in the first team.'

As the new Yorkshire president, Viscount Mountgarret, was at that time deeply involved in trying to curb the frequent verbal outbursts of his chairman, the row now became three-cornered, especially when Kirk reported Botham to the Test and County Cricket Board without first clearing his action with the full Committee. It dragged on to 3 September when Tony Brown, as Somerset's chief executive, announced: 'We have apologised to Yorkshire and made it known to Botham that his grievance about the crowd's behaviour should have been expressed through official channels rather than publicly aired. While we have regretted Botham making these remarks we believe that they are well-founded, for we have conclusive evidence from several independent and fair-minded people present on the day.'

Mercifully, when the Somerset Committee had jumped on Botham and Lord Mountgarret had jumped on his chairman the whole messy business died a natural death, but in official Somerset circles there was now some alarm about what their captain might do next. Almost certainly he had been caught by the radio interviewer in a moment when he was steamed up, and while most Yorkshiremen were embarrassed at racist taunts from the crowd at their headquarters, and Botham's loyalty to and regard for his friend were admirable, he could have chosen a more diplomatic method of voicing his displeasure. He had enjoyed so much Test glory at Headingley that his claim not to want to come back and play there could scarcely be taken seriously. He had a lot of friends and family connections in Yorkshire and was, in fact, shortly to move his home to a village no more than twenty-five miles from the ground. All this added up to the conclusion that he had spoken in the heat of the moment. It was this which worried the Somerset Committee as much as anything . . .

Gently the idea of replacing Botham as captain was 'leaked' in an attempt to test the temperature of public opinion within the county. Botham might have lost a few friends by a careless, ungrateful and ungracious attitude during his Benefit year, but he was undoubtedly idolised by a great mass of Somerset's new legions of followers. The mortal terror which gripped the Committee was rooted in the possibility of Botham asking for his release if he was deprived of the captaincy and, even worse than that, that he might take Vivian Richards with him. They had acted together in their defence of Jock McCoombe and the Committee had caved in once; suppose the two megastars were now to unite in a demand that Botham continue as captain – or else? The Committee had expected a not-over enthusiastic reaction to the idea as it began to be floated in newspapers. What they were not quite so prepared for was a bellicose blast from Tim Hudson in the *Sun*: Botham might not be interested in a tin-pot job like the Somerset captaincy. There was always Hollywood beckoning – or so the Guru seemed determined to have everyone believe. Botham himself had missed the closing games of the season through injury and was currently on holiday in Jamaica, so there had been little chance to sound him out in anything like a personal way. Hudson's broadside threw the Committee a trifle off balance and then regional television entered the lists with immediate and dramatic results.

On 1 October, HTV ran a story which indicated that Botham was thinking in terms of a year-to-year contract with Somerset rather than the two-year term the county club preferred. In official circles, this suggested that Botham was flying a kite (or his agent was), putting out an inspired 'leak' which might pave the way for subsequent negotiations. As Somerset were at that time out of touch with their captain it was all just a little disturbing, and Tony Brown, Somerset's chief executive, telephoned HTV to ask about their source of information. The following day a second piece of HTV 'Sport News' caught the eye of the Somerset officials and Committee. This speculated that there had been a rift in the close friendship between Botham and Vivian Richards and this annoyed Botham's mother who promptly rang up the HTV News Room to deny the story.

According to the HTV News Room, Mrs Botham said Ian (who had returned to England) wanted to do an interview putting this straight and, as that interview was offered exclusively to the station, naturally enough they jumped at it.

The interview, conducted by Ian Seymour, went like this:

Seymour: Well, Ian, let's start off with these – I think you are saying – malicious rumours which are sweeping around that you have had a bust-up with your great mate, Viv. What is the situation there?

Botham: Well, I was going to ring you last night, you know, I arrive back in the country last night from Jamaica and I suddenly see this on television. It amazed me. I actually genuinely believe there is someone trying to stir it up between the two of us and it's a joke. I've just spent a week with Viv in Jamaica and I think, well, blood is thicker than water, isn't it? It just seems very strange. It's frustrating.

Seymour: Totally unfounded?

Botham: Well, it's absolute news to me. Either Viv and I are the best of enemies, I don't know, but we've just spent a week together in Jamaica.

Seymour: Well, such is the name of Ian Botham, you have only been back twenty-four hours, you are automatically plastered over every single national newspaper this morning and obviously the question is: your decision to have only one year's contract with Somerset for whatever reasons – what are they?

Botham: A number of reasons really – basically because I feel at the Club now we must . . . bring in a depth of players.

I think this year it has shown extensively how weak we are once we lose key players – and I am afraid that to get quality players you have got to spend a bit of money and it's all very well saying 'youth policy' and doing this, but you have got to have some good experienced players and I think that, well, I want to captain the side, I want the side to do well, but we've got to spend money, so I'm just leaving my options open, shall we say?

Seymour: You're saying 'options'; I suppose the county would say it's a bit of an ultimatum?

Botham: Well, the county can say what they want, you know. I've been perfectly loyal, I've been perfectly honest with them for twelve years now . . . and I am not being any different here, I am not just talking about cricket, I'm talking about . . . who knows if I am going to be playing cricket in a year's time? I'm planning for the future. I've got business interests, a lot of things I've got to think about now, I've got wife, family, things of this sort, so it's all very well the cricket club saying 'Why aren't you giving us a two-year contract' but are they going to look after me in five years' time when I have packed in playing cricket?

Seymour: If you are not made captain, could you play under someone else?

Botham: Well, I think that will come out on Tuesday when we go to the meeting, but I think I'll wait and see what happens there . . . well, we've got to sit down and discuss quite a number of things.

Seymour: D'you think you will end your playing career with Somerset or would you move on to another county if the offer was right?

Botham: I'd like to end my career with Somerset. I started here, so why not finish it here? It means a lot to me, Somerset cricket, but there's an old saying, isn't there? If you haven't got the players round you, you can't do much, and I think we've this year shown it, highlighted it.

Seymour: What about the reports today that you want to be cricket's biggest earner? Has that been taken out of context? Is that really what you have been trying to say?

Botham: Well, I think if you read the actual article as opposed to what the sub-editor decides to put on the headline I think you'll find . . . the way I am looking at it is people are saying we are getting paid a lot of money and we are not doing anything so, right, my attitude is: why not give us an incentive? Why not put players on an incentive contract? Give 'em a reasonable basic and then an incentive. People in clubs say, well, they haven't got the money. I say surely in this day and age if they were to . . . get off their backsides and look around, I am sure you would get an individual sponsor for a player each year. And this is just a concept I am looking at. Clubs are always saying they have got no money; well let's look at some new ideas.

Seymour: If Somerset are to rebuild, as you are saying they must do, and as clearly all cricket hopefuls in the West Country would like to see that, what have they basically got to do – have they got to plough in just cash? Will cash bring success?

Botham: No, cash will never bring success. I think we've seen that in the football world. I think you've got to have the right blend . . . we have some very good players at Somerset but I think the one department that we are particularly weak in is the bowling department. It was a major blow, Joel's [Garner] injury, it cost him most of the season. Colin Dredge was out unfortunately for a lot longer than we anticipated but luckily he came back at the end of the season – God knows where we would have been otherwise – but, you know, the opportunity's there for the youngsters, they've got to come through. You know, guys like Mark Davis didn't have a great year but I've got a lot of faith in Mark and I think he'll come through. It's quite often the case when a guy has had a good year next year's a lot harder, but I think he'll come through and bounce back next year. But there's lots of little departments where we can improve it.

Seymour: Are there one or two of the youngsters there that you feel haven't exactly showed the potential that you expected from them?

Botham: I think half the problem is that a lot of youngsters have sort of stagnated a bit – they've been sat in the reserves. The first team's been reasonably balanced for a while now, and the major problem is that the guys have just played second-team cricket. Suddenly this year we have had a number of injuries and – bang – they're all out there and basically in the Club at the moment we've got either very experienced players or inexperienced players. There's nothing in between and this is one of the areas we've got to develop.

Seymour: Are you in yourself happy with Somerset – the way things are going there at the moment? You lost your England captaincy. We spoke within days of that and it's one of the biggest disappointments you've ever had. Now we see rumours – whatever – they may be taking the Somerset captaincy away from you.

Botham: Who are they going to give it to?

Seymour: You know, well, let's say Vic Marks, as your vice-captain. That's one option, isn't it?

Botham: Well, I just hope the Club think very hard about it because to captain any side, especially a side like Somerset where you've got a strong following, I think you've got to be a very strong person and I think you've got to be . . . I'm not saying Vic isn't . . . but I'm just wondering if he wants it. I am not really sure I see Vic as the taskmaster.

Seymour: Your agent is saying: 'Ian Botham is big news. He's a giant, we'll make him a megastar.' This has obviously played on your mind – I mean this is something – when we see figures today of £600,000 of contracts that you can actually earn in the next eighteen months, I understand –

Botham: Three months.

Seymour: Three months! Maybe you'll lend me a few bob. Er . . . that's obviously affecting really, suddenly the outlook on your life?

Botham: I think also this film thing – it's taken off as well now and we are just in the process of finalising the contracts there. There's a lot of new avenues that Tim's [Hudson] opened up for me in three months – things that, basically, that people or agents or managers in this country have been a little bit naive on. I sat down and I thought, after my first initial meetings with Tim I thought, 'You know, this guy's . . . not the crazy loon I thought he was.' . . . He makes a lot of sense and the more I listen to him and the more I talk with him, the guy is a very, very shrewd businessman . . . but not just a businessman. He's a guy I can rely on, he's a close friend, we get on very well together. It's a perfect relationship.

Seymour: What would you rather do – smash a six off of the Australians or star in a film with an opening night somewhere out in California?

Botham: Well, I've done the six . . .

Seymour: And you didn't get paid very much for it . . .

Botham: No, right.

(Not, perhaps, the most lucid exchange which has ever taken place on TV, and the Somerset Committee, no less than the public, could be forgiven if they wondered just what it was all about.)

That was Friday night, 4 October, and the Sunday newspapers were not slow to follow up a potential explosion involving the world's most exciting cricketer and the county which employed him. The phone lines between Fleet Street and the West Country were humming throughout Saturday. One of the calls went to Brian Langford, a former Somerset captain and now a Committeeman who offered to the *News of the World* the reasonable, guarded opinion that while Botham was undoubtedly a magnificent cricketer he might not be the ideal candidate for the county captaincy. On Monday Langford received a message that 'Botham was gunning for him'. But Botham once again was some way from being a little angelic boy dressed in blue. A further section of interview filmed the previous Friday was now put out by HTV on the Monday night, giving Ian's rather belligerent warning to the county about how things would have to change. It did not need any great sensitivity in the Committee to feel that the whole build-up to the meeting scheduled for the following evening had taken on an intimidatory tone. Clearly, behind the doors of the Committee Room, it was decided that quite enough slightly soiled, if not actually dirty, linen had already been washed in public and when it broke up, Botham issued an agreed statement which was decidedly low-key:

> I have asked not to be considered as captain because, as an individual who likes to give 100 per cent at all times and having given considerable thought to my position over the last couple of weeks, and bearing in mind all my commitments inside and outside the game, I cannot give the job of captain the time it requires and deserves. I am looking forward to playing for Somerset next season and minor details in the contract will be sorted out in due course.

The captaincy was offered to Peter Roebuck, the bespectacled opening batsman and a man who had known Botham since his schooldays; he accepted with delight. Roebuck, born in Oxford but a graduate of Cambridge (after schooling at Millfield), had a first-class honours degree in Law but since coming down had devoted himself to cricket, journalism and authorship. A noted wit and a gifted writer, Roebuck perhaps felt that he could 'handle' Botham in a similar way to Brearley, with a natural intellectual dominance which would manifest itself as not being a dominance at all – in short, by subtlety. Whether it *could* be done was something which would have to wait until the 1986 season, but in the meantime the Committee had those 'minor' contractual details to sort out. That involved tackling manager Hudson.

It was Hudson who won the first round of that particular contest. While informing the Committee that business commitments prevented his travelling to Taunton to discuss Botham's new contract, he publicly trumpeted that he had refused to visit Taunton and had demanded that the Committee's representatives wait upon him at Birtles Old Hall. This presented an obvious problem to the men who were nominally Botham's bosses. After a lot of discussion it was decided, with a certain pragmatism, that if the public honours were to go to Hudson/Botham the Club would at least salvage some dignity in their own way. Tony Brown, the chief executive, had friends at Mere Golf Club, ten miles from the Hudson headquarters. The two Committeemen who were to accompany him to the negotiations – Brian Langford and the Club treasurer, accountant Raymond Wright – were, like Tony, keen golfers, so arrangements were made to have lunch at Mere after their meeting with Hudson, followed by a pleasant eighteen holes on that attractive course which circles round a lake. They arrived at Birtles Old Hall in the late morning and were received by Tim Hudson's secretary, who showed them to an upstairs room where the walls were plastered with poster-pictures of Botham and Vivian Richards. The manager let them cool their heels for a time and then made his grand entrance, unrolling another poster, this time of Botham in a Rambo-style role with sub-machine gun and all! The Somerset contingent grinned at each other while the charade developed. And when Hudson fired his opening volley with a demand for a salary for his client twice as high as his current one, they rose as one man and prepared to leave.

Hudson quickly changed tack, urging the Somerset contingent not to be hasty and suggested a discussion. Brown, Wright and Langford sat down again, and when they rose Botham's new one-year contract had been agreed at a figure £1000 less than the Club had actually been willing to pay! If Hudson had won the first round, they felt (not without justification) that they had won the second and since it involved money rather than cheap publicity it was one rather more worth winning. In fact, since it was obvious that England's Selectors would always pick Botham even if he were in a wheelchair with both arms and legs broken and whatever his current form, Somerset were actually going to do rather well out of the deal. Counties whose players are required for Tests and one-day internationals are compensated to the tune of £750 per Test and £250 per one-day, and in 1986 there were to be three Tests against India, three against New Zealand and two one-day internationals against each country. That meant £5500 in Somerset's kitty in return for Botham's services. As Hudson informed the press of his 'triumph' over the negotiators, the Somerset trio played a round of golf at Mere in an equally satisfied frame of mind. They might reasonably have felt that their satisfaction had the sounder basis.

One way and another, and particularly in view of all the undignified gloating emanating from his business headquarters, Botham's image – at least amongst the saner and more intelligent members of the cricketing public – was becoming just a little more tarnished at this time. With accidental, but what turned out to be utterly brilliant, timing Ian himself changed the whole picture in a matter of days. On 26 October he started his 870-mile walk from John o'Groats to Land's End amidst an unprecedented blaze of the most favourable publicity. Now, it must be emphasised at once that his walk should not be seen simply as a gimmick, an image-building enterprise. Botham genuinely had a very strong feeling for young leukaemia victims; he had wanted to do something for them ever since a visit to the Musgrave Hospital in Taunton nine years earlier when he had been deeply touched by his first sight of the way the disease affects youngsters. It was a happy coincidence that the sponsored walk had been scheduled to take place at a time when his personal popularity had been taking a bit of a battering. It had actually been planned for two years.

His manager was something less than 100 per cent in favour of the idea, perhaps because it did not involve him in any spectacular role, and the exposure in media terms was unparalleled. Jimmy Savile, a man who knew better than most the value of personal publicity, had undertaken a similar sponsored walk a few years earlier but by comparison with the Botham effort his was virtually shrouded in mystery. By far the greatest asset to fund-raising on Botham's walk was the attention of BBC television. Almost every morning, 'Breakfast Time' viewers started the day with a view of England's greatest cricket hero, on the move in his quest to raise funds for handicapped children, chatting to one of TV's most wholesome characters, Frank Bough, who presents a picture of everybody's favourite uncle. When Uncle Frank occasionally took a break the delectable and exceedingly popular Selina Scott took over to add a different dimension to the interviewing – and allow Botham to introduce the touch of flirtatiousness which most of Miss Scott's male admirers would dearly have liked to indulge in. On top of all this came massive coverage by national and Sunday newspapers and by provincial journals when Botham arrived in their circulation areas. And finally came the personal contact with the admiring members of his public.

But, inevitably it now seemed, Ian could not avoid fouling his own nest from time to time, even on an excursion like this, as we shall see. The question we must ask ourselves is: how much should he be blamed for instances where he offended well-meaning people and how much allowance should be made for his weariness at the end of each back-breaking day, an immense, appalling weariness which must have made it so difficult to accept every invitation, to gratify every wish to shake his hands or to have him receive personally all the money that the public wanted to hand over to him? Let us take as a cross-section of public opinion amongst the people who met him (or who were unable to meet him) on that stretch of the trek which was just half-way between John o'Groats and Land's End – the area between Penrith and Lancaster.

On Sunday, 10 November 1985, the entourage arrived in the little Cumbrian market town of Penrith. There were support vehicles, walk-organisers, TV and newspaper representatives and a few of the inevitable hangers-on. Gordon and Pat Steel, whose fifteen-year-old son was a leukaemia victim, had organised a social evening at the Gateway Hotel to hand over the £1500 which had been collected there. This had been raised by auctioning articles which had been given by local firms and personalities, including the MP for the constituency, Mr David Maclean, and the chairman of the Eden (District) Council, Ernie McBain, was waiting to hand over the money. Over a hundred tickets had been sold at short notice and there was tremendous disappointment when Botham sent a message to say that he was too tired and stiff to come down from his suite. Was it fair to expect him, after a walk so far stretching over 400 miles with 20 covered that day, to appear to receive donations which so many local people had worked so hard to collect? Only Ian himself could decide whether he was capable of making one last effort that day to totter downstairs on his aching feet to meet the crowd waiting below. If he had shaken hands with one it must have meant shaking hands with all, or disappointment would certainly in individual cases have turned to resentment. He couldn't really win. And yet on the plus side of his visit to Penrith was a visit to the Fire Station to receive a cheque, the signing of dozens of autograph albums and bats, a pause in the village of Clifton to play conkers with schoolchildren – conjuring up memories of his battles with Jasper the caretaker in Yeovil, perhaps? – and a meeting with three-year-old Gemma Thompson, a tiny leukaemia victim, to whom her mother said he was 'charming' in a meeting seen by 'Breakfast Time' viewers.

On Monday he walked on, over the bleak expanse of Shap Summit where the A6 climbs to over 1000 feet and which is usually one of the first roads in England to be blocked in a snowstorm. He reached Kendal, southern gateway to the Lake District, half an hour ahead of schedule, taking the Mayor – who had planned an informal civic reception – by surprise. Councillor Richard Brayshaw dashed downstairs to shake Botham by the hand and to invite him upstairs to the Mayor's Parlour for a spot of refreshment, but the long-distance walker declined as he marched on to the South Lakeland Leisure Centre which was his target for that day. The Mayor told the press: 'I was very disappointed at not meeting him properly and taking him for a drink and a chat in the Parlour. I think a lot of people were disappointed, but he said if he stopped his legs would stiffen up. I think the man was under a lot of harassment.' Once again it is entirely possible to understand public and mayoral disappointment, but is it not just as easy to feel sympathy towards Botham? He had a few hundred yards to walk to complete his stint for that day. It would have been anti-climactic in the extreme to have broken off to spend a quarter of an hour at the Town Hall.

So on he went to the Leisure Centre where he left after a few minutes to be driven to his hotel for that night. His departure left the Centre's assistant manager Roger Burns with a crowd of people who were mostly a little upset at not being able to talk to Ian. His comment to the press was: 'We got quite a few complaints from people who had missed him. It was a great let-down for many kids who had turned up to see their hero.' Of course it was and it was good to see Mr Burns adding, understandingly: 'I can really sympathise with Botham. He was suffering and his legs were shaking and he was really cold and tired. He thanked us for offering the use of the Centre's facilities.' It didn't prevent a number of people ringing the editorial offices of the *Westmorland Gazette* to complain. One of them, a Mrs P. Thomas, was reported as saying: 'I wasn't impressed at all. We know he is doing a great thing but he should have stayed longer. Lots of children were disappointed.' No, Botham *couldn't* win – always that 'doing a great thing, but . . .'

There were more plaudits than pannings, however. Lorry-drivers stopped to wish Ian well and to make individual donations; fighter aircraft on training exercises at low level dipped their wings in salute and a couple even put on an impromptu aerobatics display; folk-dancers provided musical and terpsichorean escorts; and always there were parents of leukaemia victims waiting to thank him and to present their children. There was something almost Biblical about the progress at times. On 12 November it reached Lancaster, where there was the usual massive reception. Debbie Liver was a reporter on one of the local newspapers and on returning from her assignment of covering the arrival in Lancaster she was asked what she thought of Ian Botham.

'He's an ignorant pig,' she snapped. And, pressed for details, she went on: 'I suppose he would have been all smiles and charm if the television cameras had been there but they weren't. So he wasn't.' And beyond that she simply did not want to talk about her meeting with the great man.

Ken Frohock, who is news editor of the other local paper, the *Lancaster Guardian*, reported to his friends an entirely different reaction, however. Apart from his professional duties, Ken had been instructed by *two* nephews to bring back separate autographs for them. He offered two separate pieces of paper to Botham, who signed both – a feat no easier than making interview notes without breaking one's stride. 'Initially, I was a bit hesitant because I had heard what had happened the previous day in Kendal,' said Frohock. (Declining the Mayor's invitation and that quick about-turn at the Leisure Centre had already, in less than twenty-four hours, begun to build up into a large-scale condemnation of the walker's personal PR.) 'I said to one of my reporters, Martin Butler, "Don't be surprised if I get knocked for six." But I found him an absolutely smashing feller and so, it seemed, did most of Lancaster.'

It was here that two women from the Isle of Man waited to hand over a cheque for £600 which they had collected, schoolboys from Kirkby Lonsdale contributed £250 and the more local Ripley St Thomas weighed in with £75. Gifts large and small built up a total of £6200 from the Lancaster area. And that, really, was the story of the whole trip. The 'little people' of Britain backed Botham's effort 100 per cent; it was the industrialists and business houses which disappointed him. But let's return for a moment to the different impressions Ian Botham made upon people along the way. At various stages of the walk – Kendal–Lancaster, Lancaster–Preston, Preston–Blackburn and Blackburn–Manchester – Botham was joined by Mrs Stephanie Mains, a former nurse whose patients had included young leukaemia victims, and it turned out to be one of the more moving experiences of her life.

He is obviously a man's man, and if I had met him in

any other circumstances I might not have taken to him. But all I can say about him on the walk was that he was fantastic. I know he's very outspoken and can upset some people but I also know that he's a very caring person. As we walked past Pendlebury Children's Hospital, near Manchester, some of the little ones came out and he was in tears when he saw them. He really was. What people would see a little further along the road was Ian walking into Manchester with his arms round two blondes and I suppose that's part of his image, too. But what I shall remember is seeing him with tears in his eyes as he saw those little ones, leukaemia sufferers who had lost their hair and were obviously very, very ill. I know he cared about them.

Mrs Mains, chairman of the Lancaster district committee of the Leukaemia Research Fund, was given a target of £1000 when she went into the work in June 1985, and felt that that was an impossible figure. But between the time when Ian walked through Lancaster and Christmas – six weeks later – a total of *£10,000* was raised. 'It could never have happened without him,' said Mrs Mains.

When I took over I thought we would have the usual round of coffee mornings and that sort of thing, and a target of £1000 did not seem remotely possible. Everything changed after Ian had walked through. It was the most fantastic experience just to be involved in it in a small way. The atmosphere was unbelievable . . . people were giving us hundreds of pounds as we walked across the moors. I would have loved to go all the way to Land's End, but the back trouble which caused me to give up nursing made that impossible. And I kept thinking of Ian getting up every morning to start walking another twenty miles, then another twenty, and another. He had a bad foot infection when he was in Lancaster, but we were asked not to say anything about that.

So there we have one lady happy to judge Ian Botham on what he did for sick children and, in the light of that, to ignore anything else she might have heard or read about him. And there were many others along the road who took the same view. Even those not closely connected with the cause of leukaemia research must have got a little caught up in the family atmosphere of the walk when, during the night he spent in Lancaster, Botham's wife Kathy gave birth to their third child – a daughter to be named Rebecca and to be known as Becky – 100 miles away in Doncaster. Her mother wanted to phone Ian at once but, characteristically, Kathy would not have him disturbed at half-past three in the morning. At breakfast time, the whole country shared in the parental delight, courtesy of television, and by a happy chance it was one of Selina Scott's mornings on Botham duty. 'What are you going to call her?' came the question most people were asking that morning. 'I haven't the foggiest idea,' replied Dad. And then, inevitably: 'How about Selina?' The nation's viewers loved it. And as Ian approached Preston that afternoon the *Lancashire Evening Post* got into the spirit of the happiest day of the walk by sending out a human Babygram to greet him.

Apart from its primary objective of raising money for the most deserving of causes, apart from its excellence as a daily piece of TV which brought something fresh, sentimental, heart-warming, humorous to each morning, the Walk was an absolute natural for the feature-writers and the straight news reporters. For the former there was the possibility that Botham might be in one of his get-lost-I-have-something-better-to-do moods, in which case they could admire the strong, silent fortitude of his attitude or knock him for churlishness as the fancy took them. For the latter, there was human interest every inch of the way. And there was always the possibility that Botham might break down and have to call it off. After all, how many of us could even contemplate the possibility of walking from John o'Groats to Land's End? Most of all, as always with the sort of man who was the central character in the play, there was always an equal possibility of *a major incident*.

Those whose perhaps unworthy (and often unsought) duty it was to watch for such an occasion had to wait until the last few days of the walk before it occurred. Presumably it was worth waiting for because, on 27 November, Botham *thumped a policeman*! I was in Australia when this happened and it made headlines there – indeed it did. Botham has been a bogey-man to Aussie cricketers far too often for this to pass without notice on the other side of the world. Back home, the police were in the most difficult of situations. On any normal day they were faced with the virtually impossible job of trying to maintain law and order in an increasingly undisciplined society where, it seemed, an agitator or nut case had only to cry 'police brutality' to have the allegation plastered over every front page and TV screen in the country. Now, they had a public hero who by this time must have had the support of 99.9 per cent of the population, striking an officer who, it turned out, was a supporter of the enterprise and had, in fact, contributed to it. What could the police do? To have charged Botham with assaulting a constable in the execution of his duty would have brought down the fury of the whole country upon their heads, yet at a time when it was vitally important not to have the authority of the forces of law and order diminished in any way, the alternative was to sweep it all under the carpet. It has to be said that the Cornish Police got it right. On 29 November that best-known of anonymous figures, 'a police spokesman', announced:

> Visibility was very poor. Botham's group of between thirty and fifty people were walking out of Bodmin and they were apparently running in front of traffic and trying to stop cars. At the time police were concerned for their safety, and traffic Inspector Brian Carder advised Botham and his entourage to take particular care. Tempers flared a little on Botham's side and then a little later, further outside Bodmin, police again became concerned for their safety. PC

> Peter Fleming again advised Botham to be careful and was punched three times, around the helmet and to the body. [It is permissible to reflect for a moment that Botham must have been in a fair old state to try punching a police helmet!] Police are taking no action over the incident. Obviously tempers were frayed and people were tired. Peter Fleming is a particular supporter of the leukaemia campaign and he is not going to take any action, although it could have been construed as an assault on the police.

Good, sensible policy; good neutral terminology. Full marks to the Devon and Cornwall Constabulary.

The walk was duly completed and raised over £400,000, far more than the officially stated original target of £100,000 and far less than Ian's own rather ambitiously designated figure of £1 million. By any standards it was a magnificent effort, and strangely enough it was the *Guardian* which chose to dwell rather lengthily on the seamier side of the effort. In an article which must have caused anguish to that newspaper's cricket correspondent – who is apt to go into a highly literary swoon at the very appearance of Botham on a cricket field – it not only described the police punch-up as 'the most eye-catching of the incidents of the last few days' but drew attention to another wrangle involving a radio reporter, quoted Botham as dubbing Inspector Carder 'a wanker' and reproduced a comment from Eric Gummow, landlord of the Victoria Hotel near Bodmin, who was apparently 'bloody disgusted' when Botham departed to see his physiotherapist instead of greeting the crowd outside Mr Gummow's pub. But all in all he had had a good press during his five weeks on the road, and by the end of November 1985 he could reasonably claim to be the most popular man in Britain. It was a pretty safe bet, therefore, that he would soon do something to damage the image . . .

Throughout the summer of 1985, while the sports pages of national newspapers recorded six-hitting feats and whirlwind innings against Warwicks and others, the news pages featured stories of the showbiz fame which apparently waited just round the corner for I. T. Botham. These titbits were generously dispensed by Tim Hudson, like the good agent he was proving to be, at least in terms of publicity. To most people it must have seemed rather fatuous, since Botham the cricketer needed no synthetic boosting at all to further his career. He was, and had been for five years or more, the number one attraction and crowd-puller in the game. But this was not enough for the energetic Mr Hudson, who proclaimed: 'He's Biggles, Raffles and Errol Flynn all rolled into one.' An intriguing mixture, one might think, and is it not difficult to imagine a greater contradiction than Errol Flynn and the clean-cut hero of Captain Johns's tales of derring-do? Botham was then seen, in the imaginative eyes of Mr Hudson, as the next James Bond, and the *Sun* 'exclusively' announced that he had been guaranteed a million dollars by an Australian film producer to appear in something called *The Perpetrator* with Oliver Reed. This, for a moment, caused some of us to sit up, because the thought of O. Reed and I. T. Botham being unleashed together upon the gently nurtured populace of Australia was calculated to bring about a major disruption of Commonwealth relations, even under Bob Hawke's man-of-the-people regime. And then, we reflected, it *is* a *Sun* exclusive after all, which usually means that no one else will touch the story. And by October the *Sunday Times* was quoting Gary Rhodes – the man reputed to have offered that million to Botham – as saying from his office in Brisbane: 'I never offered Ian anything of the sort. What I did was ask for publicity stills, authentication that he was taking acting lessons or a videotape to prove he *could* act. All I got was a request for 40,000 dollars from Hudson. How can you do business with a man like that? He's mad. Any deal is off before it's started.' It must be said that that pronouncement caused profound disappointment in cricket-writing circles around the country. Ian's acting début had been, and still is, awaited with the keenest anticipation.

The *Daily Mirror* was the next newspaper to be fed an

'exclusive', and this foreshadowed Botham's transformation into a tournament professional golfer – although it has to be said that as the *Sun*'s great Fleet Street (or Wapping) rival, the *Mirror* probably printed the story with its editorial tongue firmly in the cheek. This particular miracle was to be achieved by Wilson's, the golf equipment manufacturers. Alas, their marketing director, James McAlley, told the *Sunday Times*: 'That didn't come from us. We heard about Ian's interest in the game and we gave him a set of clubs.' The faithful ghost, Alasdair Ross, had in the meantime not been idle. Under a picture of Botham dressed (or at least half-dressed) as Sylvester Stallone playing his Rambo character and wielding a grenade-launcher, Mr Ross told us that Botham would 'get a taste of life on the big screen when he visits Hollywood in December with his agent and business partner Tim Hudson'. Botham (according to the ghost) would like to have a few beers with Sylvester: 'I like his style and I'm sure he'd be very interested in the English-look fashionwear Tim and I are marketing.'

There was something touching about Botham's devotion to his partner in the way that that little sales-pitch was slipped into an otherwise unbelievably banal piece of hogwash: 'I would love to loose off a few rounds with that gun Rambo uses in the film – I don't think we can miss with a thing like that. It is a fair weight but I reckon I could fire it from the hip. It is only a little bit heavier than my bat!' But by now the whole thing was becoming something worse than pathetic. The greatest natural talent in world cricket was allowing himself to be reduced to a figure of ridicule, a little boy playing the modern equivalent of cowboys and Indians. Could he not see it? Apparently not. And he reacted belligerently to any friendly suggestion that he had something better to offer the world on the cricket field than the silver screen.

In December, after a worrying moment or two when there seemed to be a possibility that the United States would not grant him a visa because of his conviction for possessing cannabis, off he went to California; along, too, went the ghost. Having no immediate reporting to do about hordes of film producers clamouring for Ian's signature to contracts, long or short term, Alasdair Ross filed another of those *Sun* exclusives: Botham, c. and b. 0, by a Sydney car-parts salesman, Carl McGuinn, in the annual cricket match between British and Australian customers of an English-style pub, the Old King's Head in Santa Monica. But the *Daily Mail* had unkindly decided to cover the visit, too.

In an article covering almost a whole page and devastatingly headed 'Ian Who?' the *Mail* disclosed:

> There are no movie directors summoning him for screen tests and not one invitation to appear on a chat show. Instead of living it up in five-star luxury he's dossing down in the garden shed of his manager's brightly painted beach shack. His Hollywood adventure had turned into a fiasco while he was still on the plane from London. A buxom, scantily clad brunette, hired to plug his arrival by gate-crashing a lunch for 1000 British and American businessmen, was thrown out before she could even start her pitch. When Ian did arrive, only his flamboyant manager and three hangers-on were there. Hudson told Ian he would meet the local press and celebrities at a dinner party on Sunset Strip. But apart from the group who met him at the airport and a couple of photographers, the only other guests were three girls, two of whom were married to long-forgotten 1960s musicians. The evening brightened up somewhat when veteran actor Donald Pleasance dropped in to the British-style restaurant for some English grub and was dragged over for a brief introduction. However, he beat a hasty retreat.

The indefatigable Mr Hudson apparently saw no anticlimax in all this and told the *Mail*'s reporter: 'Ian will be going to the studios.'

'Which studios?'

'Universal.'

'To take the tour that is open to any member of the public?'

'Well, yes. But it *is* the VIP tour.'

Mr Hudson went on: 'Ian has three or four more years' cricket in him yet before we need to concentrate on making it in movies. But mark my words, Ian is Britain's greatest hero since Churchill and will be a superstar in the Cary Grant mould.' Even the most devoted Botham admirer would have to blink at that one – at least those who remember the smooth, suave, silky charm of Mr Grant. There being not much further business on the Hollywood agenda, Botham returned to England to be met by the *Mail*'s Amit Roy, who very quickly discovered that he was not talking to the *Daily Mail* because, apparently, the 'Ian Who?' story had been reported to him. Welcome to the Club, Amit Roy.

11 THE RECLUSE

Just as Botham had been in 1981, David Gower was completely on a hiding to nothing as he led England on tour to the West Indies in 1986. Even allowing for the unpredictable nature of cricket, even accepting the oldest of clichés that 'it's a funny game', there was no possible way in the whole wide world that England could beat the Windies. Of course, a captain setting off on tour cannot say that and there were the usual brave words – brave but totally empty, nevertheless – for the media, to be passed on to whoever might be inclined to believe them. Certainly the players knew they were in for a hard time, and the only realistic possibility of staving off defeat had to centre round the pitch at the Queen's Park Oval in Port-of-Spain, Trinidad, which is traditionally lower and slower than the other Test grounds, since that island with its great mixture of Indian and Chinese blood has for many years produced outstanding spin bowlers rather than quicker men. But in the context of Test cricket, 'slower' is merely a relative term. The West Indies' battery of Barbadian and Jamaican fast bowlers were always likely to make nonsense of it.

Botham went there with 4409 Test runs to his name at an average of 36.43 and 343 Test wickets at 26.37, although his record in both areas against the Windies was modest in the extreme. Gower himself had 5385 runs, Gooch 3027, Gatting 2246 and Lamb (a more impressive performer against Caribbean opposition) 2211. Tim Robinson, who had arrived on the Test scene so successfully in India (1984–5) and consolidated his position as an England opener against the Australians in the summer of '85, had no experience against the four-man non-stop barrage, and while his excellent back-foot technique promised, on paper, to be useful in the West Indies, there was the thought in some circles that his Nottinghamshire partner, Chris Broad, might be a better bet. There would have been a certain irony if the left-handed Broad had been chosen. After the 1984 series in which the West Indies carried out their 'blackwash' in England, it was felt that Broad had performed as courageously and as well as anyone, but since he was regarded as being less certain against spin bowling he was omitted from the tour to India and replaced by his Notts partner, Robinson. If the Selectors had followed a consistent policy line the following winter it would have been logical to pick Broad and leave out Robinson. The argument against doing so was that it would have been unfair to omit a man who had been so successful in the summer against Australia. But wasn't that exactly the way in which they had behaved unfairly to Broad at the end of the previous summer?

Graham Gooch was a certainty to return after an absence of three years while he was banned from Test cricket for having played in South Africa, and it was his selection – together with that of Peter Willey and John Emburey, who had also played in South Africa – which set the political ball rolling. Although the West Indies Board of Control were parties to the agreement that every country had a freedom of choice in selecting its Test players irrespective of political issues, the pressures which could – and now were – exerted by a number of government figures made a mockery of that agreement. In Antigua and in Trinidad political chiefs made it known that they would personally boycott the matches when the tourists played in those islands. In the more volatile atmosphere of Trinidad in particular (Antigua, it was thought, being very much more cricket-minded than politically orientated) this was certain to be seen as a go-ahead for demonstrations by those who felt strongly about the situation in South Africa and some who simply preferred a good banner-waving demo to a game of cricket. There must have been many times – there certainly ought to have been – in that uncertain atmosphere of the three months leading up to the tour when the Test and County Cricket Board considered pulling out and cancelling the tour altogether. That would have spelled financial disaster to the West Indies Board, who badly need the income from tours by England and Australia in particular to finance their domestic competitions. It was a tricky and uneasy atmosphere for the players as they set out – most of all for Gooch, Willey and Emburey, who were likely to be singled out, without credible justification, as disciples of apartheid.

First came the one-day international and the First Test in Jamaica, where there is always a fairly fiery undertow of politics in any case, and an encounter with a problem of a different kind: Balfour Patrick Patterson. He had played one game for Lancashire in 1984 on the recommendation of Clive Lloyd, and in 1985 became a more regular performer. The invaluable *Playfair Cricket Annual*, in its 1985 pen pictures of all first-class players, listed him as RHB, RFM, but the latter description slightly understated the bowling of the young Jamaican. This is perhaps best illustrated by quoting a conversation between Jack Bond, then Lancashire manager, and David Hughes, one of his trusted playing lieutenants, after an appearance by Patterson in a second-team match in which one of the umpires was David ('Bumble') Lloyd, a former Lancs captain.

'Right,' said the manager, 'just how quick *is* he?'

'Well,' replied Hughes, 'let's put it this way – when he'd warmed up and was bowling his second over, "Bumble" was backing away at square leg.'

With fifteen games against county sides in 1985, Patterson had played twice against Derbyshire, Somerset, Warwicks and Notts and, since several of his games had coincided with Tests, not all of England's batsmen had seen him. And not many of those who had were prepared for the searing pace he generated before his home spectators in Jamaica. A 24-year-old of driving ambition, he saw his opportunity to join the élite corps of West Indian quicks despite the massed ranks of contenders, and now pursued it with ferocity. Malcolm Marshall has been widely accepted for the past three years as the world's fastest bowler. Clive Lloyd now reported back to Old Trafford from the Test in Jamaica that Patterson was a yard and a half quicker than Marshall! Such terms are usually arbitrary since it is difficult, if not impossible, to establish them with any degree of arithmetical accuracy, but as a metaphorical *indication* of pace, they are valuable.

It did not matter to any marked extent that Patterson, striving for even greater pace, sprayed it about a bit and bowled a fair proportion of no balls. What concerned the English batsmen was that here was yet another manifestation of fast bowling at its most dangerous, with an added dimension. Marshall and Holding are, generally speaking, pretty accurate as well as fast; Garner is deceptively fast with the extra problem of getting bounce by his delivery from a great height. Here now was a man of even greater pace who might suffer from lapses of direction but could then whip in the straighter ball without any warning. And in terms of danger to life and limb, it doesn't matter much whether the ball is legally or illegally delivered; the perils are just the same. So here were poor old England once again up against an attack of great pace, hour after hour, day after day, with no respite – or virtually none. If Roger Harper or Vivian Richards came on for two or three overs there was the new problem of a possible lapse of concentration in sheer relief at being free for a moment or two from the torments of incessant ninety-miles-an-hour bombardment. It is impossible, really, for those of us who have never experienced the ordeal to understand what it is like. We can only offer a view based on observation with a professional eye, some more experienced than others, some more sympathetic than others, and on our conversations with the men who *do* have to contend with it. Mike Gatting, who had to return home for repairs to a badly fractured nose, would be an excellent witness.

Whether it is *cricket* in the old-fashioned sense may be open to debate, but it is difficult to see any country in this highly competitive age failing to use such a potent weapon if it were available. Equally, it is difficult to criticise batsmen with the technique, grace and charm of England's top six, who are capable of scoring high-class centuries against any other country in the world and giving enormous pleasure while they are doing so, for being unable to cope with the day-long pressures of 120-feet-per-second deliveries on some pitches where a ball was just as liable to rear at the throat as shoot around the ankles. It was a situation where sheer pace was the most potent of weapons and the West Indies had it in abundance. Occasionally it might be possible to make some progress in the one-day internationals, where the ordeal was of limited duration and where the absence of a tight cordon of close catchers made it easier – no, less difficult – to score off the edge of the bat, but this could not realistically be taken as a guide to what was possible in a five-day Test.

This high drama was always going to lead to a full turn-out of cricket reporters, and the promise of quasi-political demonstrations in Trinidad led to an equally large-scale attendance of news reporters. When the demonstrations turned out to be less spectacular than had been feared (or hoped, depending upon the standpoint) pressure upon all the newsmen from their masters back home to get *some* sort of story increased. At first the target was Gower, whose lack of form provided a talking point in much the same way as Botham's had done in 1981. The difference was that Gower did not adopt a stance of silly bravado. In one press conference after another his attitude gradually began to change from a dignified acceptance of defeat by a team who had played better, to one of bewilderment and perplexity about what he could be expected to do next. But in Jamaica, carried over at first to Trinidad, it was Gower who was the focus of media attention, and as captain he was the man who had to answer the barrage of questions at press conferences, some valid, some asinine. If his patience began to wear a bit thin it was difficult, from an objective point of view, to blame him. From the purely subjective angle, most of the questions had to be asked because every writer and broadcaster had to say *something* in his next despatch back home. With a limited number of things which could be said, and an unlimited number of reporters on hand, players other than the captain became the alternative targets.

After a day in the firing line, the last thing any player wanted was a newsman accosting him in the hotel garden, by the swimming pool, in the bar or even tapping on the door of his room. Yet the newspapermen had their problems, too. Botham was a contracted columnist for the *Sun* and, whoever wrote the stuff, it was Botham's name which appeared above the material published. The *Daily Express* was carrying pieces under the names of Gower *and* Richards, the two captains. Other papers naturally enough wanted 'quotes' of some kind. They were paying out a lot of money to have not one, but two reporters in the Caribbean, sometimes with a photographer as well, and *something* was demanded from them. On 9 March, the *Mail*'s Ian Wooldridge flew into Trinidad and reported next morning that Botham and Gooch were vowing never to tour overseas again. In typically graphic style, Wooldridge said they

> cite harassment at every turn: from political activists to prying reporters. They do not mention the temporary but horrific ordeal of facing a hit squad of large, black, fast bowlers raining bouncers around their ears but that must be a contributory factor. Botham has become a lone, reclusive figure who confines himself to his hotel room. He complains, with justification, that any move he makes in public will be distorted. He calls his room 'the bat cage' and broods there on the price of stardom. Gooch, a morose figure at breakfast yesterday, is said to be worn down by the gauntlet of insulting placards he has to run every morning to get into the Test ground. The politest describes him as 'a fascist pig'.
>
> I have seen England cricket teams disintegrate under pressure before. But never have England previously been threatened by top players confessing they are prepared to throw away their international careers

> rather than face it again. Their main charges are that even at the end of a day's play, frequently harrowing enough in itself, they are under such personal scrutiny from a large press contingent that they cannot live normal lives in off-duty hours. They fear that to be seen drinking in public or to be photographed in the proximity of any woman in the swimming-pool area will lead to a spate of tabloid publicity back home attempting to explain their shortcomings on the field. This is particularly so for Ian Botham, whose public exploits like walking the length of Britain, knocking on the dream factory doors of Hollywood and employing a manager whose sole purpose is to promote him as an internationally charismatic figure, has earned him pop star attention which now, at a low point in his cricket career, he probably regrets.

Now, some of that is not entirely fair from the normally scrupulous Wooldridge to members of his own craft. He knows that most cricket correspondents are decent people with a genuine feeling for the game and a personal liking for most players. He also knows that most of them would most willingly back off writing about matters other than performances on the field – were it not for the ever-present knowledge that not every newspaperman does his job the same way. And when news reporters (as opposed to purely cricket-writers) are around, they are subject to pressures from their news desks from which cricket correspondents are normally free. If they are told to write a particular story, by and large they *write* it. And the most tolerant newspaper in the world is not going to react too well to a rival splashing eye-catching dramas all over its pages marked 'exclusive'. It is a really desperate problem to which, in this era of circulation wars, there seems no solution. What most newspapermen would readily accept, however, is the next point made in Ian Wooldridge's article: 'The trouble is exacerbated by a disastrous decision at Lord's to allow Test players on tour to "write" highly-paid ghosted columns for British newspapers. This has done much to break down the long-standing trust between players and correspondents. Players are liable to say one thing when questioned by rival newspapers and "write" completely the opposite in the publication by which they are employed.'

That is absolutely right. BBC Radio puts a four-figure sum into the players' 'kitty' before every tour, which represents payment for all interviews carried out on the tour. Only one player has ever refused to record an interview on any tour I have made, and that was Ian Botham. It was not a controversial topic on which I wanted to talk to him – simply a five-wicket performance against New Zealand in Wellington which, to some extent, represented a return to bowling form after a fairly lengthy thin time in this department of his game. It makes it rather difficult – in some cases impossible – to explain to a programme producer back in England that a player has breached the unwritten agreement for which he has implicitly accepted payment from the BBC while his ghosted column in the *Sun* (for which he is admittedly paid a lot more money) carries his views on all kinds of topics. Even though they don't contribute anything to the players' 'kitty' there is no reason why rival papers to the *Sun* should feel less aggrieved at being deprived of quotes from the most colourful figure in a tour party.

The TCCB's decision to allow this sort of ghosted writing for one or two papers was bound to damage player–media relationships on tour. In view of all the other problems, it can only be seen as a classically stupid concession. I should add that the BBC's arrangement was never regarded as involving exclusivity; indeed I always made a point of making the recording available to any newspaperman who wanted 'quotes' from a player. It saved time for both player and newsman, while leaving us with the natural exclusivity of having the actual words uttered in the player's own voice, and that was enough.

While Ian Wooldridge concentrated on the off-the-field pressures on players in that article of 10 March, the purely cricket-writers found themselves torn between letting down

Botham lightly for a particularly undistinguished spell of bowling in the Second Test and savaging him for his performance. Almost five years to the day after his 'big baby' blast against Botham, which led ultimately to the manhandling at Bermuda airport, Henry Blofeld decided to chance his arm once again in even more emphatic terms. In the *Sunday Express* of 9 March, 'Blowers' thundered:

> England's hapless position in the Second Test was exaggerated by the apparent obstinacy and selfishness of Ian Botham on Friday at the start of the West Indians' first innings. For David Gower's side to have had an infinitesimal chance of clawing their way back into the match they had to rock the West Indies with two early wickets. Greg Thomas, whose pace had scared some of the West Indians in Jamaica, had to open downwind. And, with a heavy cloudbase, outswinger Richard Ellison was the natural choice for the other end. As it was, Botham seized the new ball with the wind behind him, put two men back for the mistimed hook and was carved up for 39 runs in five disgraceful overs. The question is: why did Gower allow Botham to take the new ball, let alone bowl five overs with it? In fact, who is captain of England? Is Gower in control of Botham's massive ego? On this showing he is not and when a player acts as Botham did now his record counts for very little. Botham was allowed to ruin whatever slender chances England still had, and clearly blew his cool while he was being flogged around the ground and put on a tiresome display of petulance. It was a disgrace, and Botham in this form has become an acute embarrassment to England. If he will not discipline himself, then he badly needs a captain who can do it for him.

Harsh words. But true. Brave words, but they needed to be said. And some of us had been saying them for some time. Cricket correspondents were not the only ones who had watched Botham for so long now bowling badly with two captains – successively Willis and Gower – seemingly having neither the inclination, in Willis's case, nor the physical and psychological weight, in Gower's, to put a stop to it. The Ian Wooldridge article which appeared in the *Daily Mail* the day after Henry Blofeld's attack in the *Sunday Express* was, as we have seen, fairly sympathetic towards Botham. One day later, on 11 March, he took a slightly different line.

> For much of the gruelling Test Match here Ian Botham has worn the disgruntled scowl of the street gang bully who has met his match. Against the great West Indian war machine he has looked a very ordinary cricketer, contributing just two runs to England's catastrophic first innings and bowling so badly at times that even his colleagues have shaken their heads in disbelief. They are fighting like dingbats here to save the Test and look to him today to renounce his showmanship, curb his impetuosity and play a long and responsible innings. Any sudden rush of blood to the head, any slapdash heroics that end in disaster, could lead to civil war in the team. Some of them look back with nostalgia to last winter's tour of India when Botham was 6000 miles away in Britain. They confide that the dressing-room was a much happier place. They do not say this within Botham's hearing. He is a tempestuous man. Writing thus of a national idol, a brilliantly gifted sportsman, a physically fearless competitor and an enigma of a personality, is a dangerous pastime. For one thing, debunking heroes is a particularly nasty British habit. For another, Ian Botham has the inherent capacity to make you look a mean-spirited fool before sunset. After all, he has scored 4455 runs and taken 346 wickets in Tests. It is to be hoped that the widespread criticism that has contributed to him becoming a reclusive figure will either inspire or goad him into action.
>
> He is probably the highest-paid cricketer, from all his sources of income, in history. He is also known to

> be one of its biggest spenders. In a sport whose stars are comparatively lowly paid, this has also failed to contribute to dressing-room harmony. The more immediate problems on this high-pressure, physically dangerous and increasingly nervy tour of the Caribbean, however, is that his team-mates are tired of what they see as his high-handed law-unto-himself attitude on the field. This suited all concerned very well when, as in the immortal Leeds Test Match against Australia in 1981, Botham could napalm a bowling attack with such devastating effect that a glaring lost cause was transformed into near-inconceivable victory in a couple of hours. That is not happening here and until something like it does, the discontent within the team will continue to simmer. Too many batsmen are getting painfully hit too often to endure any superstar attitudes from one of their colleagues. Publicly they are very loyal to Botham. Privately they are concerned that their own captain, the polite and quietly-spoken David Gower, does not appear to put his foot down.

This was all undoubtedly true. Those who have managed to retain some semblance of personal contact with individual players during a period of rapid deterioration in such relationships *know* that it is true. Such views have many times been expressed in off-the-record, off-duty conversations in the knowledge that confidences will be respected. And the emphasis on their being off the record has been not so much for fear of physical retribution at the hands of 'Beefy' as an entirely understandable and indeed laudable desire to keep the ranks closed. In India, in 1984–5, many conversations between players and press hinged on the better atmosphere in the camp as a whole without Botham's dominant presence. Virtually every newspaperman on that tour wrote a piece at the end of it which suggested, with varying degrees of emphasis, a happier and more harmonious set of relationships. It was not coincidence. There is no doubt at all that Gower was better able to lead his forces when they did not include the man who was, more than any other in England, potentially a match-winner. It was all so sad, such a waste.

Botham was unable to play that 'long and responsible innings' in Trinidad. No one who saw his dismissal could blame him too much for that. He was not out playing a flamboyant and irresponsible stroke. But as he left the field he found it necessary to indulge himself to the extent of a gesture to the press box which could best be identified as the flushing of a lavatory. If only the man could stop to think sensibly for a couple of minutes he would realise that no cricketer in post-war years has had more generous praise and approbation from the media than I. T. Botham. He was a folk-hero, and the publicity he received was appropriate to that status. His every achievement won him acclaim in newspapers, on TV and radio, as well as in the hearts of the public who long for his heroic sort of sporting figure. He set his own standards of athletic heroism. No one then decided: 'Let's cut him down to size.' No one wanted to, and for any individual branch of the media to try it would have been insane. Most of his team-mates admired him, and most of his media friends liked him. No one wanted to destroy the image.

How and why, then, did he set out so resolutely to destroy himself? The answer has got to lie in those wise words of Reg Hayter: 'He was unable to understand that when you become big news, you are big news for twenty-four hours a day.' And that is exactly the case. If he was charged with assault it was going to be reported – not by the cricket journalists who were his friends and admirers but by other reporters to whom the activities, all activities, of nationally known figures is news. If he was accused of possessing drugs it was going to be reported. If he bowled badly it was going to be reported because he had so often bowled magnificently. If he got himself out through irresponsibility at a time of crisis it was going to be reported because he was a man who had *saved* England in times of crisis. If he allowed his affairs to be handled by a man who saw him as a Hollywood star and proclaimed that vision to the heavens, it was going to be reported when Hollywood failed to be impressed. The star system works both ways not only in Hollywood but in sport as well.

The tumult and shouting of Trinidad were only a matter of days behind him when the Cornwall Police issued a statement on 17 March saying that they wished to interview Botham on his return to England about drug allegations *during the Walk*. Coming on top of everything else, it was a body-blow. There was a day of silence on the subject as far as the public was concerned (though every media-man in Barbados was now being hounded by his London office for a comment from Botham on the statement) and then on 19 March, in front of BBC television cameras in Bridgetown he issued an angry denial that he had been involved in anything illegal. With damaged ankle ligaments adding to his now almost unbearable burden of problems, Botham went into the Third Test at the Kensington Oval. In even the flintiest and most disapproving heart there had to be a twinge of sympathy for him. For his manager, Tim Hudson, there was probably somewhat less sympathy as the news now came from California that he had been thrown out of the King's Head pub (which had hosted the cricket match involving Botham four months earlier) after a small-time actor had claimed Hudson flung him against a wall and poured beer all over him. This strange departure from the path of peace and love by the multi-coloured Mr Hudson was said to be because the actor had 'leaked stories to the press'.

Barbados stages the Test which sees the greatest volume of support from Britain (the term is used advisedly since I have met many Scots and some Northern Irish watching cricket there). The parish of St James, on the west coast, and Christ Church in the bustling south-west provide a great deal of tourist holiday accommodation, and the cricket 'package' has become a highly organised way of escaping from some of our own winter weather. Indeed, one stand at the Kensington Oval is usually taken over by England supporters who are accorded a welcome of old-world courtesy by Barbados's most colourful cricket supporter, King Dial; he's a character who decks himself out in splendidly coloured outfits, smokes a corncob pipe and often changes his entire wardrobe at lunchtime. Barbados is a pleasant island and the 'Bajans' are largely a friendly and hospitable people. And a trip round the island on a Test rest day is a very worthwhile excursion, if only to see why it produces marvellous cricketers in such abundance.

There is very little in the way of artificial entertainment in Barbados; the islanders create their own diversions from their own environment, and very high on the list is cricket. As one drives around the narrow lanes between acres of sugar cane it is as well to take particular care in cornering, because around every bend is likely to be a game taking place in the middle of the road – it often provides the flattest surface around. The local leagues stage their games on pitches which would terrify batsmen at home who knew they had to face bowling merely of medium pace. I have seen a top-grade game taking place on a wicket where – if such things were within the Laws – there would have been three six-byes in an over! Young men of supple and athletic build come hurtling in, all wanting to be a Malcolm Marshall, hurling down top-speed deliveries which can fly anywhere after pitching. But you don't see the batsmen backing away, and any who did would have a short-lived career in senior cricket. They all look like Gordon Greenidge or Desmond Haynes; they bat with style and panache, and they get in line. Quite simply, it's the only way they will ever make any runs. These are the conditions in which they are brought up to play cricket, and whatever the speed of the bowling and the imperfections of the pitch, they take to it like ducks to water (to use a perhaps inappropriate simile). You would have to search a long, long time through the English countryside to see as many youngsters playing cricket as you will find in Barbados on a Sunday afternoon. And they all model themselves, with an abundance of natural ability, on their heroes. In almost every island throughout the West Indies it is possible to see something similar happen. Anyone who has seen cricket being played naturally in those islands need never ask again: 'How *do* they manage to unearth so many good players?'

The Barbados Test ended in three days and one session – defeat by an innings and 30 runs – and, once again, no one had any right to expect any other result. We had picked the best players available (given that there *might* be one or two selections which *might* be open to debate) and they had not been able to withstand the juggernaut power of the opposition. West Indian cricket has seemed to be getting better with each succeeding year over three decades, and English cricket, if not exactly deteriorating dramatically, has nevertheless been unable to cope with that improvement. In short, the gap has been steadily widening and, allied to changing attitudes by our Test players, it has created a situation where Peter Smith, in the *Daily Mail* of 26 March, actually seemed to feel he was paying a consoling compliment to our Test men when he wrote: 'England are still the second-best team in the world, as they should prove at home this summer.' (It might have seemed to be true, but it turned out to be well wide of the mark.) And so great was the overall calamity which had overtaken English cricket that no one was any longer making any individual mention of Ian Botham's performances.

The Test averages at the end of the Barbados match showed him to have scored a total of 82 runs in six innings and to be sixth of the six batsmen listed; he had taken four wickets at an average of 53.75 with a striking rate of one wicket every thirteen overs. In the course of a 1000-word inquest on the tour so far conducted by Peter Smith, Botham's name was not mentioned once. It was a long, long time since that had happened in any newspaper's report of any Test match. In fact for about a fortnight at the end of February, Botham's name disappeared completely from the news and it was the tour party as an entity which took stick on all sides as one disaster followed another – a poor showing and inevitable defeat in the final one-day international in Trinidad was the next reverse. On the day before that occurred, John Junor devoted part of his column in the *Sunday Express* to a tribute to Bill Edrich, the Middlesex and England player of the immediate pre-war and post-war years, but could not resist the temptation to use his piece to aim a violent side-swipe at the tourists: 'Even today with these artificial hips and at the age of seventy, wouldn't he [Edrich] still be more of a success in the West Indies than some of the snivelling, long-haired, money-conscious yobbos who now represent England?'

There would be no prizes for guessing the name of the man at whom that was principally directed, but it was rough – too rough, some would feel – against the others in a side so desperately up against the odds. And yet it was possible for a case to be made out by those who felt *some* of the more experienced tourists had brought it upon themselves by their attitude. And that case would certainly be strengthened by something that happened just before the return to Trinidad. Still in Barbados after the Test defeat, the party were due for a nets session which Gower, as captain, ordained should be an occasion of *voluntary* attendance. If ever there had been a need to show that the players were conscious of their need for extra practice it was now. The final one-day international gave them a chance to level at least that series of four matches. Peter May had left Barbados only a day or two earlier with an edict that the players must 'grit their teeth' as they faced the remaining three weeks of the tour, adding that he would be watching closely the performances of certain players, albeit from a distance. Alas, May was about three years too late in adopting his 'get tough' attitude as chairman of the Selectors, and it was a measure of how little the tourists were impressed by his words (or how dispirited by the trip) that only eleven of the seventeen players turned out for the session. Gower himself was missing and the practice was led by the gutsy Gatting, his nose broken and now with a broken thumb as well.

Under the headline 'England Flops Take One Break Too Many' the *Daily Mail* listed the men who missed the net practice: Gower, Gooch, Botham, Taylor, Emburey and Foster. Ellison and Robinson, although they were recovering from illness, took part. It was not a masterly defence of his position as England captain by Gower to make the session voluntary and to 'cut' it himself. Inevitably it was seen by most observers as meekly pandering to the wishes of certain players who simply wanted to spend the last few hours of the visit to the West Indies' most pleasant island enjoying themselves rather than working at the job they were being paid very well to do. Amongst the cricket-writers there was a new joke: why don't they make the nets compulsory and the Tests optional? The captain who said 'Please yourselves' and the players who decided not to practise could scarcely expect a good press even from the cricket correspondents, and certainly not from the cricket public at large, so many of whom were there in Barbados to see it all at first hand. Even so, what happened next startled everyone because of the sheer concentration of news items now aimed directly, and exclusively, at Botham.

On 30 March, the *Sunday Mirror* quoted Botham's father-in-law, Gerry Waller (who had spent a couple of weeks' holiday in Barbados) as saying that Botham had told him: 'I can't see me playing for England again after this series. I've obviously upset too many people. The knives are out for me at Lord's. They want my blood. The powers-that-be don't like me and I expect the worst.' Botham denied it. On 2 April, the *Daily Star* used the whole of its front page under an 'exclusive' strap-line and the heading 'Botham Drugs Shock' to claim:

> Cricket star Ian Botham takes drugs, his manager said yesterday. 'I'm aware he smokes dope but doesn't everyone?' said flamboyant Tim Hudson. 'Ian does not have a serious drugs problem. He does not take cocaine to the best of my knowledge.' Hudson was speaking in California before flying out to see Botham in the West Indies. He went on, 'I'm not worried about his drugs. But I am worried about his life-style and he's going to have to change it. We still have plans for Ian's Hollywood career and his cricketing days are by no means over. But I am going to warn him about

his life-style and tell him he must pull himself together or decide to go his own way.'

Police have said they want to question Botham about alleged drug-taking during his charity walk from John O'Groats to Land's End [the *Star* story went on]. Said Hudson: 'I don't know anything about those because I was in California at the time.' A big question mark hangs over Botham's future as a county cricketer. Hudson confirmed: 'He will quit three-day cricket after this coming season. From then on it will be one-day cricket and Test Matches. Let's face it. He can make four times what he is doing now. He could pack 5000 into any ground in Accrington, each paying £2 for a one-day cricket game. Even if Ian only gets 25 per cent of it he's made £2500 for a day's work. Can he make that kind of money in county cricket?'

Botham denied the story. His refusal to talk to the media was becoming a little difficult to sustain because the necessity of issuing denials was becoming almost a daily occurrence. BBC television news found themselves drawn into the unreal atmosphere of it all by showing pictures of Botham 'on the phone to his solicitor in England'. To anyone who knows the Queen's Park Oval in Port-of-Spain, the telephone he was using was very clearly one of the instruments in front of the press box – scarcely the sort of place for him to conduct a highly confidential chat with his legal adviser! But what of 'the flamboyant manager' who appeared to have been so indiscreet to the *Daily Star*? If he had been quoted correctly he was showing a curious ignorance of (a) the economics of the Lancashire League where Accrington play, the League's fixture list and the usual level of its match attendances; (b) the minds of the Test Selectors who, slavishly pro-Botham as they had proved to be, would scarcely be likely to pick him for Test matches if he was playing only one-day cricket for Somerset. Or would they?

So every one of the media personnel in Trinidad now awaited the arrival there of Tim Hudson for a clearing of the air with his colourful client. He never arrived; on the contrary, he turned up in London and on 4 April Botham announced, through his solicitor, that Hudson had been sacked as his manager. A beautiful, brief and highly spectacular friendship was over. A month, even a week, earlier anyone who suggested to Ian that his manager was less than superb would have been risking a thick ear. In Trinidad Botham went out and celebrated by taking the last three West Indies wickets to give him five for 71 – a record twenty-sixth time he had taken five wickets in a Test innings, giving him 352 in all and placing him just 3 behind Dennis Lillee. It could not prevent another West Indian win by ten wickets and the match was over in well under three days, but at least there was *something* to give rise to a slight optimism.

Before the Test began even Botham's staunchest supporters amongst the cricket-writers had been compelled to consider the possibility of his being dropped. He was so beset by off-the-field tangles and his form, by his own standards, had been so unimpressive throughout the tour that even those who, for nearly five years, had argued that for England to go into a Test without him was unthinkable now showed signs of wavering. But could this be, now, the start of the way back? It was difficult to think of anyone in cricket who had been happy about Tim Hudson's management of Ian and the smokescreen of meaningless publicity it had thrown up. Now it was over, was it possible that Botham could forget the pipe dreams of Hollywood stardom and concentrate on what he was capable of doing supremely well – playing cricket? During that weekend I met an England Selector and jointly, with equal fervency, we breathed: 'Thank God for that. Now perhaps he can get on with his cricketing life again.' Half an hour later, someone drew our attention to the *News of the World*, published that day!

The *Sun*'s sister paper had produced a series of allegations against Botham which ranged over several pages of the issue of 6 April. One of them was a claim by a former beauty queen, Lindy Field, that in a torrid session of sexual gymnastics she and Botham had broken the bed in his hotel room! If this had been the full extent of the allegations made against him there is little doubt that in the eyes of most of the world – at least the 'male chauvinist' part – Botham's heroic stature would have been increased. But the story went on to mention drug-taking, particularly cocaine. Botham immediately denied the allegations, and his solicitor instituted legal proceedings against the *News of the World*.

On 7 April, Mrs Marie Botham (mother of Ian) appeared on television news in England and movingly drew attention to the effect upon his wife and children of what had now grown to a major campaign involving a section of the media and her son. Kathryn Botham, strongly and admirably loyal, refused to give credence to the stories about her husband and on 8 April flew to Antigua to meet him. This had nothing to do with the newspaper allegations; it was a visit which had been planned before the tour began, but the atmosphere was now less than ideal for a family reunion. The whole tour had deteriorated into an utter and squalid mess. What, indeed, was happening to cricket?

The Bothams were not the only ones with problems. Tony Brown, managing a tour which was in stark contrast to his previous excursion (to India in the winter of 1984–5), had written to the West Indies Board of Control, gently and courteously pointing out that the pitches for practice and for some of the games were regarded as less than satisfactory. It was, no doubt, a legitimate grievance in normal circumstances but in the context of a series of overwhelming defeats for the tourists it was bound to be seen as a lame piece of excuse-finding. My personal reaction was that the letter was the result of player-power on the part of senior members of the tour who were unhappy at the diminishing of their professional reputations, but it was difficult to see the letter as anything but a mistake.

For Graham Gooch, there was a more acute personal problem. From the very beginning, and even before the tour had started, he had been singled out by certain West Indian spokesmen as the principal target for criticism for his visits to South Africa. This ignored the fact that other tourists had taken part in the so-called rebel series in that country in 1982–3 and had suffered a three-year ban from Test cricket in consequence. There were (and are) many people who felt that Gooch and the others had done nothing more reprehensible than pursue their careers as professional cricketers by taking up winter employment where it was offered. Prominent amongst those who did not take this view was Mr Lester Bird, the Deputy Prime Minister of Antigua, who categorised Gooch as 'giving comfort to a regime which brutalises people'. To a tin-pot, twopenny-ha'penny politician the phrase might have a certain grand ring to it; applied to a professional cricketer like Gooch it was the plainest, most arrant nonsense.

He had sought help from the TCCB and received little but soothing noises. He then wrote a letter to the Board which was carried back from Barbados after the Third Test by Peter May and delivered to Lord's. But with Easter coming up no one found it necessary to discuss the letter for a week!

The mental anguish of a player who was specifically named in the words of a Deputy Prime Minister, quoted in the island's newspaper shortly before that player had to go back to play a Test match in that island, is not difficult to imagine. Some of the West Indian islands can be unpleasantly volatile areas. Gooch had no means of knowing what the public reaction might be to the words of one of a country's leaders. If he feared the worst, who was to blame him? The worst was entirely possible. Having finally got round to reading Gooch's written request either to be allowed to reply in the same newspaper as Lester Bird, setting out his own case, or to be omitted from the party travelling to Antigua for the last Test, the TCCB sent out its secretary, Donald Carr. He held a long meeting with Gooch (together with the tour manager and captain) on 8 April, and the result was that Gooch agreed to travel to Antigua the following day.

This was far from the protection a player is entitled to expect from the TCCB. One has to ask: What pressure was put on Gooch to agree to carry on? How could a player, and especially an opening batsman, be expected to take part in a Test match with the strains the situation now created for him? If other players could publish ghost-written articles, why was one prohibited from defending himself in an article? Why, on two consecutive tours to the West Indies, had the TCCB allowed the grubby hand of politics to be placed menacingly on the shoulders of its players? Why had Lord's not long since said to the West Indies politicians: 'You have a Board of Control to administer your cricket. If you can't leave them to get on with the job without interference we shall not tour your country again until you do.' The idealists argue that this might lead to a division in world cricket between white and coloured nations, but would it not be better to face this possibility sooner rather than later? For assuredly we have been heading in that direction for at least five years. We saw the terrible sadness of the Bangladesh Cricket Board, struggling valiantly to establish themselves as an international body, when the England 'B' tour to their country was cancelled at the behest of politicians during this same winter of 1985–6. Every year the government of one country or another seeks to use cricket as its whipping-boy. If we do end up with England, Australia, New Zealand (and very possibly Sri Lanka) playing one series of Tests and West Indies, India and Pakistan playing another it will not be because the players of any one country see those of another as ideological adversaries. It will be because the politicians have been allowed to interfere just once too often. And will the world – South Africa or anywhere else – be one whit better for their interference? Gooch was the latest pawn to be used in the sinister game of chess being played out by political grand masters, and he did not get the support, or anything like the support, he was entitled to expect from his employers. Someone, sooner or later, is going to have to stand up against the baleful outside interference in the game of cricket, and the TCCB wasted a wonderful opportunity to give a lead – as well as letting down one of their players.

(The West Indies Board, in fact, were shortly to show themselves as hardly deserving much sympathy. They didn't really do much to resist outside political interference when in May 1986 they pathetically lodged an objection to the billing of Clive Rice as a South African representative in the Rest of the World XI to play West Indies in a match at Edgbaston for the Bob Geldof Sport Aid charity appeal. Steve Camacho, secretary of the West Indian Board, announced (with hypocrisy dripping from every syllable): 'We have nothing against Rice but he comes from a country which no longer plays official Tests.' South Africa no longer plays official Tests, of course, purely and simply because of political interference led by the West Indies! The South African Board had long since been given a clean bill of health by an International Cricket Conference investigating team as having done everything asked of it in making cricket there a fully integrated sport. Now, just six days before the Edgbaston match was due to be played, advertised as 'the ultimate cricket match' and designed to raise £150,000 to help starving Third World people, it became necessary to change the name of the Rest of the World side to 'David Gower's World XI'. Rice still played in the match, of course, but not as an 'official' representative in an 'official' Rest of the World side. Just how absurd this hair-splitting intervention from the West Indies Board was may be seen from the fact that the match was to be nothing more than a limited-overs knockabout frolic – scarcely the sort of fixture that needed to be solemnly recorded in Wisden as 'official' for any purposes whatsoever. So what did the mini-crisis achieve? It enabled the West Indies once more to impose their will upon the other cricketing nations of the world – and to be ostentatiously seen to have done so.)

Before the final Test began, Ian Botham and the incredibly courageous Kathy faced reporters, photographers, TV cameras and interviewers with questions about parts of their lives which (even in the goldfish bowl of life in the eighties) were nobody else's business but their own. Kathy even braved the mindboggling ordeal of a *tête-à-tête* with one of Fleet Street's most aggressive sob-sisters. Peter Willey had to return home injured and David Smith, after gallantly seizing his opportunity in Trinidad, had to miss the Antiguan Test because *he* was injured. David Gower could not decide until the very last moment whether he himself would be fit to play. In this atmosphere of a three-ring circus, England had to find some way of salvaging a little pride from the ruins of a hideous tour. Gower had already announced that he would not skipper MCC in their match against the champion county (Middlesex) to start the new English season, thus giving rise to inevitable speculation. Had he had enough (and who could have blamed him if that were the case)? Or had he seen that the time for a change was imminent and was anticipating Selectoral thinking?

By this time the England camp was divided virtually into three camps: the Botham brigade, Gower's company office outfit and the rest of the regiment. And who, after the events of the previous three months, could expect anything else? There would be those who blamed the tabloids for the unhappiness of an ill-fated tour. There would be those who looked a little deeper and saw that without the sabre-rattling and agitation of the politicians there would have been no call for the presence in the West Indies of so many reporters who were not concerned with the cricket. And there would be those who saw that if the TCCB had been less 'wet' in its failure to do anything to protect the men it sent out on tour, the whole shambles could have been avoided. At Lord's there have been too many craven attitudes for far too long. There has been a pathetic belief that if heads were tucked deep enough into the sand the problems would go away. And if and when all else failed the blame could be placed conveniently on 'the press'. Some day, perhaps, there will be an awakening in NW8 to the realisation that 'the press', and the way our newspapers follow their respective policies, is a fact of life just as a barrage of fast bowling and impertinent and mischievous interference by politicians are facts of life.

For the moment, with the blessed relief of their return to England now only a week away, England had to go into the final Test with just four bowlers and hope, somehow, to get away with a draw. Even now the cricket-writers, as dazed and bemused as the players by it all, tried to find an optimistic talking-point as Botham took two of the first West Indian wickets to fall, thus placing himself just one behind Dennis Lillee's world record. Alas, by the end of the innings he had managed no more and it had to be recorded that he had conceded 147 runs. Gower was lucky to escape no more serious criticism than a reference to his 'understandable wish to help Botham reach his record'. The captain at least earned plaudits for his first innings of 90, which enabled England to avoid the follow-on, but the relief was short-lived. Going in for the second time before lunch on the penultimate day, West Indies were obviously going to set out for a clean sweep of five Test victories, which meant as many runs as possible in the shortest space of time. Haynes and Richardson put on 100 for the first wicket and then Richards took on the captain's responsibility of stepping up the scoring rate still further.

In 1981, when the first Test ever to be staged at St John's, Antigua, had been played, nothing was more certain than that Richards was going to mark the historic occasion in his native island (and his wedding as well, which had taken place only days previously) with a century. So obvious was his intent that Viv played an utterly uncharacteristically cautious innings which duly took him to three figures. He came out the following morning clearly intent on putting the icing on the cake by adding to his score in an orgy of stroke play. Unfortunately for his plans, he started too ambitiously, going up on tip-toe to try to whack an enormous bouncer from Dilley with a vertically raised bat and succeeding only in lobbing a catch to Emburey. Five years later there was to be no mistake. Richards put himself yet again into the record books with the fastest century in the history of Test cricket, reaching 100 off fifty-six balls (the only realistic way to compare quick scoring in these days of funereal over-rates) with six sixes and seven fours, and declared at 246 for two. Botham, suffering the indignity of a six – over extra cover! – at the hands of his friend, conceded 78 runs in fifteen overs and thus was doomed to return to England still one wicket short of equalling the Lillee record. England were also left to hold out for nearly seven hours to avoid the blackwash (scoring 411 to win was an impossibility), lost two wickets for 33 before the close and the game ended in defeat on the last day by 240 runs.

As no other result to the series could seriously have been contemplated by any realist, perhaps the saddest aspect of the whole tour was that so many of those 3–4000 British supporters who had travelled to Barbados (and, in some cases, to Trinidad, Jamaica and Antigua) came back sickened by the attitude of some of the players *off* the field. Cricket-lovers come from all areas and all walks of life, and those of us who moved about the country – at dinners, meetings and social gatherings – found there was scarcely an occasion which did not involve the telling of some new horror story of players turning up for receptions in tatty tee-shirts and soiled jeans, of turning out at nets with 'boxes' worn over the top of shorts. In a place the size of Barbados it is virtually impossible for players to hide their social lives, and the sight of senior Test men wind-surfing or lounging beside hotel swimming pools when their more industrious colleagues were at least *trying* to improve their chances by a session in the nets provoked some of the supporters to near-apoplexy. Shoddy performances on the field cannot easily be forgotten if they are linked so closely with shabby behaviour off it. Veteran followers of the game to all parts of the world returned scandalised. English Test cricket seemed to have reached rock bottom in every way.

It is important, therefore, to record Tony Brown's emphatic denial of most of these stories. Players had *not*, he insisted on his return, appeared at any kind of formal reception, or even informal ones, in unacceptable forms of dress. They were at all times smartly and tidily turned out. They were 'as good as gold about that', he said. Brown also made the point that net practice was not always likely to be beneficial when the facilities were so dreadfully substandard. In some cases, no practice at all was better than what could be accomplished on the pitches provided. I respect Tony Brown; I am happy to give his views.

There remained one further problem for the TCCB to consider: the allowing of ghost-written articles in newspapers by several of the senior players on the tour. Individually, some members of the Board were ready to admit that 'it might have been a mistake'. It was something which would have to be 'looked at'. If the Board finally decided that it *was* wrong and sought to impose a ban on such activity on future tours who, one wondered, was going to tell Ian Botham that he was to be deprived of £45,000 worth of his annual income?

On rest day in the Test, Botham had recorded an interview for BBC TV's 'Breakfast Time' programme – renewing his cordial relationship with Uncle Frank Bough – in which he once again denied the sex-and-drug allegations of the Sunday newspapers and claimed there was a press vendetta against him. He was saying, one was forced to assume, that the *Mail on Sunday*, the *News of the World*, the *Sunday Mirror*, the *Sunday People* and the *Daily Star* had spent a lot of time and money over the previous two years deliberately and expensively sending teams of reporters around the world to search for people willing to tell lies. In the course of the interview he said: 'I would like to say at this point that it is not the cricket journalists. In general they have a good rapport with the players.' This would be good news to the cricket-writers. Did it mean that they could now report the fact when Botham bowled badly, or batted irresponsibly, or abused the opposition, or expectorated up and down the cricket field or ostentatiously indicated displeasure with his captain's field-placings? He admitted that he had smoked cannabis. 'I came up in the period of the 60s and 70s,' he said. 'There was a lot of it around. I tried it and it didn't do anything for me – end of story.' What, then, about January 1985?

Ian Botham scored 168 Test runs in ten innings; he took eleven wickets in 134.5 overs at a cost of 48.63 runs apiece and Michael Carey in the *Daily Telegraph* reported: 'It is sad when a player of Botham's talent is more of a liability than an asset, yet that was the case much of the time with his bowling often indifferent, his wicket too often given away and his attitude to practice a disruptive element.' Would the *Telegraph*'s cricket correspondent now be accused of joining the 'vendetta' which Ian felt had been mounted against him? In other areas of Fleet Street there was criticism, in varying degrees, of his cricket and his contribution to the tour as a whole, and it was beginning to look as though he might change the views he had expressed in his TV interview: 'You cricket-writers are all right but it's the other lot . . .' There were, in fact, cricket-writers who offered qualified support of Ian too, rightly pointing out that he had been under more than the usual amount of pressure. But Gooch had been under outside pressures too – none of them directly of his own making – and he had bravely given his answer with 51 runs in England's last innings of the tour.

Scarcely had the applause died away for the award of man of the match to Vivian Richards and man of the series to Malcolm Marshall, than Botham was to be heard in a Radio 2 interview hoping, notwithstanding any previously expressed views to the contrary ('fed up with the tour', 'would have been tempted to turn his back on England cricket but for the support of fans', 'felt like saying he didn't want to tour again'), to be with England in Australia in the winter of 1986–7! It may be argued that Ian's supreme, God-given talent gave him the right to look that far ahead. And there is no doubt that the Selectors' slavish obsession with picking him, whatever his form or his conduct on the field of play, over the previous four years had led him to expect selection come what may. Since 1982, when his Test place might sometimes have been considered in doubt if he had been anyone else but Ian Botham, he had been chosen not on what he was currently doing with bat and ball but on what he *might* do, and a lot of other players might have been forgiven if they had contemplated changing their names by deed poll. But a few eyebrows must have been raised here and and there just the same. (On 29 June, the Selectors learned from their Sunday papers what Botham thought of *them*. 'Blow, blow thou winter wind . . .')

And what of the alleged vendetta against him? Is it not just a little fanciful to picture the editorial conference of any newspaper sitting down and deciding: 'Right – we'll start a campaign *against* England's greatest cricketing talent.'? Newspapers don't decide on innocent targets for expensive campaigns of critical journalism. But since Brearley had relinquished the England captaincy, Ian had been seen in an increasingly ostentatious light to regard himself as free from the restraints which applied to other players. He had been seen not to train with the others, not to practise with the others, not to bowl with any regard for the fields set by his captain, to make it difficult (putting it at its best) for the captain to take him off when he was not bowling well, to question the judgment of umpires. True, he had been bolstered in the belief that he was fire-proof by weak-kneed selection policy and TCCB *laissez-faire*. And, it has to be said, by a certain amount of journalistic sycophancy. He had used this – perhaps really without realising it – to play off one ally against another, and some people have long memories.

Cricketers hold some writers in higher regard than others; it will probably come as a surprise to Ian to learn that writers feel exactly the same way about cricketers, not just as players but as people. Some are more worthy of respect than others, just as some writers are. The Cricket Writers' Club is today not quite the Corinthian concept of a gentlemen's organisation which was originally envisaged by Jim Swanton and his colleagues in 1946, and it has members whose knowledge of the game is not their strongest suit. More importantly, it has members with no real love of the game, no feeling for it, and that must be seen as the ultimate sin. It has members who, if you tossed a tennis ball gently towards them, would not know how to catch it (that is not merely a figure of speech – I have actually seen it happen). Once I asked a member what an overseas tour meant to him and he replied without hesitation: 'I make enough profit on my expenses to buy a new car every year.' So it is not entirely surprising that the mutual respect which existed between E. W. Swanton and Co and the players of a bygone age has gradually been dissipated.

But players and their attitudes have changed, too, and this can largely be attributed to MONEY. It is still difficult, thank God, to find a first-class cricketer who doesn't enjoy the game and its camaraderie; it is still possible, thank God, for a writer to spend an evening in the company of players from whom he can part thinking: What a thoroughly pleasant session that was. But that happens today almost exclusively in the context of *county* cricket. In Test circles it is far too often all about how much the one party can do for the other; it is difficult to think in terms of the personal relationships which were so highly prized by Jim Swanton and, indeed, by some of us in a later era. Some journalists, too, opt for the easier alternative, and if a team of investigative cricketers had flown out to New Zealand in 1984 they might well have found a number of journalists – and CWC members – taking part in activities which are held to be so reprehensible in players. The deterioration in the degree of cordiality which existed for so long between those who play the game and those who report it is the result of faults on both sides. The one common factor which one finds, with infinite sadness, is a lack of respect for the game itself.

In the second week of the new, 1986 season, Botham enraptured his Taunton admirers once again – and several million viewers of BBC 2's 'Sunday Grandstand' – by hitting Wayne Daniel, of Middlesex, for two sixes in the last three balls of a John Player game to bring off another impossible win. Two days after that he smashed the Glamorgan attack all round the Taunton ground, and then he was interviewed by Devon and Cornwall Police about the allegations of drug-use during his John o' Groats to Land's End walk. The formal police statement afterwards said that the papers had been sent to the Director of Public Prosecutions, who subsequently decided to take no action. In the meantime, lengthy exchanges had been taking place between his legal advisers and those of the *Mail on Sunday* against whom, it will be recalled, he had had a libel action pending since March 1984. On Sunday 18 May the *Mail on Sunday* took up almost the whole of its front page with an enormous headline: 'Botham – I *Did* Take Pot.' And under his own by-line Ian then wrote:

> This is one of the most difficult days of my life. I have decided that the time has come for me to be honest with myself, with the game I love, with my friends and with all those who through thick and thin have helped and supported me down the years. Over the years an awful lot has been written about me. Some of it has been true and some of it ludicrous. I have to accept, however reluctantly, that these days a Test cricketer, or anybody who becomes a major sporting personality, has a very high price to pay for all the adulation and the monetary rewards which go with success. But there was one article published by the *Mail on Sunday* on 11 March 1984, which was, in its way, the most shocking of all. It alleged that during the New Zealand tour which had just concluded – and which had been something of a disaster for the England team – I had smoked 'pot'. The Test team had actually gone to Pakistan for the second stage of the tour when I first heard what it was the *Mail on Sunday* was proposing to print. I was in the Hilton Hotel, Lahore, when I first got wind of the allegations that were being made against me. I remember that occasion as if it were some sort of nightmare. My reaction was one of horror. It was a bolt from the blue and I had no one around me whom I could properly talk to. I was a long way from home and it seemed to me that, because of the proposed article, everything that I had fought for and worked so hard to achieve would be at risk.

> I did something then that I have regretted ever since because I have had to live with the consequences of that decision. I denied that I had ever smoked pot at any time in my life and started legal proceedings against the *Mail on Sunday* for what it had said about the New Zealand tour. I know that what I am saying will shock many people, particularly those who have stood by me for so long. The fact is that I have at various times in the past smoked pot. I had been with a group of people who had been doing it and I went along with it. On other occasions I have smoked simply in order to relax – to get off the sometimes fearful treadmill of being an international celebrity, trying to forget for a moment the pressures that were on me all the time.

It was a long article which went on for another page and a half of the tabloid newspaper. Two or three hours after it had been read around the breakfast tables of Britain the England squad for the two one-day internationals against India the following weekend was announced. Botham's name was in the party. The squad had, of course, been picked the previous Friday, and, following tradition, it was made public for the first time on BBC Radio News at midday on the Sunday. What would the TCCB do now? On Monday 19 May, the Board's Executive Committee met at Lord's under the chairmanship of Raman Subba Row. The other members involved were Colin Atkinson (chairman of the Disciplinary Committee), Doug Insole (chairman of the Overseas Tours Committee), Bernie Coleman (chairman of the Marketing Committee), Tony Steven (chairman of the Finance Committee), Alan Smith (secretary of Warwickshire CCC), and Mike Turner (secretary-manager of Leicestershire CCC). It must have been, to some extent, an embarrassing occasion since Colin Atkinson was president of Somerset CCC and headmaster of Millfield School, where pupils had been expelled for involvement in drug-taking. Insole, Smith and Subba Row had all managed overseas tours in which Botham had been a member of the party. The statement issued afterwards said:

> The Disciplinary Committee are being asked to carry out a full investigation arising from statements made in the article and the player will be invited to attend this hearing which will be set up as a matter of urgency. In the meantime the Executive Committee have instructed the Chairman of Selectors that Botham should be withdrawn from the England party due to play the two Texaco Trophy matches against India and not to select him again until the investigation has been completed.

While that meeting was taking place in London, Botham was playing for Somerset against Sussex at Hove where, in a departure from recent policy, he was freely available for pictures and interviews. He now seemed to be making a sustained plea for understanding, but there was still a touch of defiance. He had not smoked a joint since his early twenties, he said, adding: 'I don't know what all the big fuss is about.'

Fed on a rich diet of TV pictures showing Ian smiting sixes out of the Test grounds of England, knocking down Australian wickets or plucking magical catches out of the air, the general public were in a mood to support the man who gave them so much pleasure either in their ringside seats or their fireside armchairs. Yes – drug-taking *was* against the law but Ian had said he only tried it casually, at that a long time ago, so how could it compare with the marvellous lead he gave to youngsters in carving out a sporting career? On Monday 26 May, I drove home from the PGA Golf Championship at Wentworth where I had heard in the clubhouse, 'Botham ought to be banned for life from every sport,' to Morecambe where, within three minutes of arriving I heard a comment of a very different kind. A lady who to my certain knowledge has never been closer to cricket than an evening twenty-overs knockabout game announced with all the feeling in the world, 'If they ban him they are a narrow-minded bunch of old fogies.'

It is, of course, always dangerous to generalise but if, on the morning of 29 May when the Disciplinary Committee met, I had been pressed to do so I would certainly have said, 'Those people who are a bit closer to cricket will certainly want to see some salutary lesson administered to Ian Botham. Those who simply watch from the sidelines and enjoy his cricket will not want to see him taken out of the game.' There is an urgent need for cricketers as good as Ian Botham in English cricket – in any cricket. The public loves a hero and his cricket has so often been heroic. But should we have it at any price? Ian did not help his own cause in dismissing the affair immediately after his 'revelations' in the *Mail on Sunday* by saying on TV that he didn't know what all the fuss was about. John Junor was absolutely right in saying that was arrogant. It was offensively arrogant and especially so to those who had been close to his cricket, to his behaviour and to his misbehaviour through so much of his career. It was indeed an insult to our intelligence. The rules of life are not just for the masses; they are not waived for those who possess outstanding God-given ability in any sphere. Indeed, it might be said that they are doubly applicable to those whose example is followed by impressionable young people in an age when standards seem to slip a little further every day.

After more than seven hours in session, the Disciplinary Committee announced that Ian Botham had been suspended from first-class cricket until 31 July for having brought the game into disrepute by using cannabis, and admitting in a newspaper article that he had done so after previously denying that he had used the drug.

Botham, and his solicitor, announced that they were disappointed at the decision of the Committee and appealed (but on 12 June the Appeals Committee found no cause to alter the decision or the suspension). I was far from alone in feeling that he had been very, very leniently treated indeed.

12 THE MISGUIDED LOYALIST

Somerset ended the 1986 season in sixteenth place in the County Championship – next to the bottom and therefore just one place higher than in 1985. In 19 innings Botham totalled 804 runs at an average of 44.66 and his 22 championship wickets cost 43.68. Although the county had more than its share of injury problems the results, and that championship position, were disappointing and the Committee had some thorough heart-searching to do at the end of it.

Botham, after the TCCB ban, returned to Test cricket at The Oval on 23 August in the final match of the series against New Zealand. He took a wicket with the first ball he bowled! It is probably true to say that a lot of people would have bet that he would do so, such is the magic of the man. Very few would have bet *against* his doing so. Certainly I would not have done; I might even have been tempted to predict the type of delivery which would get him his wicket. It was short-pitched and would have gone harmlessly down the leg side if the batsman had been a right-hander. It was, in fact, the left-handed opener, Bruce Edgar, who followed a ball well wide of his off stump as if somehow mesmerised, steering it into the hands of second slip: a wicket with the very first ball Botham had bowled after his return from a ban which many of his devoted followers actually felt to be unjust! Once again, it was the stuff the legends are made of; the reception from the crowd was tumultuous and it was not noticeably muted in the tabloid press – it was also the stuff that headlines are written about!

It was during that Test (on the Saturday of it) that the Somerset Committee made a serious miscalculation. On 25 August came the announcement from Taunton that the two mighty West Indians, Viv Richards and Joel Garner, were not to be offered new contracts. Martin Crowe, the immensely talented young New Zealander who had languished in second-eleven cricket during the two previous seasons with Somerset (although he had, of course, been playing with the New Zealand tourists through the second half of 1986), had been signed for the next three years as the county's overseas player. Looked at coldly, clinically and dispassionately, the logic of the step now taken by the Committee could not be faulted. Garner had become increasingly injury-prone and had bowled only 419 championship overs during the 1986 season, taking 47 wickets for 23.21 runs apiece. Richards had scored 1174 runs at 43.48 – good figures but not outstandingly so for a man who was widely regarded as the best batsman in the world. Richards was potentially a match-winner in any game in which he took part and he had not won too many for Somerset in that summer. Great players stand to be judged by their own standards and Richards's standards were the highest. The impression in the Somerset Committee room was very strongly that Viv was becoming increasingly a 'big occasion player', a man who raised his sights to the topmost targets only when he was sufficiently motivated, and he seemed to be finding it increasingly difficult to motivate himself.

Looking ahead to the next three years, if they re-signed the two West Indians, Somerset had to ask themselves: could Garner, in his thirty-fifth year in 1987, be expected to be any more readily available than he had been in 1986? Would the strain on his legs, carrying around that 6ft 8ins height, be less or more than it had been the previous season? And what about 1988 and 1989? With his friend, and friendly rival, Botham, likely to be missing during six Test matches in 1987 would Richards be able to motivate himself any more in 1987 than he had done in 1986? Would not the strain of touring as the West Indies captain through a long winter in Pakistan, Australia and New Zealand be likely to leave him jaded when he returned to play for Somerset in the summer of '87? Was he not likely to be absent from county cricket in 1988 when West Indies toured England? And in 1989 Richards would be thirty-seven years old with a lot more round-the-world, 12-months-a-year top-level cricket behind him . . . The Somerset Committee's view that Garner and Richards were the great and glorious past while Crowe represented a considerably more healthy future was quite unanswerable. Looking ahead, as Committees must, the decision was absolutely right. Where Somerset came unstuck was in their public relations – the abrupt, seemingly ungrateful and ungracious, dispensing with the services of two local folk-heroes. And the timing was as unfortunate as it could be, coming right in the middle of a Test where the third of Somerset's great international players, I. T. Botham, had just re-asserted himself in typically dramatic style and who now weighed in with the ultimate bombshell: 'If Joel and Vivvy go, I go.' A horrified and shocked reaction from the county membership was quite inevitable.

What the Committee should have done was to break the news gently. It should have started with a 'leak' to the media that a tricky decision would have to be made at the end of the season. It should have been followed up by a gradual 'educating' of the public about the issues involved. Stories should have appeared in newspapers pointing out that The Big Bird's fitness could by no means be guaranteed and that Richards's workload during the next three years was scarcely likely to leave him fresh enough to pile up more records and new match-winning feats for Somerset. It could all have been broached very gently to the Somerset membership in a way that would have conditioned the members to what had to happen.

County Committees are generally suspicious and wary of the media, in some cases with justification. The tabloid press in particular much prefer a thundering great row to a peaceful solution. But in this case Somerset would not have been seeking or risking headlines. All they wanted, all they *needed*, was the odd down-page paragraph here and there. It did not have to come as an official club statement – that could be saved for later when the public had had two or three months to consider the implications of the hints which had been dropped. At worst, they would have seen things in a more sensible and less emotional light; at best, the Committee would have found at least a grudging acceptance of a course the Committee members themselves knew to be necessary. Somerset have a former player, Eric Hill, who is a widely respected cricket writer; the county has a lot of friends amongst other cricket journalists. Sadly, the committee did not seek advice from any of these and made no attempt to enlist their help in breaking the news softly, and they paid the penalty in the form of a widely publicised revolt of members culminating in an extraordinary general meeting of the Club at Shepton Mallet on 8 November. Fortunately for the sanity of the game, the Committee survived a vote of no confidence by a majority representing two and a half votes to one, but by then an awful lot of dirty linen had been very publicly washed and any hope there might have been of persuading Botham that it was not necessary for him to leave the county as a gesture of support to his friends had long since vanished.

During the extensive skirmishes leading up to the point where the battle was finally joined at Shepton Mallet, and before he set out on tour to Australia, Ian had played a prominent vocal part. He used the word 'loyalty' extensively, ignoring completely the fact that the county Committee had been more than usually loyal to *him* in his brushes with higher authority. Taking into account the problems Ian had created for Somerset in recent years, the club had been *intensely* loyal to him. But he had neither the wit nor the inclination to see this. Considering that he had one or two cronies amongst the cricketing press on tour in Australia to advise him, it seems astonishing that he now uttered such puerile rubbish on the topic of Somerset's revolution and its outcome. Surely one of them would have been able to advise him that if he had nothing helpful or constructive to say (or in that particular context, nothing *regretful*, because it is always sad to see a county club embroiled in internal warfare) then he should have kept quiet?

We now saw him on our TV screens, or read him quoted in our newspapers, boasting that his team-mates, the men with whom he had grown up in Somerset, had better watch out when he played against them for his new county, whichever that might turn out to be. (He expected, he said, quite a queue of them, come 1 January 1987.) In November, a book appeared under the joint names of Peter Roebuck and Ian Botham to which the latter's literary contribution was manifestly not substantial. It had been written when the two were like David and Jonathan; the relationship seemed to have deteriorated to one more like that of Cain and Abel by the time Roebuck prepared to fly to Australia to cover the Tests for a newspaper. 'I suggest,' thundered Botham from the Antipodes, 'he stays in London. He'll be a lot safer.' What ridiculous, childish, loutish, bullying language was this from the hero of a hundred thousand schoolboys? 'God help Somerset,' he said, 'when we're playing against them.' What a pathetically infantile attitude from a thirty-one-year-old man at the peak of his profession. Can there be any wonder that standards of behaviour and attitudes to sport slip a little further every day when we see this sort of example set by an outstandingly gifted practitioner?

By mid-November it was time for Dr Jekyll to take over for a day or two from Mr Hyde, and in the First Test in Brisbane Botham scored a century of high technical quality and the usual spectacular entertainment value. Once again he was everybody's hero, as we saw his brilliant stroke play on our screens. How many of us, then, were sickened to see in the same twenty minutes of recorded highlights, this same cricketing genius mouthing obscenities at departing batsmen and running around with clenched fist like some football hooligan on the rampage? And how heartfelt was our sickness to read in Peter West's *Daily Telegraph* report that Philip DeFreitas – twenty years old and playing in his first Test match – had hastened a defeated batsman on his way with similar gestures and abuse? That is what happens when examples are set by unworthy idols.

By this time Botham had announced to the world – not bothering first to inform Somerset CCC who were, until 31 December, still his employers – that in future he would spend his Australian summers playing for Queensland. This meant, in all probability, that he would not be available to tour with England and we might expect him to stage a farewell performance of a highly dramatic nature. His sense of theatre is very strong.

His contribution to the Second Test in Perth was negligible with both bat and ball, though he did take his hundredth Test catch, another remarkable landmark in a career which, just at this moment, looked as though it might possibly go into limbo when he returned to England. Somerset had abandoned any lingering hope that he might play for them in 1987 so where was he likely to go? A little kite-flying (of exactly the type Somerset CCC should have undertaken in the matter of Richards and Garner) had now begun in certain quarters. Worcestershire's chairman, Duncan Fearnley (the man who makes Botham's bats), enthusiastically favoured an approach for his services; Don Kenyon, the county President (and a man I happened to know did not approve of Botham's attitude), urged caution, fearing that the issue might split the membership. Warwickshire showed signs of interest, then backed off. Derbyshire, ambitiously contemplating the double acquisition of both Geoffrey Boycott (who had been released by Yorkshire) *and* Botham, had clearly given little or no thought to two things: (a) the almighty personality clash which was likely to occur if the two found themselves in the same dressing-room, after Botham's idiotic and insulting remarks about Boycott during a question-and-answer session at a dinner in Manchester the previous summer (again widely publicised), remarks which led Boycott to consider legal action against Botham; and (b) the effect upon their own contracted players which such a double signing would inevitably bring.

On 11 December, Geoffrey Boycott announced he would not be joining Derbyshire in 1987, so the county was left to concentrate its full energies on persuading Botham to join *them* when he became free – on 1 January.

Since his several outbursts at the time of Somerset's extraordinary general meeting, Ian had tidied up his act considerably. The interviews he gave were pleasant-sounding and reasonable and they were on non-controversial topics. This was a pretty clear indication of good management and captaincy on the Australian tour and, with a win in Brisbane and a comfortable draw in the Second Test in Perth under its corporate belt, the party was able to tackle its duties in a pleasant enough atmosphere. In Perth, Botham pulled up in his delivery stride during the Australian second innings with an obviously painful injury to his side. The new honeymoon he was now enjoying with the media was immediately obvious. For a week before the Third Test in Adelaide, there was intense speculation amongst the cricket correspondents on whether England would risk playing Ian simply as a batsman. When he was finally unable to play and Australia piled up a first innings total of 514 for five declared, televiewers were told at home by the BBC News correspondent Michael Peschardt: 'Ian Botham was sorely missed.' The *Mail on Sunday*, after three years of industrious investigation into Botham's non-cricketing activities and much breast-beating at their discoveries, now headlined Alan Lee's weekly report: 'Aussies Revel in Botham Absence'. He was a hero again – even when he wasn't playing! Everyone seemed to have forgotten, with marvellous convenience, that his Test bowling figures in the first two matches had been four wickets for 177 runs! How, then, could anyone reasonably and justifiably claim that on the magnificent batting pitch of the Adelaide Oval, the all-rounder's presence would have made a vital difference to England's performance in the field? The answer is, of course, that no one *reasonably and justifiably* could and there must have been a fair measure of disenchantment amongst the players who *were* on parade at these what-might-have-been yearnings. But no one should ever underestimate Ian's ability to provide the unexpected, the impossible, the miraculous.

The final days of 1986 saw Botham on public display in the best possible light. Christmas Day in Melbourne found him promenading with his three young children, the complete family man, and on Boxing Day he hit the headlines once more by taking five wickets in a Test innings for a record-equalling twenty-seventh time. Without being too cynical, I cannot help but suggest that if Richard Hadlee (the previous single holder of that record) had seen the performance he could have been forgiven for throwing up his hands and crying, 'Why do I bother? What's the point of *thinking* my way through a game, relating one delivery to another, working on weaknesses I recognise in opposition batsmen? Why – when "Both" can come along and bowl out Australians with oranges?' And who could blame Hadlee? How was a half-fit, three-quarter-pace Botham returning figures of 16–4–41–5? How?

The phlegmatic Geoff Marsh, who had given England so much trouble earlier in the series, now aimed a hideous, cross-bat slog at a rank long hop and saw Jack Richards leap for a stratospheric catch behind the wicket. Allan Border, having exhorted his troops to play positively but not suicidally, chased a ball well wide of the off stump for Richards this time to dive for a catch which was almost subterranean: 'Not a great delivery from Botham; Border can't believe the stroke he played' was the most restrained Australian opinion. More colourful but no less understandable was the view of the experienced Adelaide journalist Alan Shiell: 'Botham is a freak. He now has a Test record 366 wickets but the statistics do not show how many of them he has taken with bad balls – long hops that deserve to be carted all over the place. There cannot be much doubt any more that the Australians really do have a complex about Botham and his intimidating way. Few, if any, bowlers could have got away with some of the tripe he served up, yet he returned the remarkable analysis of five for 41 off 16 overs.'

And that, of course, is absolutely right. It makes it doubly important, in my view, to study the tables at the end of this book to see where, and against whom, Ian has (and has not) reaped his richest rewards. There is no doubt at all that since 1981 he has put the 'hex' on the Australians in a way they find impossible to shake off. A man whose approach to cricket – indeed, to life – is essentially physical, has contrived to establish a *meta*physical dominance. There is no other explanation for it.

We know that an expert judge like Tom Cartwright has seen in Botham's bowling something that many batsmen cannot or will not recognise; I remember when the Australians returned from their 1985 tour of England, Dave Gilbert talked at some length about how Botham's bowling surprised so many of his team-mates in the way that some deliveries arrived much earlier than the batsman expected. But this is really the only explanation we have which stands up to examination in a sober, technical light. It cannot wholly account for the suicidal tendencies of Andrew Hilditch on that tour, for instance. Hilditch, a lawyer by profession, must be credited with sufficient intelligence to be capable of batting more sensibly than he did at Edgbaston and The Oval. Border, of all people, must wake up at night screaming at the thought of the stroke he played at Melbourne, on Boxing Day, 1986.

It is possible that the answer may rest, to some extent, in the Australian character and temperament. Theirs is the ultimate macho image as far as sport is concerned. To be fed a sumptuous diet of short-pitched deliveries (they are all 'bouncers' as far as Ian himself is concerned!) somehow seems to constitute a challenge to Australian manhood. Their batsmen stand at the crease saying to themselves, 'This is just another flaming long hop; I'm going to give it the treatment, whoever's bowling it.' But if this is some part of the explanation, it can by no means be the whole of it. At last one begins to have a little sympathy with the Selectors who for so long have insisted: 'We shall pick him, come what may, whatever his form, because he, more than anyone else, can win a game which no one else seems capable of winning.' It is rather like believing in fairies and one does not immediately recognise our Selectors as being incurable romantics. Yet once in a while Botham proves them right and the rest of us wrong in a way which defies all logic and most common sense.

In Melbourne, Botham was still troubled by his injury. He might well not have played at all. As it was, the new ball was given to 'Gladys' Small and Phil DeFreitas and in all the tumult and shouting about Botham's five for 41 (bowling as third seamer) Small's five for 48 from 22.4 overs of rather more orthodox attack was an achievement which was almost overlooked. But Botham took three slip catches as well. Plainly there is a magic about the man which transcends all logical appraisal.

In terms of his relationships with fellow members of the human race, however, there was no trace of magic. When England duly won the Fourth Test by an innings and 14 runs, his first public utterance came in the form of another sideswipe at 'the press'. This from a man whose newspaper and television publicity throughout all four Tests (even when he was not playing in one of them) was of the kind normally reserved for those on the brink of canonisation! Was there no limit to the kind of idolatry he sought?

Victory in Melbourne meant England had retained the Ashes and, while this was good for the morale of all of us after the trauma of the previous summer at home, one hoped the players would not get unduly carried away with their success. Australia had been bad enough in all conscience on their 1985 visit to the UK; now, in front of their own supporters, they had been quite unbelievably bad. Those of us old enough to have been reared on the fighting traditions of the Aussies of previous generations found it difficult to believe that any eleven of their breed could perform quite as abysmally as this. Their supporters, as ever, took the line of least resistance. If you happened to ask any given Australian, in any street of any town or city, if he knew the Test score the answer was inevitably: 'Test? What Test is that?' Oh yes. The Aussies are great winners . . . the world's worst losers.

Between the Fourth and Fifth Tests of this already long and complex tour, the Australian Board had sandwiched the Benson and Hedges Challenge – a four-cornered competition of one-day internationals involving Australia, England, West Indies and Pakistan, staged to coincide with the America's Cup which was being sailed in Gage Roads, Freemantle. The idea was to add to the festivities in Perth and to cash in on the huge crowds gathered in Western Australia. The Challenge brought a handsome and clear-cut win for England which, with the Ashes already in the bag, meant the tour was turning into a substantial triumph for Mike Gatting and his party. Botham made one spectacular contribution of the kind which makes him the game's greatest individual attraction, an innings of 69 from 35 balls in the New Year's Day game against Australia. In one over from Simon Davis he blasted 26 runs and this at the expense of a man widely regarded as the most economical limited-overs bowler in the country.

It was unfortunate that victory in the final of the Challenge should be marred by post-match violence by drunken hooligans, many of them waving Union Jacks and some carrying knives. This led to 25 arrests and a call from the police for sales of liquor at cricket matches to be either banned, or at least limited. The biggest factor in stemming the tide of violence, one was delighted to see, was a lap of honour by England players holding the trophy aloft – another big plus for the management and captaincy of the touring party. A large following of English cricket enthusiasts had made the trip to Australia to watch various stages of the tour and it was sickening to most of them to see soccer-style hooliganism taken right across to the other side of the world. It was interesting, too, to see in the crowds in Sydney, for instance, a banner proclaiming 'D.H.S.S. Tour, '86–87'. Australian newspapers were not slow to point out that this group proudly acknowledged that its presence was financed by dole-money.

But British disquiet was nothing compared with Aussie despair as the scene was set for the Final Test in Sydney. Cricket was in total disarray; the America's Cup was likely to return to the USA; tennis showed no immediate likelihood of producing a Hoad, a Laver or a Rosewall. Suddenly, although both games were out of season, Rugby Union and League players found themselves called upon to stand duty as national sporting heroes.

The beleaguered selectors, harangued from all quarters by critics with no alternatives of their own to suggest, contrived to startle the cricketing world by including in the 12 for Sydney the name of one Peter Taylor. It gave the newspaper sub-editors a field day of headline-writing: 'Peter Who?' Experienced cricket-writers speculated that a communications error had occurred, arguing that the man selected was actually *Mark* Taylor, a Sydney batsman of undoubted potential who had, in fact, impressed me 14 months earlier when I saw him playing Grade (weekend) cricket. But as the fog cleared it became clear there had been no typographical error; the selectors, with either a masterpiece of inspiration or a complete departure from sanity, had picked a man, an off-spinning all-rounder, who had played just half-a-dozen games of first-class cricket in the 30 years of his life. A week later he was hailed as the saviour of Australian cricket after being chosen as man of the match in a final Test which Australia had won! In the massive media euphoria which followed I did not find one single word of congratulation to the selectors for their omniscience.

It was, in fact, a man-of-the-match choice which must have owed more to sentiment, allied to near-hysterical relief than to cold logic. Taylor bowled very well indeed and batted stubbornly but compared with two or three other performances in the Test, his did not really stand out as the decisive factor. Without the 184 not out scored by Dean Jones in Australia's first innings, they would not have had the slightest chance of winning the game. And John Emburey's seven for 78 in the Australian second innings was off-spinning of the very highest class although Emburey himself felt he had bowled better for worse figures on other occasions. But if Taylor's selection had mystified the nation, then his man-of-the-match award now held a romantic appeal which enraptured the nation. Suddenly *every* man-in-the-street knew the Test score!

It was an interesting game which ended only in the closing stages of the final 20 overs. Australia totalled 343 (and imagine how sick that would have looked without Jones's 184) and 251; England made 251 and 264. It was a Test which involved drama, heroics, controversy and sentimentality in roughly equal measures and yet (in what was billed as the last Test he would ever play in Australia), Ian Botham played one of the most uninspired roles of his international cricketing life.

In Australia's first innings his figures were 23–10–43–0 – unusually economical figures but no wicket for the world record-holder. When England batted he strode to the wicket at 89–4, clearly determined to sort out this upstart Taylor who had just disposed of his pal, Allan Lamb, for his first Test wicket. Two offside fours came from the first two balls he received. In Taylor's next over Botham hoisted him over the fence at long-on for the only six of the innings. But Taylor showed himself to be no confused novice and Botham was immediately caught at short leg. Taylor, a likeable, intelligent, thinking bowler, disposed of Botham first ball in the second innings and, given the paranoia which grips Australians every time the big fellow gets into his batting stride, maybe that man-of-the-match selection was not so far off the mark.

The last day brought some thrilling cricket from both sides. When Botham was out, England were 102 for five and the game was to all intents and purposes, lost. Gatting, however, (playing wonderfully well on a worn and turning pitch) and the gallant Jack Richards, put together 131 for the sixth wicket which saw Border's captaincy begin to crack under pressure. As the last 20 overs began, the match looked comfortably like a draw but Gatting seemed to sense a possibility of a win even though a striking rate of something like eight-an-over was required. They started to play a few shots and Border (to the disgust of Bill O'Reilly, for one, Richie Benaud for another) took Taylor out of the firing line (six for 67 in the first innings, the wicket of

Botham again in the bag in the second) and moved out a couple of his attacking fieldsmen. At that point I would have put money on an England win. But what had to be seen as a defensive measure by Border turned out to be a stroke of genius. For Taylor, he brought on Steve Waugh, a talented all-rounder, who seems to have taken on the mantle of Doug Walters as a breaker of stands. He caught and bowled Gatting at 233 for seven and leg-spinner Peter Sleep mopped up the innings with his best figures in international cricket of 35–14–72–5. If it was to prove Ian's last Test in Australia (but who can predict what might happen in this most volatile of careers?) it ended on an utterly insignificant note for him. He had faced 14 deliveries, scored 16 runs (one six, two fours) and his second innings bowling showed 3–0–17–0.

In four Tests he had scored 189 runs (138 of them in the one innings in Brisbane) for an average of 31.50 and he had taken nine Test wickets at 32.89. It had been a low-key tour for him in every way. Even an off-duty evening at the North Sydney Rugby League Club escaped public notice although in some ways it paralleled that famous one in Manchester where he slagged off the England Selectors. This time, again in a question-and-answer session, he turned his attention (surprise, surprise!) to the British press and how they ruined his life as England captain. By now, of course, he must have been entirely convinced that no matter how much he slammed Fleet Street, its newspapers would always come back for more.

By the time the finals of the three-team World Series Cup had been reached and a tired-looking West Indies eliminated, it had been announced that Botham would, after all, be a Worcestershire player in 1987. It was a coup which delighted Duncan Fearnley who had flown out to Australia to complete it; it was news received with more muted pleasure by certain Worcestershire players wintering overseas. Botham's talent would never be denied or even questioned by any professional mind; his presence in a dressing-room and within a club was something else altogether . . .

And as the long tour drew to an end, Botham waited until

the very last moment to make any significant impression – carrying off the player-of-the-finals award when England beat Australia to make it a grand slam of success for the party.

It had been a good tour by England and one which, it was to be hoped, might now establish them with a basis for progress. It had been a tour free from public controversy which had to be seen as a tribute to the management and it had been the most resoundingly successful on the field for more years than most of us cared to think about. Botham's low profile was clearly due to a large extent by pre-tour legislation (no ghosted columns) and also to intelligent handling by Mickey Stewart and Mike Gatting. Personally, I was delighted with Gatting's success as captain. I have always found him sound and pleasant, possessed of good, honest common sense, and a damned good cricketer. It seemed churlish, as well as unperceptive, of the *Guardian* to print an article which was re-published in the *Sydney Morning Herald*, patronising the England captain with faint praise. He had done the best job of skippering a tour side since Brearley – what more did they want?

And so, in mid-February, England flew home from what had probably been Ian Botham's last tour and maybe even his final Test, depending upon the view of the Selectors. It had been pleasantly and mercifully free of unsavoury publicity. And as I moved across the Tasman Sea to New Zealand, Richard Hadlee announced that he would take part in a lately arranged tour to Sri Lanka in April–May and asked the New Zealand Cricket Board for a three-year contract. He did not want to go out of the game with Botham's name at the top of the list of Test wicket-takers!

Before we leave the '86–87 winter tour to Australia, it is worth taking another look at a matter we have touched upon elsewhere in this book – the persecution (can it reasonably be described as anything else?) of umpires by elevision. When Dean Jones had scored just five runs in at innings of 184 not out in the Fifth Test in Sydney and stralia were 27 for one, England appealed for a catch behind the wicket off Gladstone Small. As the appeal was turned down, all eyes – of players and spectators alike – turned slowly, but with immense and dramatic significance, to the huge TV screen in the ground which replayed the incident in slow motion. The telephoto lens, focusing-in close on the stroke and the catch, showed all too clearly that Jones was out. More than five hours later he was still there and the records will show for evermore that he made an unbeaten 184. If the English are to condemn the umpire for probably, almost certainly, costing them the game, should they not condemn Dean Jones as a cheat? And if they do, where does this leave the game of cricket? Herein, surely, lies the great danger of electronic intrusion into the game. What, in God's name, must an umpire feel when, having made a judgment based on his skill, his experience, his knowledge, his honesty and his eyesight, he is shown to everyone in the ground to have made a mistake?

For well over 100 years the game of cricket has existed on a basis of mutual respect between players and officials. It has been accepted that, human frailty being what it is, mistakes will occur from time to time, but, apart from personal rumination on what-might-have-been, there is no place for lingering acrimony. Decent and intelligent cricketers have accepted a philosophy that these things even themselves out. Indeed, later in the same day as Jones's escape, we saw Steve Waugh sadly making his way back to the pavilion after being 'caught' off his ribs. In terms of wrong decisions, the day had evened itself out; in terms of what course the game might have taken, who can say what the Australian total might have been if Jones had gone for five or if Waugh had *not* gone for nought? We are left with the 'glorious uncertainty' of cricket as we have always known it until the prying eye of the camera started to turn things inside out.

I am astonished that Australian cricket can find umpires willing to officiate in such conditions; I am staggered that the Board of Control allow their umpires to be so humiliated. We have seen in the past West Indian umpires hounded out of their homes by spectators who, merely on the evidence of their eyes at 100 yards distance, have taken issue with decisions. Can anyone imagine what it would be like to have every last, minute detail of a difficult and controversial decision presented on a huge screen inside the ground? How, then, do Australian umpires view the innovation? With exquisite diplomacy, Peter McConnell (one of the Test panel) says: 'I can see the advantages of the big screen as far as the public is concerned, but it doesn't help umpires. I deliberately turn my back on the replays and I don't watch TV highlights at home, either. I believe if an umpire watches and feels he has made a mistake it could shatter his confidence or influence a decision later in the game.' That's obviously good thinking but it doesn't make life any easier. When, less than a week after the Sydney Test, Kerry Packer announced the sale of his Channel 9 television and cricket 'marketing' company to another media tycoon, many tributes were paid to the way he had 'revolutionised' cricket telecasts. Packer himself was quoted in the *Sydney Daily Mirror* as saying: 'Channel 9 has done more for sports coverage than anyone else.' The *Mirror* concluded that he was right and would be sorely missed. It might perhaps have been more appropriate to comment that, apart from drastically changing players' attitudes for the worse by the initial World Series circus, apart from recruiting some commentators of pitiful inadequacy, Channel 9 had reduced television coverage of cricket to a farce.

It was good, therefore, to see Peter Roebuck, the Somerset captain (fortunately unscathed despite Botham's dark threats of retribution!) whose writing for the *Sydney Morning Herald* throughout the series was a model of literary merit combined with a practising captain's authority, offering his view of the big screen: 'This is intolerable. One of the greatest things about cricket is that the umpire's decision is final, yet here the players were treated to several views of the matter (Jones's escape) and a mistake was exposed. The umpiring has been good in this series and these replays serve only to undermine the authority and the confidence of the adjudicators.' Amen to that.

13 THE ALL-ROUNDER

Where does Botham stand in terms of all-round ability in the history of the game and in modern (i.e. post-war) cricket? Let us consult three authorities, the first of them Trevor Bailey who provided the foreword to this book:

> There is a glut of outstanding all-round talent of Test calibre at the present time – Imran Khan, Kapil Dev, Ravi Shastri, Richard Hadlee and Clive Rice. Although all would have shone in any era, could it be that with the exception of the West Indies, the general standards have fallen so that wickets and runs are somewhat easier to come by? Any capable batsman must fancy his chances of making runs against Australia, Sri Lanka and Pakistan while, apart from Richard Hadlee, Kiwi attacks look rather mundane. Conversely, any class bowler must expect to capture Australian wickets anywhere and certainly would welcome bowling against India, Pakistan or New Zealand – in England. So how does Ian measure up to the finest of his contemporaries? I rate him superior to Clive Rice in all three departments. The fact that Clive won the Silk Cut Challenge merely illustrates that one-off individual competitions, although fun and financially rewarding for the contestants, mean and prove nothing because cricket is a team sport and must be judged within that context. Richard Hadlee is a better bowler than Ian but he is not in the same class as a batsman. In fact at international (as distinct from county) level, I would be inclined to put Richard into

the category of a superb bowler and an ideal person to have lurking around in the lower order, particularly when runs are required in a hurry and the wicket is not too lively. Shastri (a slow left-armer) lacks Ian's penetration as a bowler but he has probably not reached his peak yet in that department; that could also be true of his batting, in which he can take both an attacking or defensive role. As yet he is not a serious challenger to Ian in the Test all-rounder stakes.

In style, performance and crowd appeal Kapil Dev comes closest because he is also a spectacular, extravagant batsman capable of massive hits. A fast-medium opening bowler, he does swing the ball, and he is a brilliant all-round fieldsman. Both would be an asset to any side but if allowed only one my choice would be Botham because he has been virtually responsible for winning more Tests, possesses a less volatile temperament and never admits defeat. Ian's most formidable rival for the title of best all-rounder in the world in the eighties is Imran Khan, who for a period was probably the fastest – certainly one of the best – fast bowlers in the world, a batsman of international stature and a superb fieldsman. Imran would certainly have made more runs if he had played for a team with a weaker batting line-up and while his overall figures are still very impressive they would have been even more so if he had not joined World Series [Kerry Packer] cricket and if he had not missed a number of other Tests through injury.

How does Ian Botham measure up against pre-war giants? I have selected three, not only because of their ability but because I was fortunate enough to have seen all three in action and also to have played with them – Learie Constantine, Frank Woolley and Wally Hammond. Learie would have been the perfect limited-overs cricketer: a very fast bowler, a brilliant if unconventional hitter, a fabulous fielder and, like Ian, a superb entertainer. However, in Test matches both his bowling and his batting figures are unremarkable and I would place him more in the Keith Boyce (Essex and West Indies) category.

The batting of Frank Woolley was not only memorable for the vast number of runs he scored but also for the supremely elegant, effortless way in which they were acquired. He was an international-class left-arm spinner in an era when England had almost a surfeit of them, and a classic slip. As a batsman I would obviously place Frank well ahead of Ian and it is not feasible to compare their bowling, but for Test matches I would pick Ian first if only for his rough, robust approach and ability to be at his best when all seemed lost.

Wally Hammond is generally agreed to have been, after Sir Jack Hobbs, the greatest of English batsmen, and therefore was far superior to Ian in that department. Wally will also be remembered as one of our finest slips, though it is said that he seldom, if ever, took a catch in his left hand, which must have made the job easier. In addition, he was a high-class seamer but unlike Ian he never attempted to develop his talents with the ball to the maximum. He was essentially a master batsman who was content to remain an occasional bowler, albeit a very good one, and he would never have been selected for England purely in that capacity. Therefore, Wally Hammond was never an all-rounder in the fullest meaning of the word, though he obviously could have been had he so desired.

Although impossible to compare with them because their cricket was played in a different world, it is unthinkable to discuss the merits of all-rounders without mentioning two incredible Yorkshiremen – Wilfred Rhodes and George Hirst. The former achieved the 'double' eighteen times and he became a good enough batsman to open for England at a time when the competition was strong. The latter, a fast-medium bowler, took more than 100 wickets and scored over

1000 runs in each of sixteen summers and in one of them he made over 2000 runs and took over 200 wickets, a physical feat which would certainly have tested the redoubtable Botham.

Since the war there have been three other magnificent all-rounders: Gary Sobers, Keith Miller and Mike Procter. For my money, Gary stands head and shoulders above everybody, the most complete cricketer of all time. For his batting alone he would have been an automatic choice for any Test team in any period. He had the ability to *destroy* an international attack; equally, he not infrequently rescued his side and inspired the tail. He had the ability and the concentration required to produce the really big innings. He was a marvellous player on a bad wicket; he could improvise. In addition, everything was done with grace, power and charm so that no less an expert and connoisseur than Sir Donald Bradman described one innings he played for the Rest of the World side as the finest he had ever witnessed. However, I am inclined to believe Gary's bowling was even more remarkable than his batting because he was good enough to be picked by the West Indies purely as a bowler *in three different styles* – something I do not think will ever happen again.

There are many marked similarities between Ian Botham and Keith Miller in his prime, both on and off the field. Both were headstrong extroverts, not easy to handle, and inevitably both have found themselves at odds with the Establishment. Both believed in playing hard and living life to the full. Both caught not only many brilliant catches with deceptive casualness but they also caught the imagination of the general public because they possessed that 'presence' which draws admirers from both sexes. In company with Ray Lindwall, Keith formed one of the most devastating spearheads in history and I have no hesitation in nominating him as a faster and more menacing bowler than Ian, especially with the old ball on a plumb pitch.

There would not be much to choose between them as batsmen. Both, with a little more discipline and patience, would have made more runs. It is interesting that both have Test batting averages of just over 36 (at the time of writing) which Ian should improve before he eventually retires. But against that it should be remembered that Keith usually made his runs against stronger attacks and on uncovered pitches which, at the highest level, suggests Keith was the better all-rounder, but not by much.

At his peak, Mike Procter was a genuinely fast bowler who bowled very big inswingers and was good enough to have opened any Test attack. He was also worth his place in a Test eleven as a punishing middle order batsman. It is hard to judge just how well he would have done in Test cricket if he had played as many games as our other candidates, but as a South African, sadly, he was restricted by politics to only seven Tests. But the forty-one wickets he captured at 15 apiece suggest he would have taken very many more, while forty-seven centuries in a comparatively restricted first-class career indicate he could well have made a large number of runs. Although Mike made a bigger impact as an all-rounder for Gloucestershire – for several seasons his county, with good cause, was known as Proctershire – than Ian has done at Somerset, he did have the advantage of not being absent on Test duty for half the season and thus he did not suffer the anti-climax of returning from an exciting Test before a capacity crowd to a three-day county game in front of a few spectators. I would not like to have to choose between this pair. If it came to it, I would probably say Botham – by a neck.

The Bailey view, while undeniably expert, is that of the present-day bystander – the opinion of a man who has done it himself but in his own age. Consider, next, the view of a man who is one of Botham's greatest rivals in modern cricket, Richard Hadlee, another member of that exclusive club of 300-Test-wicket-takers, and in fewer Tests spread over a much longer period. Hadlee, although a useful batsman, did not really come into the reckoning as an all-rounder until his second or third season in English county championship cricket. As a New Zealander he was, in fact, an *amateur* cricketer until he joined Notts in 1978, but by 1984 his batting had developed to the point where he became the first man in English cricket to complete the first-class double of 1000 runs and 100 wickets since 1967. As we have seen, in character, style and temperament he is just about as far removed from Ian Botham as it is possible for two cricketers to be, which enables him to look at his rival with detached, clinical appraisal.

> I have always thought, sure – he's got a lot of natural talent and ability, and I get the impression that he's relied a bit too much on that. I don't know whether he has put the groundwork in or not. I know he has had a lot of pressure from the media about one thing and another and that is certainly not helping his performances, but I have always felt that he has been a pretty inconsistent, unreliable sort of player although at times *brilliant*, either with bat or ball to win or turn a match with an inspired performance. I don't think he has looked after himself as he might have done.
>
> In his early days he was a genuine swing bowler. He got guys out by nicks or by bowling them out. I think he got to the stage too early in his career when he lost his swing, lost the spring of his approach to the wicket, the way he ran in. Then he tried to come in and bounce it at everybody. When I look at his record of 354 Test wickets (at the time of writing) and then look at Dennis Lillee with 355, to me there is no comparison between the two. To me, Lillee is the greatest in my time, possibly in the history of the game as far as *the art* of bowling is concerned. Trueman is a legend in his own right; I didn't see him play so I can't judge him. Michael Holding is one of the most gifted fast bowlers around – a superb, rhythmic action

and a guy that genuinely bowls the ball to get you out . . . he'll swing the odd one, he'll nip it around, he'll bounce you or glove you.

Now, 'Both' is not that sort of bowler in my opinion. He's a guy who gets a lot of wickets with what I call 'carrot' balls – a miscued pull shot when he's trying to bounce you, a full-blooded drive which is brilliantly caught in the gully or the covers. Obviously, he'll get the odd bloke bowled or lbw, but he's anywhere and everywhere. He's probably trying to do too much instead of coming in there on the basic principles like Lillee, Holding, perhaps myself to a lesser degree. You know – you *think* the guy out. I've always thought that bowling an over is like having six shells in the chamber of a gun, and whilst every ball is a potential wicket-taker it doesn't work out that way. You are trying to get the bloke into a certain position so that the third ball or the fourth ball is the one that you are looking to get you the wicket. In other words, if the guy is going forward at you all the time you encourage him a bit, then you give him one a bit shorter and suddenly he's looking to get back; the ball jumps on him, bounces a bit and he might nick one. I don't know whether 'Both' thinks like that. He's looking to do anything and everything, and it's amazing how many wickets he's got in that way.

As a batsman he's the type who is looking to dominate right from the outset and he'll play the big shot early in his innings. He's not the type of guy who will graft; even if the team's in trouble he'll look to play it his own way. I think a team can afford to have a player like him and really give him a free licence (within reason) to play a natural sort of game. If you are an attacking player you are better off playing that sort of innings and if you fail, well, bad luck. There are going to be other days when you produce the goods. Obviously, if you are in a situation where you are trying to save the match, then, maybe, you've got to graft. That's basic thinking. But he will play the big shot, the big lofted drive over the bowler's head, the big shot over the covers, the pull shot, the drop-kick shot and I think a lot of that has probably come through playing with Viv [Richards], actually, and I think that the rivalry with him is probably greater than with me or Imran or Kapil. I think those two have got so much respect and probably love for each other, if you like, that one's trying to outdo the other.

I remember a game here [Trent Bridge], a Sunday League match, Notts playing Somerset, and Somerset scored 250 in forty overs. 'Both' and Viv were batting together and they were having a race to a hundred. Viv was going well right at the start and when 'Both' came in he was so far behind that he just had to get ahead of Viv. And so they were hitting fours and sixes and they were having a right old conversation out there in the middle – 'I'm going to outdo you, sort of thing; you got 12 off that over, I'll get 15 off the next' – and that's the way it was. I think he looks for that sort of situation to produce the goods. Technically, I think 'Both' hits the ball pretty straight. He hits it in the air quite a lot but he hits it so hard that you've still got to catch it. Stackpole had that theory, didn't he? – even if he nicked it he had given it the full flow of the bat. 'Both' really gives it a whack, probably one of the hardest-hitting batsmen I've seen, along with Viv as well. I think 'Both's' career developed around Viv being at Somerset, so that it is reflected in his modern-day play.

From Tom Cartwright, who had probably a greater influence than anyone else upon Botham as a young player, we get this view:

As a batsman I always thought of him as a hitter. I still think of him as a hitter, a very clean hitter when he is striking it well. I think the worst thing that could possibly happen to him is for him to be put in a batting position, number one to five, and get him to go in *thinking* like a batsman. I am not putting him down in saying that but I think he is a spontaneous cricketer. You give him any situation and he will react spontaneously, and most of the time he will do it well – sometimes better than anybody has ever done it before. And I think that about his batting. If he is batting at number six or even seven, then if you are in the cart he can go in and if it's his day he can transform something that looked ridiculous into a winning position. His catching, again it's all spontaneous, something that he does by reaction. If you get him thinking, then I think that negates what he has to offer. I felt that when he was a boy – I didn't want anybody to cramp him. There were several senior players who wanted him jumping on and I used to say to them 'Leave him alone. I will deal with him.' Because I thought he was like a breath of fresh air coming into the Somerset dressing-room – like a big soft puppy, really. People tend to think that he doesn't need to believe in himself but he does, he does. He needs somebody to boost him.

Now, when his bowling went wrong he had got very big round the middle and he was still trying to bowl with the same action. Of course, he couldn't and consequently he developed some back trouble which was crippling him. I feel – and it's something which upsets me – that he has never achieved the levels of ability as a bowler that he should have. When you look at his one-day figures they are appalling, they really are. You know that's just a lack of discipline. It sounds silly when you know he is going to break the world record for Test wickets. I used to have raging arguments with Closey who would say, 'You're going to be a *fast* bowler, lad,' and I would say, 'Closey, he'll never make a fast bowler because he hasn't got the action. He's going to make a very useful lively fast-medium bowler and he could be very good, but he'll never, never bowl quick if he lives to be ninety.' And I used to grab Ian as we were going out on to the field and say, 'Never mind what he [Close] says to you. Just say yes or nod your head and then run in and bowl fast-medium.' That was an on-going thing for several years, and Closey never knew!

And it was necessary, very necessary because Ian's easily led and if Closey said to him, 'You can be the fastest thing in the world,' he'd think he could. I used to get on to him about his bouncers but all the same, he does get people out. The thing that I've noticed is that with batters all over the world, and certainly in county cricket here, he doesn't bowl it quick but what he does is bowl it [the bouncer] with a good line – off stump or just outside – and they still try and hook him. And that's how he gets them out. His line is almost unerring and I've been bothered at the number of batsmen round the world who haven't picked this out. If he *was* quick then he wouldn't get so many of them out, because I think they would have found they couldn't cope. But just below that top pace, they still think they can hook him.

I have always felt that he had an awful lot of natural talent. As a boy he was built like a man and, properly channelled, it was always going to be good. I'm just disappointed that he hasn't achieved his full potential as a bowler. In years to come it won't matter. People will just look at the figures and say, 'He must have been great.' But the people around today never really rate his figures in relation to the bowling ability they are actually seeing. Quite rightly. Now I think that could have looked better, his presentation could have been so much better. Probably, at international level he has played against men who were not the best in the world, not the same sort of levels that bowlers have played against in the past. But I think there was that little bit more to be dragged out of him and it has never been dragged out of him, really. But he *has* done what was necessary in his time.

14 THE 'WASTER'

In 1984 the BBC's radio sports unit produced a series of programmes which brought together for conversation pairings of prominent public figures who had never previously met. It provided some interesting and entertaining chats under the general title of 'Let's Get Together', and none more significant than one, edited by my good friend Trisha Lowcock, which featured Ian Botham and Group Captain Sir Douglas Bader, the RAF's most charismatic figure. One passage from that half-hour exchange of views tells us, I feel, more about the character of I. T. Botham than almost anything else in his thirty years up until now. It went like this:

> *Bader*: You're a very young man, Ian, very well-known but there's a lot of life left for you, and when you get older you will remember something which really influenced your whole life – as going to the Royal Air Force College influenced my life both in and out of the RAF . . . the chaps I was with there and the way one learned to behave and everything else. That was the major influence in my life. When you get to my age and look back . . .
>
> *Botham*: There's certainly one that sticks in my mind more than anything else. I can remember when the headmaster had me in his study, myself and a friend [Robin Trevett] for the umpteenth time and he said, 'You two are nothing but wasters. You will make nothing of your careers. You'll just drift away. You'll be the people that society wants to forget.' And ever

> since he said that to me there has been a determination, something inside me which said, 'I'll show you.' And it's quite funny – the lad I was doing it with, he's become quite successful in his career and I keep in touch with him and we went down to the local pub in Yeovil and who should walk in but the headmaster. Rob walked over and he rubbed it in more than me because I just stood there and had a drink. But Rob got out his wallet and said, 'Right. What would you like? A bottle of champagne? Please have it. I am the most successful waster you'll ever meet.' It was a very funny evening. We laughed and joked about it. Perhaps in many ways I owe something to him, I don't know.

There seems to me to be a terrible significance about Ian's memory of that encounter in his headmaster's study. He had so nearly got it right, because he still thought about it so many years later, but because he hadn't got it *quite* right the episode may be seen as a disaster. He saw the Trevett gesture in the pub as a triumph – that appalling gesture which indicated a belief that the contents of his wallet made him richer than a wise headmaster. Viewed in its very best light, the incident can only be seen as a pitiful instance of tawdry vulgarity. To Botham and his friend it was a triumph – and there lies the tragedy. They did not see that they had cheapened themselves, not diminished the headmaster; they hadn't *understood* what he had said to them ten years or so earlier. What a twisted sense of values the episode reveals. It was the contents of the wallet, the size of the bank account, which mattered as far as they were concerned – that was their measure of a successful life. Ian had remembered his headmaster's words but had not grasped their meaning. The admonition had remained in his mind as a challenge and, so far as it went, that was good, but he had misunderstood the whole essence of the homily. Success to him was measured by the money he had made and the public adulation he enjoyed – not the quality of his contribution to the society he lived in. In his efforts for sick children we can see the basic decency of the young man trying to fight its way through, but even in doing that he somehow contrived to tarnish the image from time to time. His electrifying leap to star status was always going to take a lot of handling, and it needed a sober and responsible mind to handle it. Other people have been saddled with a similar burden in an age where we build up our heroes overnight and then are just as quick to topple them. Some have been able to cope with instant fame; some have failed.

In so many of Ian's attitudes and utterances over the past five years it is possible to see that he came to despise the media where the image had been reflected. Yet he was willing to take thousands of pounds a year for lending his name to a job he was not capable of doing himself, i.e. writing a newspaper column. Did this, then, cause him to despise even more the men who contributed so generously to his income? And was it wrong of him to feel that way? These are questions we have to ask *ourselves* because newspapers do not readily hand out thousands on which there is no return. The papers with the largest circulations are often those with the most dubious standards of journalism, and cheque-book journalism is despised most heartily by newspapermen themselves, certainly in those echelons of the craft where the real writing is done and cheque books are something used to pay the household bills. What, therefore, we may ask, is the responsibility of those millions of members of the public who rush to buy copies of the *Sun*, not merely for the titillation of Page 3 but to be able to tell their friends who *don't* buy the paper, 'Ian Botham says . . .' Are *they* free from blame? Should not they take a share of the responsibility?

In so many ways Ian Botham is quite simply a product of modern society with its many imperfections. He has given immense pleasure to countless thousands through an application of his outstanding talent; he has on other occasions disappointed and dismayed his fans by using that talent in an irresponsible manner. He has worked magnificently to help sick children in a way which excited the admiration of everyone, and he has admitted using drugs at the very time when drug-taking amongst young people – the sort who admire Ian Botham so much and so unreservedly – is a matter of the most acute public concern. He has been generous and sportsmanlike to team-mates and opponents in many of his epic encounters; he has been cheap and boorish to others when personal pique has got the better of good sense and common decency. He has been allowed to get away with behaviour on the field which would have been unthinkable in another generation – the generation of the very people charged with maintaining standards today. Consequently he has shown respect for authority only when he believed it was entitled to expect respect.

Ian is not the first to find difficulty in coping with the status of the superstar, and he will not be the last to believe that favourable publicity is his right and that unfavourable comment can be dismissed, that the rules of the game of Life are made for *other* people. Are we, then, too hard on our heroes? Do we expect too much of them? Have we expected more of this man than he has been capable of giving? These, too, are questions we must all ask ourselves because the Ian Bothams come all too rarely upon the stage of international sport, and when they do they are important to us all. There are those who will feel that his headmaster's worst fears were realised and that an imperfect understanding of what was required to make a good and productive life has resulted in the wastage of a truly great talent. There will be others who look at his figures – at his bowling, batting and fielding – and say the rest doesn't matter, that Ian Botham was a phenomenon we were privileged to see just once in our lifetimes. Which view will be the right one?

APPENDIX
THE FIGURES

A statistical survey of Botham's career up to the end of the 1986 tour to West Indies follows. It has been prepared, in marvellous detail, by Wendy Wimbush who scores for BBC Television during an English summer and then departs, lucky girl, to do a similar job in Australia during *their* summer. Her tables will no doubt fascinate those who enjoy looking at their cricket in arithmetical terms. For those who (like me) experience some difficulty in finding their way through such charted minutiae it may be of interest to focus our attention on selected highlights of a career which have a special reference to some of the points made in our story.

For instance, in 41 Tests up to and including the Australian series of 1981 Ian Botham's 202 Test wickets were achieved at a striking rate of one every 48.06 deliveries. After that, in 43 Tests, he took a further 152 wickets at a rate of one every 62.55 balls. In that earlier period he conceded 44.12 runs per 100 balls bowled; in the latter he conceded 55.81 per 100 balls. This may, perhaps, be taken as evidence to support the Brian Close forecast (that the bowling would get 'no better') and Ian's critics' contention that his bowling has, in fact, declined during the second half of his Test career.

Let us now look at his performances (*vis-à-vis* the Freddie Trueman comparison of performances for county *and* country). In 1977, Ian took 10 wickets for England in 73 overs and 70 for Somerset in 535.5, but the following year, now fully established as a regular – indeed, England's *most* regular Test bowler, he bowled 218 overs in Tests and took 37 wickets against 369.5 overs for Somerset and 58 wickets. By 1982 we find him bowling nearly as many overs (244.2) for England as he was for Somerset (247.2), taking 27 Test wickets compared with 39 county victims, and in 1985 he bowled nearly 100 overs *more* for the national side (251.4) than for Somerset (154.4). He took 31 Test wickets and only 13 for his county in 1985. During nine seasons at the top of his profession his bowling performances for his county have declined in direct ratio to the amount of bowling he has done for England.

These are points which depend upon how you look at them – the England Selectors' delight may have found few echoes in the committee room at Taunton. So let us turn to less gloomy and contentious matters. Ian reached 1000 Test runs against India at the Oval in 1979. He had done it in 21 Tests and with it came the double (1000 runs and 100 wickets) because two Tests earlier (at Lord's) he had claimed his 100th victim.

His 150th wicket came the following year and his delight could not have been greater because it was his greatest friend, Vivian Richards, caught by Peter Willey at the Oval (his 29th Test).

Next came 200 wickets (Marsh, caught by Gatting) at the Oval in 1981 (41 Tests), followed by 2000 runs during the 1981–2 tour of India and Sri Lanka (42 Tests). He reached 250 wickets and 3000 runs during the same match (the First Test, and his 55th) against Australia at Perth on the 1982–3 tour. The victim was Allan Border. The 1984 home series with the West Indies might have been a dismal one from England's point of view, but at Lord's Botham completed 4000 runs (in 70 Tests) and at the Oval he took his 300th wicket (Dujon, caught Tavaré) in his 72nd Test. The 'triple double' was unique in Test cricket history.

At Port of Spain, Trinidad, during the ill-fated 1986 tour he took his 350th wicket.

If the 1985 season was depressing for Somerset in the results achieved, there was no shortage of entertainment value when their captain was available. He hit 1530 runs for an average of 69.54, with 5 centuries and 9 fifties.

He struck 10 sixes against Notts at Taunton, 8 against Glamorgan (Taunton), 1 against the Australians (Taunton), 8 against Hampshire (Taunton), 5 against Gloucs at Bath, 2 in the First Test (Headingley), 5 against Surrey at the Oval, 1 in the Second Test (Lord's), 8 against Leics (Taunton), 12 against Warwicks (Edgbaston), 4 against Essex (Taunton), 10 against Northants (Weston-super-Mare), 2 in the Fifth Test (Edgbaston) and 4 against Lancs at Old Trafford – a record 80 six-hits in 27 first-class innings.

I. T. BOTHAM First-Class Career

Year	M	I	NO	HS	Runs	Av	100	50	Ct	St	Ov	Runs	W	Av	5w/ 10w	B
1974	18	29	3	59	441	16.96	–	1	15		309	779	30	25.96	1/–	5-
1975	22	36	4	65	584	18.25	–	2	18		605.3	1,704	62	27.48	1/–	5-
	40	**65**	**7**	**65**	**1,025**	**17.67**	**–**	**3**	**33**			**2,483**	**92**	**26.98**	**2/–**	**5-**
1976	20	35	5	167*	1,022	34.06	1	6	16		563.4	1,880	66	28.48	4/–	6-
	60	**100**	**12**	**167***	**2,047**	**23.26**	**1**	**9**	**49**			**4,323**	**158**	**27.36**	**6/1**	**6-**
1977	17	27	3	114	738	30.75	1	5	15		665.5	1,983	88	22.53	6/1	6-
Pak/NZ	**77**	**127**	**15**	**167***	**2,785**	**24.86**	**2**	**14**	**64**		†	**6,306**	**246**	**25.63**	**12/2**	**6-**
1977–78	9	12	4	126*	397	49.62	2	1	7		210.4	691	35	19.74	3/1	7-
1978	17	20	–	108	538	26.90	2	1	11		605.2	1,640	100	16.40	10/1	8-
Aus	**103**	**159**	**19**	**167***	**3,720**	**26.57**	**6**	**16**	**82**		†	**8,637**	**381**	**22.66**	**25/4**	**8-**
1978–79	9	14	–	74	361	25.78	–	3	14		239.3	848	44	19.27	2/–	5-
1979	15	20	1	137	731	38.47	2	1	21		436.4	1,318	46	28.65	3/–	6-
Aus/India	**127**	**193**	**20**	**167***	**4,812**	**27.81**	**8**	**20**	**117**			**10,803**	**471**	**22.93**	**30/4**	**8-**
1979–80	6	10	1	114	331	36.77	2	–	5		242	532	34	15.64	4/2	7-
1980	18	27	–	228	1,149	42.55	2	6	24		453.3	1,387	40	34.67	–	4-
WI	**151**	**230**	**21**	**228**	**6,292**	**30.10**	**12**	**26**	**146**			**12,722**	**545**	**23.34**	**34/6**	**8-**
1980–81	8	14	–	40	197	14.07	–	–	8		224.2	790	23	34.34	–	4-
1981	16	24	2	149*	925	42.04	3	4	19		574.2	1,712	67	25.55	4/1	6-
India/SL	**175**	**268**	**23**	**228**	**7,414**	**30.26**	**15**	**30**	**173**			**15,224**	**635**	**23.97**	**38/7**	**8-**
1981–82	11	15	1	142	760	54.28	2	5	7		317.2	928	25	37.12	1/–	5-
1982	17	29	1	208	1,241	44.32	3	7	7		491.4	1,517	66	22.98	4/–	5-
Aus	**203**	**312**	**25**	**228**	**9,415**	**32.80**	**20**	**42**	**187**			**17,669**	**726**	**24.33**	**43/7**	**8-**
1982–83	9	18	–	65	434	24.11	–	2	17		319.4	1,033	29	35.62	–	4-
1983	14	21	–	152	852	40.57	3	2	10		232.2	728	22	33.09	1/–	5-
NZ/Pak	**226**	**351**	**25**	**228**	**10,701**	**32.82**	**23**	**46**	**214**			**19,430**	**777**	**25.00**	**44/7**	**8-**
1983–84	7	10	–	138	409	40.90	1	2	8		193.5	589	16	36.81	1/–	5-
1984	17	26	1	90	797	31.88	–	7	7		449.4	1,562	59	26.47	4/–	8-1
	250	**387**	**26**	**228**	**11,907**	**32.98**	**24**	**55**	**229**			**21,581**	**852**	**25.32**	**49/7**	**8-**
1985	19	27	5	152	1,530	69.54	5	9	17		406.2	1,376	44	31.27	1/–	5-1
WI	**227**	**430**	**31**	**228**	**13,816**	**34.62**	**29**	**65**	**252**			**23,628**	**911**	**25.93**	**51/7**	**8-**
1985–86	8	16	–	70	379	23.68	–	1	6		180.5	671	15	44.73	1/–	5-

*Not out. † 8 ball overs/inc. 8 ball overs

HS: 228 Somerset v Gloucestershire (Taunton) 1980
BB: 8-34 England v Pakistan (Lord's) 1978

BOTHAM TESTS v ALL COUNTRIES

ppo-tion	M	I	NO	HS	Runs	Av	100	50	Ct	St	Balls	Runs	W	Av	5w/ 10w	BB
us	29	49	2	149*	1,422	30.25	3	6	44		7,361	3,556	136	26.14	8/2	6-78
VI	19	36	–	81	757	21.02	–	4	16		3,447	2,079	58	35.84	3/–	8-103
Z	13	20	1	138	771	40.57	3	3	13		2,996	1,342	58	23.13	6/1	6-34
d	14	17	–	208	1,201	70.64	5	5	14		3,371	1,558	59	26.40	6/1	7-48
ak	7	11	–	108	407	37.00	2	2	9		1,540	777	33	23.54	2/–	8-34
L	2	2	–	13	19	9.50	–	–	–		485	269	10	26.90	1/–	6-90
OTALS	84	135	3	208	4,577	34.93	13	20	96		19,200	9,581	354	27.06	26/4	8-34

BOTHAM TESTS IN ENGLAND/OVERSEAS

ests	M	I	NO	HS	Runs	Av	100	50	Ct	St	Balls	Runs	W	Av	5w/ 10w	BB
ngland	46	71	1	208	2,551	36.44	8	11	49		10,398	5,301	209	25.36	17/2	8-34
verseas	38	64	2	142	2,026	32.67	5	9	47		8,802	4,280	145	29.51	9/2	7-48
OTALS	84	135	3	208	4,577	34.67	13	20	96		19,200	9,581	354	27.06	26/4	8-34

BOTHAM TESTS IN ENGLAND

Year	M	I	NO	HS	Runs	Av	100	50	Ct	St	Balls	Runs	W	Av	5w/ 10w	BB
A 1977	2	2	–	25	25	12.50	–	–	1		438	202	10	20.20	2/–	5-
P 1978	3	3	–	108	212	70.66	2	–	4		455	209	13	16.07	1/–	8-
NZ 1978	3	3	–	22	51	17.00	–	–	2		853	337	24	14.04	3/1	6-
I 1979	4	5	–	137	244	48.80	1	–	10		1,074	472	20	23.60	2/–	5-
WI 1980	5	9	–	57	169	18.77	–	1	2		786	385	13	29.61	–	3-
A 1980	1	1	–	0	0	–	–	–	–		188	132	1	–	–	1-
A 1981	6	12	1	149*	399	36.27	2	1	12		1,635	700	34	20.58	3/1	6-
I 1982	3	3	–	208	403	134.32	2	1	1		561	320	9	35.55	1/–	5-
P 1982	3	6	–	69	163	27.16	–	2	1		905	478	18	26.55	1/–	5-
NZ 1983	4	8	–	103	282	35.25	1	1	3		677	340	10	34.00	–	4-
WI 1984	5	10	–	81	347	34.70	–	3	5		980	667	19	35.10	2/–	8-1
SL 1984	1	1	–	6	6	–	–	–	–		336	204	7	29.14	1/–	6-
A 1985	6	8	–	85	250	31.25	–	2	8		1,510	885	31	27.58	1/–	5-1
TOTALS	46	71	1	208	2,551	36.44	8	11	49		10,398	5,301	209	25.36	17/2	8-

HS: 208 v India (Oval) 1982
BB: 8-34 v Pakistan (Lord's) 1978

BOTHAM TESTS OVERSEAS

Year	M	I	NO	HS	Runs	Av	100	50	Ct	St	Balls	Runs	W	Av	5w/ 10w	BB
NZ 77–78	3	5	1	103	212	53.00	1	1	5		808	311	17	18.29	2/–	5-73
A 78–79	6	10	–	74	291	29.10	–	2	11		1,268	567	23	24.65	–	4-42
A 79–80	3	6	1	119*	187	37.40	1	–	3		1,039	371	19	19.52	2/1	6-78
I 79–80	1	1	–	114	114	–	1	–	–		293	106	13	8.15	2/1	7-48
WI 80–81	4	7	–	26	73	10.42	–	–	5		872	492	15	32.80	–	4-77
I 81–82	6	8	–	142	440	55.00	1	4	3		1,443	660	17	38.82	1/–	5-61
SL 81–82	1	1	–	13	13	–	–	–	–		149	65	3	21.66	–	3-28
A 82–83	5	10	–	58	270	27.00	–	1	9		1,283	729	18	40.50	–	4-75
NZ 83–84	3	4	–	138	226	56.50	1	1	3		658	354	7	50.57	1/–	5-59
P 83–84	1	2	–	22	32	16.00	–	–	4		180	90	2	45.00	–	2-90
WI 85–86	5	10	–	38	168	16.80	–	–	4		809	535	11	48.63	1/–	5-71
TOTALS	38	64	2	142	2,026	32.67	5	9	47		8,802	4,280	145	29.51	9/2	7-48

HS: 142 v India (Kanpur) 1981–82
BB: 7-48 v India (Bombay) 1979–80

BOTHAM TESTS 1977–1981

Year	M	I	NO	HS	Runs	Av	100	50	Ct	St	Balls	Runs	W	Av	5w/ 10w	BB
A 1977	2	2	–	25	25	12.50	–	–	1		438	202	10	20.20	2/–	5-21
NZ 77–78	3	5	1	103	212	53.00	1	1	5		808	311	17	18.29	2/–	5-73
P 1978	3	3	–	108	212	70.66	2	–	4		455	209	13	16.07	1/–	8-34
NZ 1978	3	3	–	22	51	17.00	–	–	2		853	337	24	14.04	3/1	6-34
A 78–79	6	10	–	74	291	29.10	–	2	11		1,268	567	23	24.65	–	4.42
I 1979	4	5	–	137	244	48.80	1	–	10		1,074	472	20	23.60	2/–	5-35
A 79–80	3	6	1	119*	187	37.40	1	–	3		1,039	371	19	19.52	2/1	6-78
I 79–80	1	1	–	114	114	–	1	–	–		293	106	13	8.15	2/1	7-48
WI 1980	5	9	–	57	169	18.77	–	1	2		786	385	13	29.61	–	3-50
A 1980	1	1	–	0	0	–	–	–	–		188	132	1	–	–	1-43
WI 80–81	4	7	–	26	73	10.42	–	–	5		872	492	15	32.80	–	4-77
TOTALS	35	52	2	137	1,578	31.56	6	4	43		8,074	3,584	168	21.33	14/3	8-34

HS: 137 v India (Headingley) 1979
BB: 8-34 v Pakistan (Lord's) 1978

BOTHAM TESTS 1981–1985-6

Year	M	I	NO	HS	Runs	Av	100	50	Ct	St	Balls	Runs	W	Av	5w/ 10w	BB
A 1981	6	12	1	149*	399	36.27	2	1	12		1,635	700	34	20.58	3/1	6-95
I 81–82	6	8	–	142	440	55.00	1	4	3		1,443	660	17	38.82	1/–	5-61
SL 81–82	1	1	–	13	13	–	–	–	–		149	65	3	21.66	–	3-28
I 1982	3	3	–	208	403	134.32	2	1	1		561	320	9	35.55	1/–	5-46
P 1982	3	6	–	69	163	27.16	–	2	1		905	478	18	26.55	1/–	5-74
A 82–83	5	10	–	58	270	27.00	–	1	9		1,283	729	18	40.50	–	4-75
NZ 1983	4	8	–	103	282	35.25	1	1	3		677	340	10	34.00	–	4-50
NZ 83–84	3	4	–	138	226	56.50	1	1	3		658	354	7	50.57	1/–	5-59
P 83–84	1	2	–	22	32	16.00	–	–	4		180	90	2	45.00	–	2-90
WI 1984	5	10	–	81	347	34.70	–	3	5		980	667	19	35.10	2/–	8-103
SL 1984	1	1	–	6	6	–	–	–	–		336	204	7	29.14	1/–	6-90
A 1985	6	8	–	85	250	31.25	–	2	8		1,510	855	31	27.58	1/–	5-109
WI 85–86	5	10	–	38	168	16.80	–	–	4		809	535	11	48.63	1/–	5-71
TOTALS	49	83	1	208	2,999	36.57	7	16	53		11,126	5,997	186	32.24	12/1	8-103

HS: 208 v India (Oval) 1982
BB: 8-103 v West Indies (Lord's) 1984

BOTHAM TESTS v AUSTRALIA

Year	M	I	NO	HS	Runs	Av	100	50	Ct	St	Balls	Runs	W	Av	5w/ 10w	BB
1977	2	2	–	25	25	12.50	–	–	1		438	202	10	20.20	2/–	5-21
1978–79	6	10	–	74	291	29.10	–	2	11		1,268	567	23	24.65	–	4-42
1979–80	3	6	1	119*	187	37.40	1	–	3		1,039	371	19	19.52	2/1	6-78
1980	1	1	–	0	0	–	–	–	–		188	132	1	–	–	1-43
1981	6	12	1	149*	399	36.27	2	1	12		1,635	700	34	20.58	3/1	6-95
1982–83	5	10	–	58	270	27.00	–	1	9		1,283	729	18	40.50	–	4-75
1985	6	8	–	85	250	31.25	–	2	8		1,510	855	31	27.58	1/–	5-109
TOTALS	29	49	2	149*	1,422	30.25	3	6	44		7,361	3,556	136	26.14	8/2	6-78

HS: 149* (Headingley) 1981
BB: 6-78 (Perth) 1979–80

BOTHAM TESTS v WEST INDIES

Year	M	I	NO	HS	Runs	Av	100	50	Ct	St	Balls	Runs	W	Av	5w/10w	BB
1980	5	9	–	57	169	18.77	–	1	2		786	385	13	29.61	–	3-50
1980–81	4	7	–	26	73	10.42	–	–	5		872	492	15	32.80	–	4-77
1984	5	10	–	81	347	34.70	–	3	5		980	667	19	35.10	2/–	8-103
1985–86	5	10	–	38	168	16.80	–	–	4		809	535	11	48.63	1/–	5-71
TOTALS	19	36	–	81	757	21.02	–	4	16		3,447	2,079	58	35.84	3/–	8-103

HS: 81 (Lord's) 1984
BB: 8-103 (Lord's) 1984

BOTHAM TESTS v NEW ZEALAND

Year	M	I	NO	HS	Runs	Av	100	50	Ct	St	Balls	Runs	W	Av	5w/10w	BB
1977–78	3	5	1	103	212	53.00	1	1	5		808	311	17	18.29	2/–	5-73
1978	3	3	–	22	51	17.00	–	–	2		853	337	24	14.04	3/1	6-34
1983	4	8	–	103	282	35.25	1	1	3		677	340	10	34.00	–	4-50
1983–84	3	4	–	138	226	56.50	1	1	3		658	354	7	50.57	1/–	5-59
TOTALS	13	20	1	138	771	40.57	3	3	13		2,996	1,342	58	23.13	6/1	6-34

HS: 138 (Wellington) 1983–84
BB: 6-34 (Trent Bridge) 1978

BOTHAM TESTS v INDIA

Year	M	I	NO	HS	Runs	Av	100	50	Ct	St	Balls	Runs	W	Av	5w/10w	BB
1979	4	5	–	137	244	48.80	1	–	10		1,074	472	20	23.60	2/–	5-35
1979–80	1	1	–	114	114	–	1	–	–		293	106	13	8.15	2/1	7-48
1981–82	6	8	–	142	440	55.00	1	4	3		1,443	660	17	38.82	1/–	5-61
1982	3	3	–	208	403	134.32	2	1	1		561	320	9	35.55	1/–	5-46
TOTALS	14	17	–	208	1,201	70.64	5	5	14		3,371	1,558	59	26.40	6/1	7-48

HS: 208 (Oval) 1982
BB: 7-48 (Bombay) 1979–80

BOTHAM TESTS v PAKISTAN

Year	M	I	NO	HS	Runs	Av	100	50	Ct	St	Balls	Runs	W	Av	5w/ 10w	BB
1978	3	3	–	108	212	70.66	2	–	4		455	209	13	16.07	1/–	8-34
1982	3	6	–	69	163	27.16	–	2	1		905	478	18	26.55	1/–	5-74
1983–84	1	2	–	22	32	16.00	–	–	4		180	90	2	45.00	–	2-90
TOTALS	7	11	–	108	407	37.00	2	2	9		1,540	777	33	23.54	2/–	8-34

HS: 108 (Lord's) 1978
BB: 8-34 (Lord's) 1978

BOTHAM TEST v SRI LANKA

Year	M	I	NO	HS	Runs	Av	100	50	Ct	St	Balls	Runs	W	Av	5w/ 10w	BB
1981–82	1	1	–	13	13	–	–	–	–		149	65	3	21.66	–	3-28
1984	1	1	–	6	6	–	–	–	–		336	204	7	29.14	1/–	6-90
TOTALS	2	2	–	13	19	9.50	–	–	–		485	269	10	29.90	1/–	6-90

HS: 13 (Colombo) 1981–82
BB: 6-90 (Lord's) 1984

BOTHAM ONE-DAY INTERNATIONALS

Year	M	I	NO	HS	Runs	Av	100	50	Ct	St	Balls	Runs	W	Av	5w	BB
WI 1976	2	2	–	20	21	10.50	–	–	–		36	57	2	28.50	–	1-26
Pak† 1977–78	3	3	2	17*	43	43.00	–	–	–		167	101	4	25.25	–	3-39
Pak/NZ 1978	4	4	–	34	69	17.25	–	–	1		222	120	5	24.00	–	2-17
Aus† 1978–79	4	2	–	31	44	22.00	–	–	2		144	104	4	26.00	–	3-16
Pru Cup 1979	5	4	1	22	65	21.66	–	–	2		318	168	6	28.00	–	2-38
Aus/WI 1979–80	9	9	–	37	114	12.66	–	–	2		492	290	12	24.16	–	3-33
WI/Aus 1980	4	4	1	42*	78	26.00	–	–	2		252	185	3	61.66	–	2-45
WI 1980–81	2	2	–	60	87	43.50	–	1	–		90	56	1	–	–	1-32
Aus 1981	3	3	1	24	42	21.00	–	–	–		198	125	5	25.00	–	2-39
I/SL 1981–82	5	5	1	60	155	38.75	–	2	1		258	175	8	21.87	–	2-20
Ind/Pak 1982	4	3	1	49	63	31.50	–	–	4		238	175	9	19.44	–	4-56
Aus/NZ 1982–83	13	12	–	65	235	19.58	–	1	5		530	467	21	22.23	–	3-29
Pru Cup 1983	7	4	–	22	40	10.00	–	–	4		480	288	8	36.00	–	2-12
NZ/Pak 1983–84	4	4	1	18*	52	17.33	–	–	1		169	97	5	19.40	–	2-7
WI 1984	3	3	–	22	39	13.00	–	–	1		168	125	3	41.66	–	2-67
Aus 1985	3	2	–	72	101	50.50	–	1	2		174	106	4	26.50	–	2-38
WI 1985–86	3	3	–	29	51	17.00	–	–	1		132	122	3	40.66	–	2-39
TOTALS	78	69	8	72	1,299	21.29	–	5	28		4,068	2,761	103	26.80	–	4-56

†8 ball overs

HS: 72 v Australia (Old Trafford) 1985
BB: 4-56 v India (Headingley) 1982

BOTHAM ONE-DAY INTERNATIONALS IN ENGLAND

Year	M	I	NO	HS	Runs	Av	100	50	Ct	St	Balls	Runs	W	Av	5w	BB
WI 1976	2	2	–	20	21	10.50	–	–	–		36	57	2	28.50	–	1-26
Pak/NZ 1978	4	4	–	34	69	17.25	–	–	1		222	120	5	24.00	–	2-17
Pru Cup 1979	5	4	1	22	65	21.66	–	–	2		318	168	6	28.00	–	2-38
WI/Aus 1980	4	4	1	42*	78	26.00	–	–	2		252	185	3	61.66	–	2-45
Aus 1981	3	3	1	24	42	21.00	–	–	–		198	125	5	25.00	–	2-39
Ind/Pak 1982	4	3	1	49	63	31.50	–	–	4		238	175	9	19.44	–	4-56
Pru Cup 1983	7	4	–	22	40	10.00	–	–	4		480	288	8	36.00	–	2-12
WI 1984	3	3	–	22	39	13.00	–	–	1		168	125	3	41.66	–	2-67
Aus 1985	3	2	–	72	101	50.50	–	1	2		174	106	4	26.50	–	2-38
TOTALS	35	29	4	72	518	20.72	–	1	16		2,086	1,349	45	29.97	–	4-56

HS: 72 v Australia (Old Trafford) 1985
BB: 4-56 v India (Headingley) 1982

OTHAM ONE-DAY INTERNATIONALS OVERSEAS

Year	M	I	NO	HS	Runs	Av	100	50	Ct	St	Balls	Runs	W	Av	5w	BB
Pak† 1977–78	3	3	2	17*	43	43.00	–	–	–		167	101	4	25.25	–	3-39
Aus† 1978–79	4	2	–	31	44	22.00	–	–	2		144	104	4	26.00	–	3-16
Aus/WI 1979–80	9	9	–	37	114	12.66	–	–	2		492	290	12	24.16	–	3-33
WI 1980–81	2	2	–	60	87	43.50	–	1	–		90	56	1	–	–	1-32
/SL 1981–82	5	5	1	60	155	38.75	–	2	1		258	175	8	21.87	–	2-20
Aus/NZ 1982–83	13	12	–	65	235	19.58	–	1	5		530	467	21	22.23	–	3-29
NZ/Pak 1983–84	4	4	1	18*	52	17.33	–	–	1		169	97	5	19.40	–	2-7
WI 1985–86	3	3	–	29	51	17.00	–	–	1		132	122	3	40.66	–	2-39
TOTALS	43	40	4	65	781	21.69	–	4	12		1,982	1,412	58	24.34	–	3-16

†8 ball overs

HS: 65 v New Zealand (Adelaide) 1982–83
BB: 3-16 v Australia (Melbourne) 1978–79

BOTHAM ONE-DAY INTERNATIONALS v AUSTRALIA

Year	M	I	NO	HS	Runs	Av	100	50	Ct	St	Balls	Runs	W	Av	5w	BB
1978–79†	4	2	–	31	44	22.00	–	–	2		144	104	4	26.00	–	3-16
1979	1	1	1	18*	18	–	–	–	–		48	32	–	–	–	–
1979–80	4	4	–	10	21	5.25	–	–	–		210	129	5	25.80	–	2-33
1980	2	2	–	4	6	3.00	–	–	–		120	69	–	–	–	–
1981	3	3	1	24	42	21.00	–	–	–		198	125	5	25.00	–	2-39
1982–83	5	5	–	29	80	16.00	–	–	–		186	177	7	25.28	–	3-29
1985	3	2	–	72	101	50.50	–	1	2		174	106	4	26.50	–	2-38
TOTALS	22	19	2	72	312	18.35	–	1	4		1,080	742	25	29.68	–	3-16

†8 ball overs

HS: 72 (Old Trafford) 1985
BB: 3-16 (Melbourne) 1978–79

BOTHAM ONE-DAY INTERNATIONALS v WEST INDIES

Year	M	I	NO	HS	Runs	Av	100	50	Ct	St	Balls	Runs	W	Av	5w	BB
1976	2	2	–	20	21	10.50	–	–	–		36	57	2	28.50	–	1-26
1979	1	1	–	4	4	–	–	–	–		72	44	2	22.00	–	2-44
1979–80	5	5	–	37	93	18.60	–	–	2		282	161	7	23.00	–	3-33
1980	2	2	1	42*	72	72.00	–	–	2		132	116	3	38.66	–	2-45
1980–81	2	2	–	60	87	43.50	–	1	–		90	56	1	–	–	1-32
1984	3	3	–	22	39	13.00	–	–	1		168	125	3	41.66	–	2-67
1985–86	3	3	–	29	51	17.00	–	–	1		132	122	3	40.66	–	2-39
TOTALS	18	18	1	60	367	21.58	–	1	6		912	681	21	32.42	–	3-33

HS: 60 (St Vincent) 1980–81
BB: 3-33 (Melbourne) 1979–80

BOTHAM ONE-DAY INTERNATIONALS v NEW ZEALAND

Year	M	I	NO	HS	Runs	Av	100	50	Ct	St	Balls	Runs	W	Av	5w	BB
1978	2	2	–	34	37	18.50	–	–	1		108	67	2	33.50	–	1-24
1979	1	1	–	21	21	–	–	–	–		72	42	1	–	–	1-42
1982–83	8	7	–	65	155	22.14	–	1	5		344	290	14	20.71	–	3-40
1983	2	2	–	22	34	17.00	–	–	1		144	89	3	29.66	–	2-42
1983–84	3	3	–	18	34	11.33	–	–	1		127	54	5	10.80	–	2-7
TOTALS	16	15	–	65	281	18.73	–	1	8		795	542	25	21.68	–	3-40

HS: 65 (Adelaide) 1982–83
BB: 3-40 (Melbourne) 1982–83

BOTHAM ONE-DAY INTERNATIONALS v INDIA

Year	M	I	NO	HS	Runs	Av	100	50	Ct	St	Balls	Runs	W	Av	5w	BB
1981–82	3	3	1	52	82	41.00	–	1	–		150	101	4	25.25	–	2-20
1982	2	1	–	4	4	–	–	–	3		120	78	5	15.60	–	4-56
1983	1	1	–	6	6	–	–	–	–		66	40	1	–	–	1-40
TOTALS	6	5	1	52	92	23.00	–	1	3		336	219	10	21.90	–	4-56

HS: 52 (Cuttack) 1981–82
BB: 4-56 (Headingley) 1982

BOTHAM ONE-DAY INTERNATIONALS v PAKISTAN

Year	M	I	NO	HS	Runs	Av	100	50	Ct	St	Balls	Runs	W	Av	5w	BB
1977–78†	3	3	2	17*	43	43.00	–	–	–		167	101	4	25.25	–	3-39
1978	2	2	–	31	32	16.00	–	–	–		114	53	3	17.66	–	2-17
1979	1	1	–	22	22	–	–	–	1		72	38	2	19.00	–	2-38
1982	2	2	1	49	59	59.00	–	–	1		118	97	4	24.25	–	3-57
1983	2	–					–	–	2		144	87	2	43.50	–	2-36
1983–84	1	1	1	18*	18	–	–	–	–		42	43	–	–	–	–
TOTALS	11	9	4	49	174	34.80	–	–	4		657	419	15	27.93	–	3-39

† 8 ball overs

HS: 49 (Old Trafford) 1982
BB: 3-39 (Sahiwal) 1977–78

BOTHAM ONE-DAY INTERNATIONALS v SRI LANKA

Year	M	I	NO	HS	Runs	Av	100	50	Ct	St	Balls	Runs	W	Av	5w	BB
1981–82	2	2	–	60	73	36.80	–	1	1		108	74	4	18.50	–	2-29
1983	2	1	–	0	0	–	–	–	1		126	72	2	36.00	–	2-12
TOTALS	4	3	–	60	73	24.33	–	1	2		234	146	6	24.33	–	2-12

HS: 60 (Colombo) 1981–82
BB: 2-12 (Headingley) 1983

BOTHAM ONE-DAY INTERNATIONALS v CANADA

Year	M	I	NO	HS	Runs	Av	100	50	Ct	St	Balls	Runs	W	Av	5w	BB
1979	1	–							1		54	12	1	–	–	1-12

BB: 1-12 (Old Trafford) 1979

BOTHAM G Cup/NatWest Trophy

Year	M	I	NO	HS	Runs	Av	100	50	Ct	St	Ov	Runs	W	Av	5w	BB
1974	3	2	1	19	34	34.00	–	–	–		33	103	2	51.50	–	2-24
1975	2	2	–	21	22	11.00	–	–	1		24	85	3	28.33	–	2-46
1976	1	1	–	3	3	–	–	–	–		6	24	1	–	–	1-24
1977	2	2	1	91*	116	116.00	–	1	2		21	60	4	15.00	–	2-23
1978	5	5	1	80	137	34.25	–	1	3		56.5	227	8	28.37	–	2-44
1979	4	3	1	29	62	31.00	–	–	2		43	133	4	33.25	–	3-15
1980	1	1	–	3	3	–	–	–	–		12	21	3	7.00	–	3-21
1981	1	1	–	45	45	–	–	–	–		11	58	1	–	–	1-58
1982	3	3	–	85	136	45.33	–	1	2		31	109	1	–	–	1-59
1983	5	3	1	96*	121	60.50	–	1	4		42.4	115	7	16.42	–	4.20
1984	3	3	1	30*	45	22.50	–	–	–		30	107	6	17.83	–	3-35
1985	3	2	–	64	101	50.50	–	1	2		31	120	1	–	–	1-42
TOTALS	33	28	6	96*	825	37.50	–	5	16		341.3	1,162	41	28.34	–	4-20

HS: 96* v Middlesex (Lord's) 1983
BB: 4-20 v Sussex (Hove) 1983

BOTHAM B & H

Year	M	I	NO	HS	Runs	Av	100	50	Ct	St	Ov	Runs	W	Av	5w	BB
1974	3	3	1	45*	66	33.00	–	–	2		31	145	3	48.33	–	2-33
1975	5	3	–	11	22	7.33	–	–	1		51	172	8	21.50	–	3-56
1976	4	4	1	43*	56	18.66	–	–	1		41.4	121	6	20.16	–	2-24
1977	4	4	–	20	53	13.25	–	–	4		42	135	4	33.75	–	2-20
1978	5	4	–	54	93	23.25	–	1	5		55	148	12	12.33	–	4-16
1979	4	1	–	0	0	–	–	–	1		32	78	5	15.60	–	3-23
1980	4	3	–	33	51	17.00	–	–	2		11	48	–	–	–	–
1981	7	7	3	57*	153	38.25	–	1	1		75.1	261	6	43.50	–	3-23
1982	7	4	–	42	83	20.75	–	–	3		60	212	15	14.13	–	4-52
1983	3	3	–	14	18	6.00	–	–	3		30.2	104	7	14.85	–	4-27
1984	5	5	1	48*	131	32.75	–	–	6		55	212	10	21.20	–	4-51
1985	4	3	–	48	116	38.66	–	–	2		41.5	147	5	29.40	–	3-15
TOTALS	55	44	6	57*	842	22.15	–	2	31		526	1,783	81	22.01	–	4-16

HS: 57* v Kent (Taunton) 1981
BB: 4-16 v Oxford & Cambridge Universities (Taunton) 1978

BOTHAM JPL

Year	M	I	NO	HS	Runs	Av	100	50	Ct	St	Ov	Runs	W	Av	5w	BB
1973	2	2	–	2	4	2.00	–	–	1		7	36	1	36.00	–	1-14
1974	12	9	2	30	122	17.42	–	–	2		64.3	281	7	40.14	–	2-16
1975	16	14	3	38*	188	17.09	–	–	4		117.2	511	21	24.33	–	3-34
1976	15	14	1	46	315	24.23	–	–	2		116	509	24	21.20	–	4-41
1977	11	10	–	69	254	25.40	–	2	4		82	321	12	26.75	–	2-16
1978	9	6	1	52	154	30.80	–	1	5		64.5	238	14	17.00	–	3-30
1979	9	8	2	55*	174	29.00	–	1	8		61.4	231	15	15.40	–	4-10
1980	11	11	2	38	210	23.33	–	–	8		63	329	11	29.90	–	3-32
1981	9	8	3	106	251	50.20	1	1	7		50	198	12	16.50	–	3-11
1982	10	10	2	105	351	43.87	1	1	5		72.5	390	15	26.00	–	4-47
1983	10	9	–	85	358	39.77	–	3	1		63.3	255	11	23.18	–	4-22
1984	8	8	–	73	235	29.37	–	1	2		49.3	216	9	24.00	–	2-11
1985	8	8	2	58	238	39.66	–	1	5		46.5	215	12	17.91	–	3-28
TOTALS	130	117	18	106	2,854	28.82	2	11	54		859	3,730	164	22.74	–	4-10

HS: 106 v Hampshire (Taunton) 1981

INDEX